PORTALS AND e-BUSINESS INTEGRATION

Emerging Business Technology Series

CORPORATE PORTALS AND e-BUSINESS INTEGRATION

Mark M. Davydov

McGraw-Hill

New York   Chicago   San Francisco   Lisbon   London
Madrid   Mexico City   Milan   New Delhi   San Juan
Seoul   Singapore   Sydney   Toronto

Library of Congress Cataloging-in-Publication Data

Davydov, Mark M.
    Corporate portals and e-business integration / by Mark M. Davydov
       p. cm. — (Emerging business technology series)
     ISBN 0-07-137179-6
     1. Electronic commerce. I. Title. II. Series.
    HF5548.32.D38 2001
    658'054678—dc21   2001018036

McGraw-Hill

A Division of The McGraw·Hill Companies

1 2 3 4 5 6 7 8 9 0 AGM/AGM 0 9 8 7 6 5 4 3 2 1

ISBN 0-07-137179-6

This book was set in Sabon by MM Design 2000 Inc.
Printed and bound by Quebecor World/Martinsburg.

Many thanks to Nancy Warner for her development work on this book.

McGraw-Hill books are available at special quantity discounts to use as premiums and sales promotions, or for use in corporate training programs. For more information, please write to the Director of Special Sales, Professional Publishing, McGraw-Hill, Two Penn Plaza, New York, NY 10121-2298. Or contact your local bookstore.

 This book is printed on recycled, acid-free paper containing a minimum of 50% recycled, de-inked fiber.

Contents

Preface

There is hardly any dissent about the notion that Internet-based trade (or, as it is being mainly called, "e-business") is one of the most remarkable business paradigms of our time, and more and more companies bet on its applications as a key imperative for their success. With vast potential for transforming the global enterprise, it is also a source of fascinating problems of the best kind for both the business community and information technology (IT) industry to work on. These problems are apparently difficult and require new methods for resolution.

New software technologies for e-business are coming on the market almost every day, and companies are starting to realize that they urgently need a unified approach for sustaining that "flood" of technologies and supporting the process of continuously enhancing e-business infrastructure. Otherwise, the high risk is ending up with incredibly costly and ineffective IT capability—the new-age "Internet legacy."

The quantity of literature related to e-business seems to grow hour by hour, mostly in the trade journals. It has become difficult to get to know the subject from its principles, and one of the prime purposes of this book is to remedy this, to a certain degree. In addition, few books have been written that discuss the relationships between two concepts that have become dominant themes in e-business transformation: one is the corporate portal and the other is integration. The books that attempt to address this subject fall well short of what is most needed by companies today.

This book does not propose to cover the entire field of corporate portal technology. It does not even cover half of it. What it does do is bring attention to the potential this technology has in a business-computing environment and how it can possibly change the very way we work and do business. This book is unlike any other book available because it focuses specifically on providing a single source that describes the "big picture" of e-business integration (What is business to business really? What is it trying to accomplish? What are the pieces and problems involved? What does or doesn't enterprise application integration do, and how does it fit into the overall picture?). The aim of the book is to construct a story about employing the most powerful tool of the current state of the art in e-business technologies—corporate information portals—with a solid business perspective on potential results.

While it is not about e-business technologies per se, the book discusses almost every element of the e-business technical environment with which corporate IT organizations have to deal, such as transaction processing, collaborative processing, business intelligence processing, the Internet and corporate intranets and related content management processing, business-to-business processing, corporate extranets, and Web-based information assistants (corporate portals) for providing a unified, customizable Web-browser interface to business information.

I have made certain sacrifices in order to maximize the effectiveness of key messages of the book, and the major one has been to restrict myself almost entirely to general, high-level coverage of many technical details. Thus, there is little discussion of such technologies as middleware, object brokering, networking, database management systems, data warehousing, and so on. Nor have I spent much time or space on the relationship of XML (eXtensible markup language), a new evolving meta-data standard and integration language of e-business, to corporate portals. Basically, I have tried to stay reasonably close to core material of the sort which most IT professionals involved in the area of e-business applications might aspire to know.

This entire book is designed to educate senior business and IT management of corporations, government agencies, banks, and other organizations on how to establish and successfully operate e-business functions using the corporate portal framework.

The book has been written from my perspective as a practicing enterprise architect whose extensive work experience has been in systems architecture.

Consequently, I have devoted this book to a particular type of IT professional—enterprise architects. Enterprise architecture has developed a reputation for being hard to comprehend as well as extremely important. Nevertheless, it may be interesting to note that the level of technology preparation required to read this book is limited to some general Internet or Web concepts and terminology—for example, the Internet, browser, Web site, content publishing, HTML, and so on. I'm anticipating that both academic and software industry researchers will find it interesting, considering the multifaceted approach taken to describe the subject of portals. Students, especially those of Masters level and above, will also benefit from access to the material.

The main question is not whether this book about corporate portals could be useful, but how, and to what end, and why is it important? The ideas and approaches that are described here deal with various aspects of organizational change influenced by the new digital economy, taken from business, information systems, and software engineering perspectives. Together they address the major concepts and issues in systems thinking and business process improvement critical to the development of effective strategies for enabling business processes for the new economy. The net effect is a book that is really useful—one source that can help any business and IT professional understand the fundamental structure of the IT environment for e-business built on a unified portal platform that integrates the Web infrastructure with mission-critical enterprise applications.

Acknowledgments

First and foremost, I must give praise and many thanks to my wife, Maria, and my son, Dimitry, for encouraging and tolerating me while writing this book. Maria and Dimitry, I could not have done any of this without your encouragement, patience, and understanding. You mean everything to me!

I wish to thank Michelle Williams for presenting the opportunity to write this book, and I would like to thank everybody else at McGraw-Hill for the patience and hard work in producing the book. Also, many thanks to Nancy Warner for editing and revising the manuscript.

I would like to thank my friends and colleagues at Galileo International, Southwestern Bell, Edward Jones, Royal Bank of Canada, American Management Systems, Oracle Corporation, IBM, the University of Alabama, and the University of Wollongong for giving me the opportunities to work in dynamic and challenging environments, to get involved in demanding endeavors, many times indirectly, and especially for giving me the opportunity to express my ideas, views, and opinions. Specifically, I would like to thank Jim Lubinski, Chuck Barnhart, Frank Auer, Mary Skaates, Babetta Gray, Jim O'Shea, Jim Elias, Dale Rentrop, John Collins, Bob Kramer, Kincey Potter, Steve Mutschler, Stephanie Haas, Edward Gould, Joel Grosh, Mark Zochowski, Phil Groff, and Chriss Todd. Special thanks to Mike Honer of Preferred Resources for constantly reminding me about who can and can't be successful in the IT field and why, and to Mike

Wise of Bank of America and Margie Skiljan of Midland Systems, Inc., for their friendship, encouragement, and appreciation of my work.

Also, special thanks to the reviewers of this book, including Tyler McDaniel of Hurwitz Group, Gretchen Teagarden of Salomon Smith Barney, and Tom Spitzer of EC Wise.

It is also my pleasure to thank the staff at *Intelligent Enterprise*, especially David Stodder, editorial director; Justin Kestelyn, editor in chief; Claudia Willen, communities director; and Jeanette Burrieski, associate editor, for giving me the opportunity to contribute to one of the best industry publications.

Obviously, this book could not be produced in a vacuum. I'm particularly grateful to the practitioners, researchers, engineers, and developers who contributed to the concept of portals and shared their knowledge about the issues in the field. The work of many of them is referenced in the book and is mentioned among resources in the book's bibliography section.

Finally, I would like to use this opportunity to acknowledge the memories of my teacher and role model, Semyon A. Kosberg, a legendary engineer and rocket designer, who valued the ability to comprehend more than any other professional quality, and my colleague and friend Bill Kraha, with whom I was sharing many of my ideas.

Introduction

"Beware of all enterprises that require new clothes"
   —Henry David Thoreau, *Walden* (1854), I, Economy

"Nothing was ever achieved by accepting reality"
   —Jeff d'Arcy, Generic Software Evangelist

Imagine a world where much of human knowledge is no longer trapped inside "silos" of all kinds of enterprise applications and legacy systems, or hidden away within millions of desktop systems. Imagine a world where a user can visit a Web site that knows who he or she is, what content he or she wants, how the information should be presented on his or her desktop, and which communities he or she wishes to join. Imagine a world where, using a single browser-based application, users are able to publish all of their documents; to access corporate policies and procedures and human resources/benefits information; to participate in product development teaming; to coordinate scheduling, resources, and shipments; to manage business operations; to provide customer support; and much more.

None of these is a farfetched scenario for today's corporations. In recent years, the technology landscape on the Internet has undergone significant changes, revolutionizing the way people and companies communicate.

To a great extent, Web sites with static HTML documents that dominated the Web in the past decade have been displaced by Web sites with dynamic content, database-based search capabilities, and analytic applications. There has been an enormous shift of expertise and market power away from Web-based information publishing technologies toward information searching and information dissemination technologies. The latter have increasingly affected corporations' Internet strategies. Some have created Web sites that have become powerful information management services in their own right, more like Yahoo! or Lycos, performing information aggregation, "personalization," and distribution to internal and external users.

Many corporations have developed capabilities in customer-oriented business intelligence within the scope of customer relationship management instruments, such as customer knowledge and customer interaction management. In order to be successful in the new economy, corporations must have a far more sophisticated understanding of customer needs, and of the tools to manage them.

The task of managing Internet access in corporations has become more complex as the variety of products proliferate, both on and off their information technology plans. The whole focus of managing enterprise information on the Internet is shifting. Originally, researchers and analysts emphasized broad-based and generalized decision processing and the mass dissemination of corporate information to internal employees as the primary focus for the Web; now, they call for collaboration, and for highly targeted and personalized distribution of content, bundled with multiple types of specialized expertise-oriented services for managing internal and external business processes.

At the heart of this phenomenon is an interesting technological concept: a single, Web-based interface ("window") into the world of disconnected and incompatible data sources and applications spread across private and public networks. This interface is termed a *portal*.

Although its definition is still evolving and new "flavors" of portals are being introduced almost every day, there are clear indications that this concept, especially as it relates to the corporate space, is destined to become the primary enabling platform for taking the next step in the Internet evolution. Using portals as a single, integrated means of access to corporate information and services will allow the creation of new "joined up-and-across" organizations capable of fully exploiting tremendous e-business opportunities.

The challenge for those developing corporate portals and running enterprises that are portal-enabled is to fully understand the principles that are involved. The issues involved are not just technology issues, but include the majority of business and management aspects: leadership and culture, architectures (business and technology), management practices and processes, and organizational models.

All of these factors make the topic of integrating e-business functions using portal technologies one of continual excitement, a case study that never ends.

This introduction presents the structure of the book. We will start off the discussion by trying to set a frame of understanding about key business imperatives/concepts to consider in order to achieve a successful e-business transformation (Chapters 1, 2, and 3). Technology aspects of integration (Chapter 4) are then investigated, showing that there is an architecture and technology gap, especially with respect to "virtual" enterprises. The discussion in Chapters 5, 6, and 7 introduces and details the corporate portal concept and associated commercial tools and products. A focus is placed on the technology's state-of-the-art definitions and standardization tendencies for corporate portals, and especially on the unification and enterprise integration principles inherent in portals with respect to e-business needs and practice. Chapter 8 presents the best practices of portal implementations. Finally, the last chapter, Chapter 9, concludes the discussion by focusing on the future of portals, thus facilitating the elaboration of a comprehensive portal-based information system for companies in the new economy.

E-business is fueled by technology, but it is not about technology. It is about solid and effective business strategies. And nothing is more important to establishing a successful business strategy than strong and progressive leadership, which is based on flexible thinking and coming out of the box to try new and different approaches without fear of failure. The world is moving too quickly to be held back by "the approaches that have been used successfully in the past" or by the mindset that "it is the way we have always done this."

Leading-Edge e-Business Solutions and Strategies

What makes this book significant among the many expositions about the new digital economy and computer-mediated business environments that have appeared daily over the last couple of years? Perhaps it is the special look into the fundamentals of the vast revolutionary process that we have been describing using a litany of e-buzzwords: e-commerce, e-business, e-services, e-market, and so on, and calling it all "the e-biz."

When you open the book for the first time and glance through its Table of Contents, you may wonder whether Chapter 1 overlaps with other books about electronic business (e-business). This may be because you have browsed through several other books in one way or another related to this "hot" topic. Oh, yes! You might think that every author feels compelled to start his or her book with a basic definition of e-business and its fundamentals. You may wonder why the book doesn't plunge right into the main subjects, *portals* and *e-business integration*, to get things moving along and to develop your key understandings through the subjects' specifics along the way. This is because the purpose of Chapter 1 is not to provide a basic definition of the concept of e-business and its fundamentals. Not only do businesses today have a basic understanding of what they are, but the majority of companies have individual employees or even whole units dedicated full time to e-business development. Nevertheless, as a large number of research studies and industry surveys have shown, although companies realize the power of leveraging electronic connections on the Internet, they still need substantial help and specific guidance to figure out the best way to embrace this new way of doing business. This is why the main purpose of this chapter is to put the entire book's discussion into a frame of "guidance," by focusing on underlying strategic business imperatives that are instrumental for achieving a truly successful e-business transformation.

Are you charged with driving your company's e-business strategy? Are you responsible for making sure your company is ready to do business in the new digital economy? Or do you need to make your current e-business infrastructure better? If so, then you certainly feel enormous pressure. E-business is making greater demands on everyone to increase job responsibilities and expand skill sets.

All of us have seen the spectacular success of the most visible Internet companies, such as Amazon.com, E-Trade, eBay, and Tripod, and the many world-class corporations that have successfully transitioned to the new digital economy, such as IBM, Hewlett-Packard, Federal Express, Sprint, Wells Fargo, and others. What are the key lessons that could be learned from this success? What is the best way to explain or summarize the most critical success factors?

To help you answer all these questions, this chapter examines several business imperatives that, without any doubt, can be viewed as the most critical factors in the current successes of the various cited enterprises. As you develop your own e-business strategies and implementation plans, you need to use them as a direction or, putting it more firmly, as an overreaching "focusing theme," ensuring that all of the stakeholders involved in your firm's e-business planning processes have a clear understanding of their key points.

What Is a "Strategy of Choice" for e-Business?

Above all, e-business is fast becoming the most challenging arena within which companies have to operate successfully in order to survive in the global marketplace. The effectiveness of any e-business program depends on its ability to avoid the often extreme "ups and downs" of e-business development. Because of the constantly increasing speed at which business and technology decisions have to be made, it is absolutely critical to avoid costly mistakes and wasted effort. At the same time, companies must move forward and cannot afford to go slowly. Today's reality is that firms which have not made aggressive moves to offer services via the Internet are "doomed" in terms of competition, because the new economy crowns winners more quickly than the traditional economy.

I'm assuming that the majority of readers know what e-business is; however, a brief deliberation about the definition would probably be helpful here. As has often happened in the history of fundamentally new concepts (for example, computer and telecommunications technologies), when the concepts are actually introduced, there are no agreed-upon terms to refer to them or to adequately describe their attributes. This is especially true in the case of e-business. Actually, it is difficult, if not almost impossible, to put forward a "single-sentence" definition for e-business. Even experts and industry analysts struggle with its exact meaning. Of course, we can always define e-business very loosely, for instance, as "doing business electronically," but such a treatment of the concept will definitely limit our understanding.

Initially, the term *e-commerce* appeared to describe the process of handling business transactions between two or more parties (mostly companies and consumers of their products) via computer; then IBM coined a usage of the term *e-business* that included business-to-business (B2B) transactions. Unfortunately, too often the terms are used interchangeably.

Broadly speaking, *e-business* is an umbrella term used for describing an all-encompassing concept of enabling the exchange of business information and automation of commercial transactions over the Internet. It includes on-line marketing and on-line retailing of products and services by companies directly to consumers. It covers procurement and distribution of products at the wholesale level, and the related exchange of information in the form of business-to-business transactions. It also encompasses sophisticated business-to-business interactions and collaboration activities at a level of enterprise applications and business processes, enabling business partners to share in-depth business intelligence, which leads, in turn, to the management and optimization of interenterprise processes such as supply chain management (SCM).

There are currently three models of e-business:

- Business to business (B2B)
- Business to consumer (B2C)
- Business to employee (B2E)

In all of these e-business models, information exchange occurs over the Internet, using the universal global data network and multiple Internet-based systems and technologies, such as content syndication and publishing tools, Web browsers, Web servers, and so on.

Regardless of whether a particular e-business implementation represents the B2B, B2C, or B2E model, there are certain common factors, illustrative of the concept as a whole, that have to be clearly identified in order to realize and sense the overall challenge of e-business transformation. What are they?

First, e-business is intensively dynamic in terms of growth. To be precise, the growth rates of e-business activities are astronomical. The concept started less than a decade ago as an interesting experiment with new media for information publishing, and it has quickly become a multitrillion-dollar market. Second, it is primarily information based—information flows have become as critical as cash flows. Third, its environment (often referred to as the *e-business ecosystem*) is mostly virtual rather than physical, as indicated by the virtualization of value chains and the rise of a new organizational form—the virtual enterprise (VE). The main focus of the VE is on obtaining a closer intimacy with suppliers, partners, and customers, and deriving value (rather than physical assets) from information, knowledge, and relationships. Finally, it is extremely complex with respect to the variety of technological and organizational issues that will have a profound impact on many aspects of your company's business—most importantly, how your company deals with the implementation of information technology (IT) and the role IT should play in its business strategy.

Strategy of choice is a term used to describe an outcome of the internal planning process that is instituted by a company in order to determine how a particular function or activity should be best accomplished. The genesis of this process lies in the examination of the best practices of leaders in the company's industry or a similar industry. This gives the company an important perspective into the "state of the art" in relation to specific initiatives that it has decided to undertake. By focusing on best practices, the company can identify problem areas and obtain the detailed knowledge needed for improving decision making, business planning, or system-development activities in order to ensure a successful implementation of the initiatives. Many new ideas usually evolve from these examinations.

From there, the company develops its own strategy of choice—a set of strategic approaches that depend upon the outcome of the examination of best practices, specific company characteristics, and the nature of the initiatives. Correctly understanding the nature of the initiatives is extremely important in order to derive a strategy that ensures success. It also helps to justify the investments in the strategy because one can sense the degree of future uncertainties and how much a rigorous financial analysis has to be tempered by emphasis on the strategic value of the initiative itself.

The reality of e-business is that arriving at such an understanding is a difficult challenge, since these initiatives touch the actual underpinnings of existing business models. None of the well-known, large-in-scope, multifaceted, technology-based concepts that substantially affected industries in the United States and around the world in the past (for example, total quality management, business process reengineering, and so on) had to deal with business fundamentals to the same degree as the concept of e-business.

Macrolevel versus Microlevel Business Issues

Let's take manufacturing, for example. In recent years, manufacturers have realized that significant strides in the optimization of manufacturing processes and the integration of the entire enterprise are necessary in order to be competitive in the global economy. As a result, enterprise resource planning (ERP) systems have been increasingly adopted as the strategy of choice. With ERP systems and similar initiatives, the main issues and problems of strategic planning have concentrated, to a large extent, not at a macrolevel, but rather at a microlevel (around 80 to 85 percent of all issues). Typically, dealing with issues at a macrolevel is forcing companies to redefine the entire conventional business order. In contrast, for ERP implementations, the goal is to improve the current business model versus entirely redefining it, more specifically, to ensure that business strategies, production practices, people and plant operations, management direction, and IT are all aligned with the key manufacturing and commercial priorities.

When the main issues and problems of strategic planning are concentrated at a microlevel, the examination of best practices could be extremely helpful because, at this level, the experience base has been synthesized in the form of generic business models that can be applied successfully to almost any enterprise. These generic business models are even coming embedded within the software. The best examples here are implementations of one of the most popular ERP systems on the market: SAP's R/3 system for discrete and process manufacturing that are based on workflow models embedded in the system.

The world of e-business is completely different. Most of the effort is at a macrolevel. It's not just about a particular type of system, like ERP, any longer. It's not just about choosing the right technology, or streamlining business processes and IT. It's actually about the entire transformation of the conventional business order. It's about disrupting industries, inventing new industries, redefining existing business models, reinventing versus reengineering business processes, and changing organizational forms and corporate cultures. It's about shifting from a classical view of management activities grouped around back-office systems (planning, organizing, directing, and controlling) to one that groups activities around producing systems to better serve the customer. As businesses are moving their existing processes (for example, order entry) onto the Internet, the change in management activities becomes very apparent, forcing businesses to concentrate on "front-office" functional areas (for example, call centers, storefronts, one-on-one meetings, and Web sites) where customer interactions occur. New business models are needed to take advantage of such interactions. In turn, by shifting the business emphasis from back-office applications toward customer-facing applications, the delineation between front- and back-office systems has diminished, creating a substantial need for a wholly unified enterprisewide computing environment.

Accomplishing all of the cited business moves correctly is proving to be the biggest challenge. In many cases, companies are entering the new e-business environment with the most basic problem—they do not have a clear understanding of what is the best approach for such transformation. What are typical or generic business processes that need to be included or considered when developing e-business solutions for a particular industry or a particular firm? Is there a generic business model that can be used as a foundation to help designate the scope of solutions? What type of business processes and resources need to be different from a business model perspective outside of the e-business environment? How should the development of a business plan for e-business be approached when there appear to be so many momentous variables, like what and how to sell, what not to sell, what and how to buy, and what not to buy? What about supply and distribution channel issues, limited historical data, corporate culture, staffing, and so on? What is the typical road map and timeline for establishing a sufficient Web infrastructure and integrating it with back-end systems? Are these moves typically done simultaneously or sequentially? These and many, many more unknowns are associated with e-business. But the first and most important question facing any company is whether to get into e-business at all.

E-Business Formulas

Naturally, as a result, companies, especially traditional "brick-and-mortar" firms, have been experimenting with different formulas. Some have a separate e-business strategy that sits apart from their everyday business activities. Some are embracing the concept across the entire enterprise. Some are establishing separate e-business subsidiaries or even totally independent on-line entities. Some are forming joint ventures with "dot-com" start-ups. Finally, there are examples of a "brick-and-mortar" company "demolished" to become an entirely Web-based business. Let's take a look at a few cases. At the time of this writing, Merrill Lynch and SINA.com have created a joint venture to provide on-line asset management services for wealthy Chinese-Americans and other Asian individuals. Barclays Bank has joined a string of companies in deciding to demolish parts of its traditional business so that it can move into the Internet age. It has closed 171 branches.

There is a growing apprehension, however, that we are only at the beginning of these experiments, although there are many clear signs that some are definitely producing nothing but trouble. Also, these experiments have brought a realization that there are no generic business models that can be applied to individual companies in the midst of e-business transformation. Even companies in the same industry, of the same size, and with similar culture and management practices cannot expect to find an e-business model that fits them all nicely.

At the same time, it is becoming apparent that we have an important opportunity to establish common, reusable strategies and business objectives that represent the best practices of the industry within the scope of a comprehensive e-business strategy. Even if many companies today cannot depend on bringing in from outside a comprehensive strategy to ensure an acceptable level of e-business success, taking a holistic point of view based on common "elements" can still foster very successful results.

Forward-thinking organizations and leading industry analysts (for example, Gartner Group, Forrester Research, The Patricia Seybold Group, and so on) are beginning to organize and standardize industry best practices in order to create and maintain a comprehensive model of the "strategy of choice" for e-business. The need to consider these matters seriously is growing every day.

In the meantime, to build a successful business on the Internet, it is imperative that companies have an "e-management" methodology in order to fully understand the real challenges of this new environment and be able to deal with them. At a minimum, such a methodology entails a rigorous set of activities designed to accomplish two key steps:

- Gaining an understanding of the characteristics of the Internet, including its dynamics and evolutionary trends.

- Examining the critical success factors and specific strategies that the particular competitor or leading companies in other industries undertook to fit into the new environment.

By completing these two actions, a company will be able to determine its optimal business strategy for managing an e-business transformation.

The remaining sections in this chapter are geared toward helping you in this endeavor. But before we proceed, let's briefly discuss a high-level taxonomy of e-business implementations as it relates to the evolution of the concept.

High-Level Taxonomies of e-Business Implementations

There are many examples of such taxonomies. Figure 1.1 depicts a vision of the evolution of e-business constructed as a summary of various reports on the subject published by the Gartner Group.

The Gartner Group uses the following four characteristics to define the evolution of e-business:

- **Content and Its Delivery Mechanism**—provisioning of mostly marketing and product description information, and predefined (bidirectional) transaction exchange between tightly coupled partners.

- **Context as an Offering and Enabling Infrastructure**—establishment of electronic marketplaces in a context of enhanced marketing and sales, and new electronic channels as elements of supply-chain management.

- **Interactivity and the Degree of Application Integration**—linking electronic marketplaces to enterprise applications and enabling interactive business-to-business transaction processing.

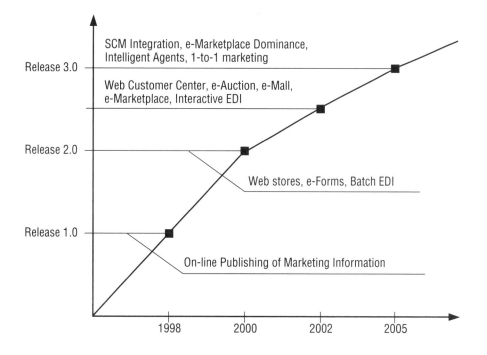

Figure 1.1: E-Business Evolution—A Function of Content and Integration

- **Channel Masters**—establishment of highly adaptive enterprises with one-to-one marketing and mass customization capabilities as well as optimized processes for electronic marketplaces.

As you can see from Figure 1.1, using the language of software vendors, we are all on or near the "E-business Release 2.0" point, which is characterized by the dominance of synergistic content offerings, primarily batch electronic data interchange (EDI), and "e-form"-based Web sites.

Figure 1.2 depicts a similar vision in terms of the evolution of e-business, but it is constructed from a different perspective, using ideas presented by Don Tapscott in his book *Blueprint to the Digital Economy: Creating Wealth in the Era of E-Business* (McGraw-Hill, 1998).

Don Tapscott's contention is that the key to e-business is building innovative business community relationships and, as a result, the progress of e-business should be described from the point of view of such relationships. Therefore, according to Figure 1.2, we are all on the upgrade path to

Release 2.0 (somewhere on Release 1.x). This point in the evolution of e-business is characterized by the transition from the period dominated by Web sites and storefronts to a period dominated by electronic marketplaces and business-to-business applications distributed across partners.

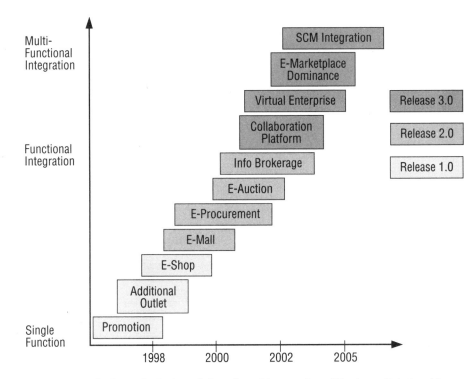

Figure 1.2: E-Business Evolution—A Function of Integration of Business Relationships

A very important point should be highlighted here. Many observers consider the best e-business strategy at this time to be the ability to drive a considerable number of customers to a company's Web site (by disseminating information about products and services) and to enable buy–sell transactions. As we transition to Release 2.0, however, a much broader strategy is required to ensure the success of the new e-business models that are emerging in areas such as e-brokerage, content syndication, and trading-group collaboration (the latter is depicted in detail in Chapter 4).

Enabling Internet Business—Delivering a Compelling Message to "Buy, Sell, or Engage" to the World

According to economists, the fundamental view of commerce is that businesses exist for the principal purpose of making profit through a process of satisfying a desire or a need expressed by an economically viable customer. There are multiple forms for delivering the satisfaction—for example, through physical objects (commonly referred to as "goods") and nonphysical objects (all kinds of intangible products or "services"). The whole process (from the point of identifying a desire or a need to delivering the satisfaction—for example, moving goods and services from where they are to where they are most valued) is an act of creating a chain of value, formulated through a point-to-point connection between participating parties. For all of that, it's clear that economically viable customers are the keys to such connections.

Now, let's focus on important extensions of this traditional view of business brought about by the Internet. What really happens when you bring your business into a global network such as the Internet?

Obviously, all the traditional rules of engagement still apply on the Internet; for example, you still have to establish a presence and create or provide something that is able to satisfy a desire or a need. However, we can clearly identify two extremely important extensions of this traditional view. First and foremost, the Internet provides an incredible acceleration of the process. Because of its computer-driven nature and its inter- and intraconnectivity, it has practically eliminated all significant barriers of distance and time. Second, it establishes new forms of value chains, in which value is captured as digital information. More and more, the delivery of satisfaction is taking place in the form of knowledge-based, information-rich digital services conducted across networks.

Such analysis brings an important kind of notion in regard to e-business that requires a further exploration. We're on the threshold of a major paradigm shift in regard to the value of goods and services in which businesses amplify value by managing the content of e-business interactions (for example, catalogs of product information, customer information, intellectual property of know-how, and so on) as assets. From the customer perspective, such assets become less capital investment and more subscription services. We also have to take into account the possible creation of a new form of value chain, the so-called *reintermediated chain*—for example, an arrangement through which the customer can obtain goods and services not directly from the producer, but through an aggregated source. At the time of this writing, more than 300 distributors, wholesalers, and consolidators (for example, FarmChem, a Midwest distributor of agricultural chemical parts such as sprayers, pumps, meters, and so on), who were getting "cut out of the loop" by the dot-com companies, have been successful not only in retaining their market share, but also in increasing it through innovative e-business applications.

As a result, the basic name of the game from a perspective of enabling e-business is to have a comprehensive strategy that covers activities along the following principal dimensions:

- Identifying the elements that provide the most cost-effective possibilities for value amplification, directly by amplifying the content (as "goods and services") or, from the producer perspective, through value-added functions that, in turn, increase the value of the "base" content.

- Building the necessary technology infrastructure services, which I call "enabling infrastructure services," for example, choosing and implementing all the technology you need to realize the possibilities mentioned in the point above.

- Constructing and delivering a compelling message about your capabilities, as they relate to both points above, to all your partners, especially customers (in this context, *compelling* refers to "a significant value-based proposition to your partners that, at the same time, is profitable to you").

While, in general, a systematic approach to the identification of chain elements could lead to a huge number of elements for follow-up economic evaluation, in practice, attention should be concentrated on the analysis of the following two major categories of such elements:

- **Primary**—Elements that *directly* impact economic equations of value chains—for example, elements associated with the following production-oriented functions:

  - Marketing and sales

  - Inbound or outbound logistics

  - Procurement

- Development

- Finance

- Operation

- Base infrastructure

- Technology infrastructure

- Customer service

- Human resource management

■ **Support**—Elements that *indirectly* impact economic equations of value chains, although the actual impact of such elements from an e-business perspective is extremely significant; this category includes structural and process-oriented elements, specifically:

- **Connection and Interaction Topologies**—One-to-one, one-to-many, many-to-many schemas (ways) of communicating and interacting among parties involved in the value chain (buyers, sellers, cooperative members, and so on). They cause us to view value chains in terms of ways we interconnect with each other, enabling us to leverage the real value.

- **Componentization**—Service-coupling schemas across a number of steps of the value chain; it is what I call "smart packaging." The premise here is this: across networks anything can and will be outsourced. As a result, the primary evolving trend is that e-business will become a series of building blocks and that these building blocks will become increasingly intelligent services. What makes them "intelligent" is the embedded knowledge, making the service capable of being always available, self-organizing, appliancelike, self-learning, and so on. That causes us to concentrate on:

  1. Combinations of the value chain elements that could be involved in such services.

  2. Core competencies and the ability to leverage people as a knowledge-producing source.

- **Virtualization**—Organization-coupling schemas across value chains, that is, all kinds of ways in which business processes are organized and inter-connected on an extended enterprise basis. Again, the primary trend is really clear here. The mature state of e-business is a world in which companies exist as parts of electronic business communities and these communities are extended between the supply side and the demand side. In other words, it all becomes a world driven by customers (for example, the particular company's customers, its customers' customers, and so on). Entire value chains are going to be "virtual enterprises," meaning that trading partners will exercise effective control of much greater assets than each of them owns individually.

To a large degree, this discussion has primarily focused on the "roadwork" aspects of how to effectively design a particular e-business model of operations. It's all about formulating the "value proposition" portion of your "e-business message to the world." Now, let's address briefly the remaining portion of the message, the portion that deals with "goals of engagement" aspects. The best way to look at it is in terms of your goals and objectives toward a particular e-business model, and the types of roles that you can best play in the value chain (for example, as a buyer, seller, or broker). Let's say you have put up a Web site with storefront functions—in other words, an "e-shop." What is your "message" in this case? The primary goals of e-shops are to promote a company and its products or services and to allow a company to obtain a low-cost distribution channel. Therefore, your "message" is first that you are seeking demand and second that you are interested in "closed" or maybe "semiopen" value chains—chains with one seller and multiple buyers. To help you to gain a better understanding of what this all means, Table 1.1 provides a summary of the functional relationships between "goals of engagement" and specific e-business models, examples of which can be found on the Internet today.

Table 1.1
Summary of Relationships Between Business Goals and e-Business Models

Functional Relationships/Goals	E-Business Characteristics
Seeking Demand	E-Shop: Promotional Content, Additional Outlet, On-Line Ordering, On-Line Order/Account Status
Seeking Suppliers	E-Procurement: On-Line Catalogs, PO/Requisition Consolidation, e-Payment
Seeking Movement of Goods or Parties/Facilitated Distribution	E-Auction: Electronic Bidding E-Marketplace: Third-Party Intermediation, Product/Service Aggregation E-Mall: Collection of e-Shops

Striving for the Customer—The High-Stakes Battle for On-Line Customers and Market Share

No one needs to tell you that succeeding in an e-business initiative means making your customers the central focus of your business objectives on the Web. It's e-Business 101 nowadays. It is no longer a question of whether to do it, but how to do it best.

But the topic of "focusing first on the customer" is a large topic that, as you know, is worth at least one entire book on its own. So, unfortunately, its treatment will not be very broad in this book.

As a result, the only strong advice this book can give you is probably what you already know. Don't try implementing an e-business solution without a comprehensive plan for a customer relationship management (CRM) program; it would not work. It should be a long-range plan that defines all aspects of selecting, prioritizing, and implementing the most promising areas in which you can improve all facets of the "acquire, retain, and grow" customer relationship processes. Although, in general, a CRM program covers a broad scope of customer relationship areas, some of which may belong primarily to traditional ("brick-and-mortar") business processes, it is only from a comprehensive long-range CRM plan that you can establish a customer-focused roadmap needed for e-business and evolve a set of near-term (6- to 12-month horizon) operational objectives.

Nevertheless, this book can perhaps provide you additional benefits in regard to forging a CRM plan by discussing the enormous challenge the Internet has brought into the CRM landscape, turning it into a "war zone."

As many observers have proclaimed, the Internet is a great equalizer. Why? It's because of the benefits of global reach and unlimited connections. But the same benefits could become liabilities by projecting an illusion of "easiness" in regard to customer relationships. Yes, on one side, as Cisco Systems likes to put it, "Customers get connected and businesses get interested; businesses get connected and customers get interested; and the more nodes that are connected to the Internet, the more benefits that are provided for customers and businesses." But on the other hand, with all these choices, attracting customers to the needed "connection" and keeping them there is a challenge, and one which often carries a staggering price tag. Moreover, customers could be easily misguided by situations in which, for example, a big company and small company are promoting the same product, or a small company is promoting an imitation product.

Facing such a metamorphosis, leading companies have been assigning high priority to CRM activities that focus on making it much easier than ever before to communicate and establish a close relationship with scores of potential and existing customers. Trying to address this need, and specifically targeting e-business, software vendors that specialize in CRM solutions have concentrated their activities in the following main areas:

- Making customers "smarter" (that is, empowering the customer in the digital economy) on a broad basis and, specifically, providing all the necessary elements (for example, ease of use, security, confidentiality, and so on) to make customers feel more comfortable doing business on line.

- Enabling companies to manage customer satisfaction effectively and efficiently by providing all the necessary elements (for example, profiling, content syndication, personalization, and so on) to allow all of the companies' on-line interactions with their customers to be based on the context of who the customer is and what his or her needs are.

Although there are many CRM products on the market today with different degrees of sophistication (as it relates to the mentioned areas), the key idea is the same. You enhance the chances for improved customer satisfaction by managing the fulfillment of performance promises and the quality of the interaction with the customer on the Internet. The quality of the interaction with the customer is based on the understanding of what the customer really wants, which, in turn, leads to better fulfillment. The more intensive the Internet-based contact, the more chances are introduced to accomplish the following four main goals:

1. Getting to know the customer's needs (for example, using detailed information about customers to market to them in an aggressive, highly targeted, and personalized way).

2. Convincing customers to initiate revenue-generating transactions (for example, buying goods or clicking on banner ads).

3. Decreasing customer migration rates through increased customer involvement (for example, building customer loyalty by making it easy for customers to do business with the company on the Internet).

4. Becoming attractive for potential customers through personalization (for example, enabling one-to-one marketing by offering several types of content or selling products aimed at different target customers).

Solutions with a comprehensive set of "getting-to-know-the-customer" functionalities will play an essential role in enabling e-business because only such solutions allow organizations to manage the customer relationship efficiently and effectively.

Blurring Lines at Corporate Boundaries— Engineering the Virtual Enterprise

In an earlier section, the notion of "virtualization" was introduced as one of the most exciting and overreaching organizational schemas of the future. Fundamentally, e-business is, first and foremost, about breaking all kinds of "walls"—internal corporate "walls" that exist between functional departments, but, more importantly, external "walls" that limit companies' willingness and actual abilities to engage in new business relationships and accept new ideas.

These new business relationships are evolving in multiple directions as electronic business communities in the form of open trading marketplaces, or VEs, in which buyers, sellers, and brokers of goods and services come together to exchange information, obtain specific knowledge, and conduct transactions. Hand in hand with new Internet technology, these new organizational forms offer partners the largest set possible of market opportunities by linking unbundled parts of the value chain that have been optimized to provide the efficient service demanded by consumers through flexible collaboration between independent market-driven entities.

Shattering traditional organizational principles in manufacturing, construction, consumer goods, and other industries that concentrate on providing goods or services, the VE paradigm will forever change the business landscape. Long-lasting business alliances, which make up the bulk of today's commercial world, will simply go away, to be replaced by all kinds of temporary (potentially, relatively short-lived) partnerships of small- to medium-sized firms engaged in dynamic, project-oriented relationships.

Therefore, companies that want to be successful in the twenty-first century will have to master the principles of such an organizational paradigm, its behavior model, its information flow patterns, and the information technology environment and infrastructure that help support its collaboration requirements—as well as start using all of this to their competitive advantage. This is the stuff of business strategy for the future.

Currently, leading companies have been experimenting with the following three models of VE that, practically speaking, represent the concept at its different stages of evolution toward a total VE behavior. Many companies have profited by a modular usage of these models already.

Extended Enterprises

The *extended enterprise* concept is based on an organizational form that is a union of scattered functions that are fulfilled within a group of cooperating organizations. The main objectives of the union are to cut down costs and response delays, to increase responsive behavior and flexibility toward customer demands, to optimize logistics, and to increase the value added by each organization involved in both intraenterprise process-related transactions and in the extended enterprise as a whole. A broad-based analysis of best practices in relation to such models suggests that the most critical success factor here is the establishment of the "leading company" role, with concrete responsibilities to ensure consistency of business processes through a full command of processes and information systems.

Customer-Focused Partnerships and Joint Ventures

The primary focus here is on direct liaisons between suppliers and customers. Typically, this model is engineered to closely resemble the so-called built-to-order marketplaces, which permit, among many things, fulfilling market needs for "customized" mass-produced goods by implementing very responsive organizational formats. It requires a new organizational structure to be built based on a VE-focused framework of enterprise integration, which establishes new relationships between the different functions and units. The new structure must include all those parts of partner organizations that are considered "chains" of SCM-dependent internal and external relationships.

Alliances and Enterprise Communities

This organizational form is not new, although it has extended in multiple ways for e-business through the introduction of so-called *e-marketplaces*. It is based on the old principle of "increasing power by gathering." Globalization of industries and intense competition are forcing even competing companies to gather and work together in order to cut costs, to cover a wider range of services, or to strengthen their sales forces. Effective alliance management is becoming a key critical success factor for such forms of VE. This includes not only "matching up" partners, but also many important features for decision making—in particular, alliance enforcement (for example, enforcing its governing rules), ensuring consistency of purpose, and partnership learning.

This generalized classification only provides a first guidance. It is possible to combine and derive these models, and to invent many variants.

The concept of VE holds great promise for revolutionizing the ways we organize and interconnect on an extended enterprise basis. But between the theory of VE and the actuality of VE creation and use lie many rocky roads upon which it is very easy to stumble. VE initiatives should not be undertaken without iterations, tests, and measurements to determine the best possible scenarios in each of the following essential areas:

- **Formalization of Organization and Management**—The tactic for control of close collaborations between companies and organizations, addressing both people and organizational issues of extended enterprises.

- **Business and Systems Integration**—The process of integrating the whole life cycle of a product or service from initial conception to final disposal at a business process level and facilitating the integration of global activities (supplying, transforming, marketing) concurrently to overcome frictions of distance, time, and work cultures.

- **Pervasive Collaboration**—The ability to provide universal real-time access (anytime, anywhere—at home, in the office, on the road) to human experts, as well as to knowledge, information, design tools, decision-support tools, and so on.

- **Technology Adoption**—The strategy of implementing a broad base of information technologies in ways that enable all the capabilities (this is far more difficult than it was when boundaries for integration resided within the same organization).

Understanding the Impact of Technology

Although the previous sections have touched on the subject of IT only in broad strokes, at this point in our discussion it should be clear that in this heady age of "e-verything," IT is forging a complete transformation of the most fundamental business concepts. It impacts every aspect of companies' lives—how companies do business, how industries get established, how new markets get established and how companies enter these new markets, and so on. Therefore, as a company progresses down the e-business strategy road to the "strategy of choice" vision, obtaining and maintaining a proper sense of direction toward IT is becoming one of the primary concerns.

The technology developments that unfold in the world of e-business can be thrilling and disorienting. One understandable reaction is to wonder: What is the more important factor for achieving success in the new economy—the "e" part (specifically, focusing on the technology side) or the "business" part (specifically, making e-business the primary way of doing business)?

The answer is both. The economics of e-business begin, of course, with technology—the Internet, the "central nervous system of the world." The Internet, with its global data network and low-cost, easy-to-use tools, has opened up e-business opportunities for everyone. You don't have to be a big corporation with a well-known brand or a company with lots of available financial and human resources to start playing the "game." There is no question that technology is making the vision of e-business possible, customers' experience more convenient and enjoyable, and many companies wealthier in the process.

But the real power of the Internet is not its rich technological environment. The real power of the Internet is its products—information and communication that enable you to build and maintain stronger relationships with your customers and business partners.

E-business, as a new dynamic business model, is driven by information, and more specifically, by information exchange that connects people, processes, and organizations, leading to better communication, cost savings, and other "well-advertised" business benefits. The real appeal of e-business is its ability to disseminate highly targeted and segmented content (goods and services), creating superior customer value as well as economic value. Rather than simply focusing on Internet-based hardware and software, organizations that undertake an e-business initiative must start simultaneously investing in business and organizational process changes that unlock the true value of these new technologies.

Over the past few years, even as the hype over the role IT plays in e-business has been dominated by the louder voices of "cheerleaders," a new, more pragmatic view has taken shape. The following discussion seeks to articulate some of the important principles behind that view, which I have come to call "e-technorealism."

The term *technorealism* was introduced by many contemporaries to force a critical frame of thinking regarding technology in general, as well as the role that tools and interfaces play in human evolution and everyday life. Integral to this frame of thinking is an understanding that any substantial technological transformation (for example, the automobile), while important and powerful, is a "mixed blessing" that comes with profound benefits as well as substantial costs.

Applying such a perspective to today's emerging Internet-based technologies is extremely important because it puts us on guard for unexpected consequences that must be addressed by thoughtful design and appropriate use. Once all the fanfare about Internet-based technologies dies down, success in a company's e-business strategy ultimately will boil down to one stark reality check: how much value the company is able to derive from managing the contents of e-business interactions as assets.

What follows is a set of evolving basic principles that could infuse a proper dose of "e-technorealism" into a company's IT strategy. Such an infusion is necessary in order to arrive at a pragmatic view of the issues related to enabling e-business with IT.

- **Enterprise architecture drives the implementation strategy of Internet technologies**—In e-business, too much is happening too fast or a "strategy-first" approach. Rather, organizations should develop an enterprise architecture that defines the "overreaching" technological blueprint, based upon specific adaptive and highly effective strategies.

- **Clear understanding of technology terms and formal definitions *does* matter**—In a world overloaded with buzzwords, nothing will make sense if people don't understand technology terms and fundamental definitions. Nowadays, in the IT industry, when you start to raise questions about basic concepts, you ask 10 people and get 21 answers. Understanding concepts is the key and puts you high on the learning curve.

- **A company does not differentiate itself by Internet technologies per se, but by how effectively it uses them to amplify value**—Following the hottest trends and introducing the "latest and greatest" technologies to bring up fancy Web storefronts that focus on making good impressions or performing transactions does not create competitive advantage. It is only those efforts aiming at enabling powerful on-line information dissemination services that are capable of strongly differentiating companies from their competitors. Popular Web sites such as Yahoo! or Lycos provide excellent models for the types of services that have to be enabled, most importantly, facilitating information aggregation, "personalization," and targeted distribution of information to internal and external users, especially customers.

- **IT cannot afford to have a "strategic investment plan" on its own—** Unfortunately, in order to demonstrate a commitment to e-transformation, many companies are establishing a separate strategic investment plan for IT that, in most cases, forces them to reallocate or cut critical investments in other areas. This is one of the biggest mistakes that a company can make while strategizing for e-business. The overall application of IT to e-business should be categorized as "enabling infrastructure services" within a company's overall strategic investment plan, one that should include a comprehensive set of underlying business model reengineering efforts required to support IT initiatives. Only then can tighter coupling between enterprise functions be ensured.

- **Internet technologies cannot "sit" nicely apart from their everyday counterparts and everyday IT business as a whole—**Too often, companies have a separate strategy geared toward Internet technologies, and dedicated teams, sometimes even outside of traditional IT organizations that are trying to figure out that strategy. This is another example of the biggest mistake that a company can make in its strategizing for e-business. It is not possible to achieve a successful e-business transformation without setting a very precise "frame of business" for the entire IT—that is, establishing an "integrated business environment" (IBE). An IBE should consist of systems support for the integration of back-end enterprise systems, such as enterprise resource planning (ERP), with front-end, customer-facing systems and tools mostly governed by Internet technologies. Moreover, IBE should include the systems needed to support collaboration and decision making between different organizations and teams. Finally, IBE should include systems support for the integration of strategic planning, marketing, product definition, and all other critical business processes into the overall information supply chain so that all information exchange activities are integrated into the e-business model. In a nutshell, the "pithy" message here is "Think one goal, one strategy, one team."

■ **Integration is not just the "plumbing" between systems, processes, and people**—The Internet is driven by the flow of information, and because of this, the interfaces—and the underlying integration technologies that make information visible between systems, processes, and people—are becoming enormously important. However, let's take a look at the preceding principle, which briefly introduced the concept of IBE. IBE is much more than just the flow ("pumping") of information. It is what I would call "Internet plus." It has characteristics of an "integrated communication workflow model." In order to understand such models, let's use coronary networks that are pumping blood as an analogy. There are two very important components in coronary networks: the heart (the organ responsible for pumping blood throughout the body) and cardiac enzymes (complex, unification-based substances capable of speeding up certain biochemical processes in the cardiac muscle—abnormal levels of these enzymes signal heart attacks). Similarly, IBE needs a "unification-based" engine or platform for managing the information flow and the information dissemination process, or else the whole e-business infrastructure will become disorganized and ineffective.

■ **Internet technologies for e-business are not neutral**—There is a widespread misconception, fueled by technology vendors and all kinds of systems integrators, that Internet technologies are completely free of bias—that they don't promote certain kinds of techniques and processes as far as e-business behaviors are concerned. In truth, technologies come loaded with both intended and unintended "views" toward e-business. For example, every tool provides its users with a particular vendor's view of how e-business interactions and information dissemination should be happening. As a result, when evaluating technological solutions, it is important to consider the biases of various technologies and to seek out those that reflect your company's specific views on e-business behaviors.

■ **Internet technologies are revolutionary and ordinary at the same time**—To a large degree, Internet technologies represent a combination of extraordinary application development tools with easy-to-use user interfaces, rich graphics, three-dimensional visualization, artificial intelligence, powerful publishing and content production, and a range of other "technological wonders." Yet as more and more applications that use such technologies become production-type systems, this new generation of IT not only increasingly resembles in all its complexity the previous one, the client-server, but even supersedes it. For every empowering or enlightening aspect of Internet technologies, there are also dimensions that are rather ordinary and basically routine—for example, managing all aspects of the development life cycle (especially move-to-production aspects), performance monitoring, capacity planning, and so on. But, in the case of e-business, these routine tasks are more complex and time-consuming than before. Remembering this principle could be very helpful when dealing with IT staff issues.

■ **Technology standards and interoperability issues are too important to be entrusted to software vendors alone**—Internet-focused software firms have demonstrated their substantial interests in enabling and preserving those open standards such as XML (eXtensible Markup Language) that are essential to a fully functioning interactive network. Unfortunately, the truth is that they are not necessarily ready to ensure interoperability at the levels that e-business requires. E-business requires moving beyond proprietary solutions with "embedded" standards toward optimized, standardized kinds of building blocks. The good metaphor here would be the toy Lego. Basically, the key strategy behind Internet-based software should be modularity, resembling that of a child's Lego set: Different building blocks of such software should fit together in any combination to support the specific needs of a particular process group or application. Therefore, flexibility to the highest degree, the ability to "lock, dock, load, and go"—this is the urgent message that customers should be sending to software vendors.

■ **Information is not knowledge; proliferation of information is a serious challenge**— "Information overload" is a phrase we hear more than ever. As the Internet pervades more of our lives, we find numerous indications that decision makers are starving for information in a glut of messy data. You may know the situation by the name "cyberspace data smog." We must not confuse the thrill of acquiring or distributing information quickly with the more daunting task of converting it into knowledge. To be useful, information has to be organized, summarized, and customized from the content interpretation standpoint. "Just enough, just in time" is the key.

Seeing e-Business Infrastructure as a Living System That Is Part of a Large, Expanding, Networked Ecosystem

Basically, the entire discussion in Chapter 1 has one particular goal—to dispel some very common misunderstandings about the nature of e-business and its value proposition, and clearly communicate one of the main lines of this book—that, first and foremost, e-business is information age business. As a result, the amount of knowledge and data relevant to Internet-based interactions and the processes that govern those interactions is rapidly becoming more valuable than physical assets exchanged over the Internet.

From the IT evolution perspective, until very recently, information age principles have been the domain of "legacy" data architecture-centric concepts such as information resource management (IRM), information engineering (IE), and so on, which unfortunately are now almost forgotten. As such, the majority of what is published and accepted about the e-business technological infrastructure has been very much Web-centric and not data-centric.

Information age ideals, however, demand us to bring "data centricity" back into the Internet. Managing e-business infrastructure from data-centric perspectives represents a major opportunity for IT organizations to have a positive impact.

It is possible and necessary, I think, to analyze the processes underlying e-business relationships from data-centric perspectives to see whether such an approach will suggest larger issues and management strategies inherent in this new communications environment that we call "cyberspace."

I define cyberspace as that conceptual information-based ecosystem where all data ("potential information") is stored. It also is that infrastructure environment where all information workers exist and function. If we accept the notion that cyberspace is an ecosystem, then in order to better comprehend its principles, we can turn to the models suggested by general systems theory, that is, cybernetics. *Cybernetics* is a science that covers, as its domain, the design or discovery and application of the principles of regulation and communication in systems of any nature that are capable of receiving, storing, and processing information for regulation and control. Given the emphasis on the concepts of process, system, environment, and user participation, cybernetics was able to gain substantial influence as a theoretical model for articulating the systematic relationships and processes among feedback, loop-driven systems including computers, networks, and humans.

Cybernetics tells us that information is "energy" that needs to be consumed and processed by a system in order for it to survive, to reproduce its key elements, and, as part of a larger ecosystem, contribute to that system in ways that enhance other systems or members of the ecosystem at large. In the case of cyberspace, information workers draw data resources from the Internet, process that data, and release it as information back into that ecosystem environment where other workers utilize it. The success of utilizing the information from a standpoint of enhancing the ecosystem at large, as in any system that includes people and organizational structures, depends upon effective resolution of issues introduced by tightly coupled collaboration between three major components of the system:

- Financial aspects (for example, investments, costs, and profits)

- Technological aspects (for example, the entire infrastructure domain of the system)

- Organizational aspects (for example, personalities and their specific roles and zones of influence and responsibility)

Cybernetics also tells us that introducing an evolutionary architecture is the best process for managing these major components effectively. It proposes the model of nature (precisely the model of ecosystems) as the generating force for architectural form. The profligate prototyping and awesome creative power of natural evolution are emulated by creating virtual architectural models that respond to changing environments. Successful developments are encouraged and evolved. Architecture is considered as a form of artificial life, subject, like the natural world, to principles of morphogenesis (for example, encapsulation, inheritance, polymorphism, and so on—very much like the object-oriented principles widely talked about nowadays), generic coding, replication, and selection. I have to quickly point out that for information systems architectures, an architect's "blueprint" is a set of generic instructions ("ideas") that are dependent on a particular environmental context for their interpretation, whereas in other systems (e.g., construction), an architect's blueprint is a specific one-off set of plans.

Stressing the importance of enterprise architectural models to e-business success is another major line of this book. It is no accident that it is the number-one principle on the list of principles of "e-technorealism" presented in an earlier section. The enterprise architecture model is an inherent growth strategy that defines both the manner in which the enterprise elaborates its business rules and the resulting business model.

It is ironic that many e-business initiatives actually lack the methodological incisiveness that generic systems theory analogies imply. Only through a comprehensive architecture is it possible to introduce the badly needed form of component-based rationalization and methodology that embraces a generic approach, a modular coordination, and a perception of technology infrastructure as a toolkit of parts. Unfortunately, to the contrary, the systems development profession—and the IT industry as a whole—has failed to embrace this concept at the proper levels and learn from architecture's influence and the progress it has made in many technology-intensive industries (for example, aircraft and automotive). Systems development remains a "free-lancing" activity. It still has not made the transition to a truly modeling-intensive industry with adequate research and development capabilities. Systems development has been left largely to individual programmers who make choices of proper design and prototyping that, usually, are done in an uncoordinated and "artistic" manner. Such an approach brings inevitable failures with serious consequences (the topics of e-business architecture and related recommendations are covered in detail in Chapter 2).

E-Business Challenges and the Dynamics of Today's Markets

In order to round off Chapter 1, one more point needs to be discussed. E-business is a challenge for all companies, but it is particularly difficult for the following two categories:

1. Small and small-to-medium businesses in highly competitive, but mostly traditional markets (for example, consumer goods, retail, financial services, and so on) that are trying to create a substantial Internet presence in order to stay competitive.

2. Businesses of any size, large or small, which operate in high-velocity markets. These markets are emergent (blurred boundaries, competition, viable business models), transforming (major shifts in technology, government regulation, and so on), or hypercompetitive (oligopoly of aggressive competitors). Many high-profile companies, products, or people (that readers have heard of, know about from personal experience, or

can easily identify with) represent high-velocity markets. The Dell Computer Corporation, Acer in Canada, Brøderbund Software, Inc., and many new faces of colliding and competing players in the electronic brokerage and high-energy network services (for example, Internet Virtual Private Networks or I-VPN) industries illustrate the important kinds of strategic challenges managers face in transitioning to the digital economy in these markets.

What are the strategic challenges facing the cited types of companies? In the case of small companies in traditional markets, the biggest challenges involve struggling to attract customers to the company's Web storefront, ensuring customer loyalty, and determining the best role to play in the value chain as a member of an e-market. For these companies, finding effective solutions to these challenges is a big challenge in itself because of constrained financial and, most importantly, human resources needed to acquire expertise.

In the case of high-velocity markets, the e-business challenges are even bigger because of the following two critical factors introduced and imposed by the dynamics of such markets:

- Key performance driver is the ability to change (most importantly, technologically)—to adapt, to construct temporary business relationships, to anticipate new market opportunities, and perhaps even to set the pace of change.

- Key performance metrics are time-driven: time pacing, rhythm (for example, life cycle), past and future, and so on.

For the companies cited, the ability to change and time management are the two most critical success factors in e-business transformation. Again, embracing the concept of enterprise architecture to drive implementation strategies is the number-one priority here.

Strategic Technology Blueprint for e-Business

By the time you finish this book, there will have been multiple high-profile examples of e-business failures, involving mostly dot-com companies. For example, in Europe, Boo.com, a fashion goods e-commerce site, and Net Imperative, a trade news and comparison-shopping site, are no longer in business, accumulating between them over $1 billion in debt. In the United States, Reel.com, a video and DVD site, on-line event planner eParties.com, and Toysmart.com, a highly publicized site for toys, educational materials, and Disney games, have closed their doors after running short of money and investor interest.

Nevertheless, no one should interpret such events as evidence that, fundamentally, the concept of e-business is wrong or it's one more "silver bullet" that will disappear soon. On the contrary, e-business will continue to grow with unprecedented speed, and many more companies will enter the race, especially traditional "brick-and-mortar" firms. The Internet has created a new, completely electronic economy. As with any economy, this one has unique business and financial models, strategies, structures, politics, organizational cultures, combatants, regulations, opportunities, challenges, and real problems. In this sense, as the new digital economy is gaining steam, there will be a lot of big winners. Unfortunately, though, there will be more losers, primarily due to deficient business and technology strategies, poorly managed implementations, failures of business process reengineering, unclear views or misjudgments of what customers really want, and the use of inadequate technology (or the misuse of technology altogether).

Chapter 2 continues the discussion started in Chapter 1, with a specific emphasis on providing additional insights and a better understanding about critical aspects of designing your company's strategic technology blueprint for e-business transformation.

Where Do You Start?

An e-business strategic technology blueprint (architecture) defines all the technologies, application systems, components, and interfaces that enable and support an e-business model. As was articulated in Chapter 1 (within the context of e-business), although IT is the prime driver, IT development (as well as IT planning) depends upon a vastly broadened look at changes in business practices influenced by the new e-business models. Such a look allows us to culminate with detailed requirements for a technology solution needed to enable a successful transformation to the new economy. In other words, the process of designing a strategic architecture involves going from business objectives to technology infrastructure choices, not the other way around.

As a result (see Figure 2.1), the cited process is a step-by-step hierarchical process with a feedback loop, consisting of four categories of macrolevel analysis (assessment) of:

- **Business Objectives**—Examination of specific company goals based on the chosen e-business model, combined with primary impact factors and strategic ideas for improving competitiveness and increasing efficiency.

- **Best Practices of Technology Leverage for e-Business**—Examination of how leading corporations are leveraging IT and new Internet tools to achieve significant business value.

- **E-Business Strategic Technology Architecture (EBSTA) and Its Functional Levels**—Definition of all the technologies, application systems, components, and interfaces that enable and support an e-business model.

- **Justification**—Analysis of financial and nonfinancial benefits.

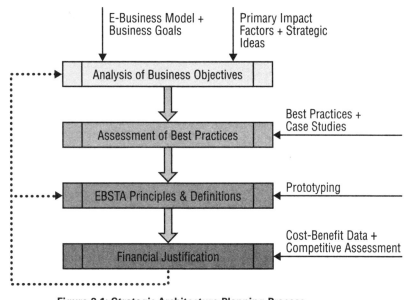

Figure 2.1: Strategic Architecture Planning Process

These few steps comprise a methodology, that is, an organized process, to perform strategic IT architecture planning. When sufficient understanding of macrolevel impacts of e-business, combined with knowledge about specific business objectives, is obtained, an architectural background is generally superior. Within such a background, we shall be able to formulate an effective technology architecture, reinforcing changes in business practices and in the underlying information technologies.

An effective EBSTA provides two crucial benefits in regard to e-business transformation. First, it enables more rapid time to market, better investment protection against technology shifts, scalability, robustness, adaptability to change, and, ultimately, an e-business environment that is business-oriented, rather than technology-centric. Second, it aligns the technology infrastructure to the business model and business processes; ensures that the various components of technology, systems, and processes work cohesively; and provides a roadmap for its implementation.

Macrolevel Analysis of Business Objectives

The economics of e-business are driven by the desire to improve competitiveness at as low a cost as possible. In recent years, three of the most influential principles of competitiveness have become well established for companies in any industry and in any type of business:

- **Product Differentiation**—In the on-line economy, especially in emerging and high-volatility markets, in order to capture increased market share, it is absolutely vital that product differentiation be achieved and maintained through constant attention to innovation in essential value, brand development, and value adding with complementary products and services.

- **Intermediation Capabilities**—The inherent pressure of the Internet to transform many products and services into commodities, the disintermediation of traditional distributors, and the evolution of new distributors (reintermediation) who are specifically organized for new ways of doing business are fundamental unbalancing factors in terms of competitiveness and differentiation. A distribution strategy that leverages new intermediaries or establishes a company itself as a new intermediary is among the most important factors to incorporate into a strategic business plan for e-business.

- **Customer Service and Customer Base Development**—Clearly, providing the best possible customer service has been always one of the most well-known methods of achieving differentiation. With the Internet, this factor has become even more influential because the balance of power is shifting toward the customer. True customer loyalty, although it is now much harder to obtain and sustain, is a function of convenience: the availability of full self-service, with an easy way to get human assistance if needed, and, most importantly, having a sense of being served "personally." It is therefore necessary to personalize the experience of customer support as much as possible, starting with little things, like programming the Web site to address customers by name, and working up to providing content and services based on knowing the patterns of customer behavior. Refining customer support tactics literally person by person, in real time, using personalization technologies, is a necessity, not an option.

Realization of all these principles leads many companies to accept that e-business represents the greatest opportunity and the greatest challenge that they have to urgently address. Responding to these challenges requires the support of a solid and innovative technology infrastructure that is capable of ensuring the success of a company's differentiation strategy to drive profitability in the digital economy.

In addition to differentiation, many other business objectives must be addressed, focusing on maximizing profitability through increased efficiency.

In e-business, quite simply, the best areas for improving efficiency are fulfillment (make it faster) and transaction costs (make cost per transaction cheaper). As a result, there is no better strategy than to examine each type of business-to-business or business-to-consumer transaction within a company's value chain and assess whether it should and could be done more efficiently in an Internet environment.

There is general consensus that, from the perspective of e-business, both technological and methodological development of companies will set more and more demands on the flow and management of information. Effective information management will be one of the key factors in maximizing profitability. This means know-how and real-time accessibility of information. Extending beyond the traditional organizational boundaries, a vast number of technologies can be used to allow in-depth cost analysis of performance across the enterprise, down to single transactions and single positions. This analysis can incorporate a variety of factors and can be performed on a real-time basis, capturing volatile market conditions that affect the value of the cost components. Successful companies already utilize such technologies as a strategic means of increasing efficiency. The in-depth cost analysis of performance across the enterprise forms an essential tool in the development of processes in companies, allowing the elimination of unnecessary processes and simplifying the entire operation. An effective technology infrastructure maximizes profitability by decreasing inefficiencies in business processes and monitoring costs at all interaction points of the value chain.

In many cost-sensitive industries (e.g., manufacturing), when addressing the issue of defining a strategy for improving efficiency, many managers look to information technology for easy answers without rethinking their conventional product development, manufacturing, and distribution strategies. There is strong consensus that the strategy process has to be balanced by a business process reengineering force—the evolution of new business processes and models that are tailor-made for the digital world.

Looking at Business Processes and Relationships

The term *business process reengineering* (BPR) has been put aside since the popularity of the Internet soared. Many people wish it would be forgotten altogether. After all, not very many such projects have really succeeded (mostly because we did not want them to succeed in the first place). It is because we were afraid to change. If you think we can afford to not embrace BPR now, with the Internet, however, you are totally mistaken. BPR is poised for a big comeback. E-business transformation cannot be accomplished without the close alignment of the technology infrastructure to the business model, and business processes cannot be transformed without BPR.

Clearly, in the past, the majority of BPR projects have failed, largely because of a lack of employee support and the massive personnel retraining required; technology challenges have also contributed to failure. BPR requires linking incompatible computer systems across the enterprise, enabling the sharing of information easily and cheaply. Luckily, the same is required for e-business.

For a company to succeed with an e-business transformation, BPR needs to be fully embraced. BPR should be viewed as a pervasive and powerful approach to effecting the transition strategy, innovation, and performance improvement objectives in the enterprise.[1] Although the current implementation of many Internet technologies (such as Web-based storefronts, electronic ordering, electronic catalogs, and so on) is triggering the redesign of business processes (for example, sales and marketing, procurement, order management, and so on), too often it is after the fact. The end result is lost opportunities and less-than-expected outcomes from new technologies.

What should be happening before the Internet technologies are brought in? There should be detailed analyses of existing business processes to determine the proper ways to integrate the new Internet technologies into process redesign and to ensure that such technologies are not simply "injected" into a potentially insufficient process. Such an approach facilitates the focused use of technology in process redesign and establishes a framework for close alignment of the technology infrastructure to the business model and business processes.

Prior BPR efforts have shown that much better results in terms of technology alignment are obtained when the majority of business processes involved in commercial relationships (for example, procurement, purchasing, logistics, sales, marketing, manufacturing, customer support, and so on) are analyzed as an integrated whole, as opposed to being assessed individually. When processes are assessed in an integrated fashion, all-important interrelationships, such as logical synergies between redesign alternatives, complementary technologies, human interactions, information flows, and so on, are taken into consideration. Understanding these relationships is very important in order to focus redesign activities on those process activities that offer the greatest potential to leverage new Internet technologies.

Best Practices of Technology Leverage for e-Business: From Architecture to Strategy

According to META Group's analysis,[2] "While most near-term Global 2000 EC strategies will target value chain initiatives (procurement, EDI/XML, externalization, dynamic trading network evolution, extranets, business collaboration), complex sell side (for example, Web branding, affiliations, order management, Web-based distribution) and customer relationship-focused efforts (for example, bill payment/presentment, multi-brand communities, integrated self-service) initiated in 1999–2000 will drive investment through 2003."

In light of this statement, the following discussion will focus on examining how leading corporations are leveraging IT and new Internet tools to achieve significant business value. Nevertheless, this examination is not meant to be inclusive of every practice that an organization should be adopting with regard to IT strategies. Rather, it is meant to highlight the critical (most used) strategies that can help companies achieve significant improvement of efficiency across their organizations within multiple e-business models and across a variety of industries (e.g., telecommunications, consumer products, legal, public utilities, software vendors, and so on).

Before we proceed, one important statement from Chapter 1 has to be reiterated here. Although many companies have made dramatic improvements in efficiency and differentiation—often gaining double-digit increases in profitability—I do not know of one instance where measurable successes have occurred without overhauling a company's strategic planning processes and simultaneously merging them with the strategic technology architecture planning process to reflect the e-business economy-accelerating business cycle. Moreover, long-term business strategy becomes an on-going, iterative, event-driven process, driven by the architecture and fed by the continuous evolution of Internet technologies.

Figure 2.2 illustrates in broad strokes the relationship between business value and time to implement Internet technologies (and their cost, as a result) for the most popular areas of process improvement:

- **Intranets and Web-Based Document Management**—Implementation of self-service intranets to replace manual, paper-based processes and the paper forms in human resources, training, marketing, purchasing, and so on is often the first area where Internet technologies are introduced to improve effectiveness, especially in companies that depend upon document management as a core business process (for example, insurance, financial services, legal, health care).

- **Sales Force Automation**—Internet-based automation of information-intensive sales processes that handle prospects, contracts, custom deals, pricing, and other activities that facilitate sales can deliver significant ROI.

- **Order Management**—Electronic self-service ordering and electronic catalog management are among the most popular areas for all companies that sell products or claim processing companies (for example, insurance and health care).

- **Inventory and Configuration Management**—This is very popular area for leveraging Internet technologies, especially for large multinational companies that sell products worldwide.

- **Electronic Bill Presentation and Payment**—Bill presentation and electronic payment are favorite areas for customer care-focused companies in telecommunications and financial services industries.

- **Customer Support**—Web-based and integrated with intelligent problem knowledge bases and problem management applications, self-service customer support services generally provide very high business value. This category includes all kinds of on-line services, such as 24-hour service and support information, the ability to check product availability and track accounts or stock portfolios, the availability of timely news and service updates, and so on.

- **Distribution and Service Channel Automation**—Implementation of extranet-based systems is highly beneficial to any company that sells products or services through a network of dealerships, franchises, or brokers.

- **Financial Reporting, Analysis, and Decision Support**—Web-based integrated reporting systems can give decision makers access to real-time or consolidated information, customized to present the right information to the right decision maker at the right time.

- **Value Chain Integration**—Overall, analyses of best practices have shown that the single greatest efficiency to be gained by Internet technology deployment is value chain integration. Through this strategy, each point of information flow is optimized (for example, bidirectional, secure passing of quality data is guaranteed) across all transaction points from the end customer up the value chain through all the suppliers. Value chain integration allows for substantial improvement of profitability by affecting multiple factors simultaneously (for example, tremendous cost savings, increased sales opportunities, improved customer service, and so on).

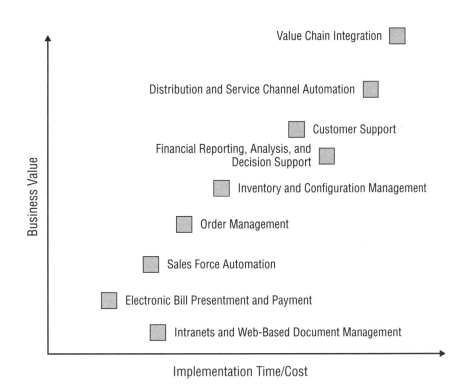

Figure 2.2: Relationship between Business Value and Implementation Time

Clearly, much has been written about how leading companies have been benefiting from Internet technology deployment. Again and again we have been hearing about such examples as Dell Computer or Amazon.com. The hype around these and similar companies that succeeded "big" in the new economy is so extreme that it is appropriate to ask the question: Is it really the case that Internet technologies are delivering astonishing results? The answer is a definite "Yes!" What makes it possible, though, is really not the technology itself. It is when businesses are putting a lot of rigor into examining their business processes and business models to determine how they can leverage information technology to gain a competitive edge. It is when they are tapping into solid e-business technology architecture. It is when they are adopting new differentiation strategies through close integration of their architecture with their overall business strategy. Only then do these businesses find that they can provide better products and services, and even new products and services—faster and at a lower cost.

The Notion of e-Services

Over the past decade, there have been a number of important advances in computer-based technologies, such as high throughput networks and distributed processing infrastructure capable of supporting a wide collection of underlying protocols and standards, including transmission control protocol/Internet protocol (TCP/IP), Internet interobject protocol (IIOP), remote procedure call (RPC), distributed computing environment (DCE), Common Request Broker Architecture (CORBA), and remote method invocation (RMI). These advances have led to many new tools, processes, techniques, and commercial technologies that brought to light a revolutionary concept of assembling software-intensive solutions: component-based development. More and more, we see organizations turning to components as a way to encapsulate critical application functionality for automating business processes within autonomous "building blocks" that can be easily integrated and deployed in order to build new services to support emerging business processes.[3]

Component-based development has encouraged a "component" view of the Internet as a deployment target for highly autonomous service-oriented systems of all kinds, supporting commercial transactions, information gathering and dissemination, and many forms of specific on-line services.

As a consequence of these technology drivers, what a company may expect from IT as a competitive advantage and as a significant asset is quite different now than it was only a few years ago. In fact, evolving views of the Internet as a growing ecosystem of building blocks, and the understanding that these building blocks will become increasingly intelligent services offered commercially by various companies, are having a deep impact on many aspects of business in the beginning of the twenty-first century.

It didn't take long until a new concept (model) for "commercializing" autonomous service-oriented systems was born, termed *e-services*. Hewlett-Packard (HP) introduced the concept of "e-services" a couple of years ago, and since then it has been refined and extended by many leading software and hardware vendors with substantial presence in the marketplace, such as Sun Microsystems, IBM, and Ariba.

In terms of a formal definition, HP contributed the following[4]: "An e-service is any asset that you make available via the Net to

(1) drive new revenue streams

[and/or]

(2) create new efficiencies."

In their most abstract form, "e-services" are very simple to understand (see Figure 2.3).

From a broad-based perspective, HP has envisioned that any resource accessible on the Internet by people, businesses, or even "things," fulfilling a well-defined function, is an e-service.[5] HP has referred to such a future state of the Internet as "Chapter Two of the Internet," in which businesses are pluggable, turnkey, modular, "on the fly," and able to work universally across platforms and hardware—essentially a highly service-oriented Web versus a "do-it-yourself" Web limited to a monolithic, "Web browser–Web server" system.

In its "Chapter Two of the Internet," HP is predicting that the following technology trends will dominate the Internet's landscape for the next three to five years:

■ The extinction of Internet service providers (ISPs) and the proliferation of application service providers (ASPs) through so-called applications-on-tap services for key business functions and the use of a "pay-as-you-go" software revenue model. Companies would not own and run their own mission-critical software; it would be "rented" from the ASP on an as-needed basis, creating a new breed of service provider and potentially reducing a company's overall operating costs.

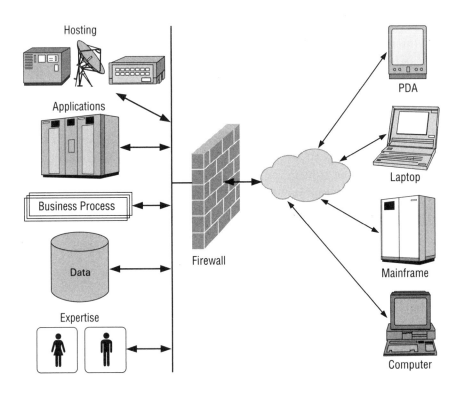

Figure 2.3: E-Services

- The proliferation of new e-services portals in accordance with three major categories: loyalty, vertical, and horizontal portals. E-services portals are envisioned to be massively interconnected Web portals that communicate not only with the content providers who comprise the "base" of the sites, but also with the companies and services those providers rely on to get customers what they want. In the model of e-services, these next-generation portals are intended to act as virtual all-encompassing shopping and service malls, and much more. Let's use an "apartment-renting" portal as an example. Once a customer decides to rent an apartment using such a portal, not only will that portal make sure that the actual apartment will be "free for occupancy" at an agreed date, but it will also communicate that transaction to the other content providers on the portal, giving them an opportunity for a transaction (for example, dispatching orders for transferring utility and phone service).

■ The birth of special types of intermediaries devoted exclusively to the dynamic brokering of e-services, providing "on-the-fly" commercial arrangements for delivery of such services. Envision a world where consumers and businesses will send out requests for services like travel or banking via the Internet. These requests will be accumulated by brokers who, in turn, will connect with companies that offer corresponding e-services and would like to bid to fulfill these requests. Then brokers will return results to the corporate or individual consumer, without requiring any effort on the consumer's part. E-services brokers will have a universal interface: one profile, one log in, and one "face" to the user.

If you are paying much attention to all the talk in the press and the almost boundless enthusiasm in the stock markets for all kinds of e-service offerings, it is easy to get an impression that e-services are something really "new" among the other "hot" concepts of e-business. But in reality, e-services are the representation of an evolution of already established concepts. It is very important to realize that e-services, like everything else in e-business, are about the delivery of information. Any company that would like to offer an e-service has to own or have access to a valuable material that others cannot offer at a lower price. There still is and always will be a need for brokering systems ("intermediaries") that help a user get the information he or she requires at the lowest price. Brokering systems for e-services are the next step in the evolution of well-known "Internet intermediaries" or "aggregators," such as search, news, and community Web sites (Yahoo!, for example, is perhaps the best known intermediary). In many fundamental respects, e-services portals and many other new "portals" emerging every day in all spheres of public life and business, from arts and sciences to vertical industries, are quickly becoming the new "standards" for forms (in terms of shape and type) of presenting distinguished competencies and applications of IT as commercial offerings to the e-business market, forms with higher intangible elements of delivering value and user satisfaction.

The application of e-services has taken the concept one step further, giving birth to the notion of "appliance-based" computing (ABC) popularized intensively by HP.[6] ABC can be viewed as the next level in the evolution of distributed computing, in which the services traditionally provided by general-purpose PC-class computers (for example, laptop, desktop, and workstation-class computers) can be supported by a set of cooperating devices and services. An important difference between ABC and other types of distributed computing is that ABC is exclusively Web-based.

The basic ABC model is shown in Figure 2.4.

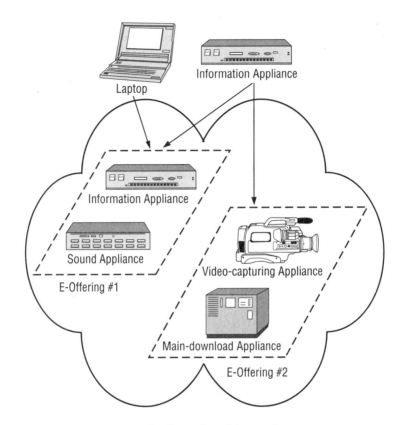

Figure 2.4: Appliance-Based Computing

ABC uses the Web to connect services and appliances (Web devices). An appliance is a device that supports either a singular (very concrete) or a limited set of similar singular tasks, basically a subset of functions from a general-purpose PC. Devices can be accessed either via a Web browser or though peer communications with another device. One important class of appliances has to be mentioned here—information appliances (IA). An information appliance is a device that supports a concrete information-based function: text, graphics, image, video, or sound processing. In ABC, appliances and e-services (for example, specific functions that can be realized using those appliances, like music download) are grouped together based on a physical relationship or configuration. Such groups can be viewed as "offerings." A user receives various offerings, which are then used in a variety of ways.

The core elements of future e-business are e-services and appliance-based computing. While it could be argued that these concepts are very abstract or basic, their value is to ensure that businesses can operate on the Internet as pluggable, turnkey, modular, and "on-the-fly" entities, choosing their focus and delivering appealing and valuable offerings to consumers. Therefore, they must be seen as fundamentals.

E-Business Strategic Technology Architecture

Technology architecture is an umbrella term (another "buzzword") for a formalized approach to systems development. This approach establishes an image of software applications and computing infrastructure that is needed to provide required information solutions that cross and help melt organizational boundaries (in other words, a "concept car" for enterprise systems). Such architectures are not designed simply to meet the specific system needs of a short-term business strategy. Rather, they are geared to a long-term goal, represent a broad perspective, and are designed as a frame to provide a common and flexible base for all the applications in the early stage of their life cycle.

As we arrive at the point of looking at the issue of EBSTA in detail, we have to note the following facts. Although, since the 1980s many organizations have been developing and implementing enterprise architectures using formalized, conceptual architectural concepts (commonly referred to as "reference architectures"), most of this experience is out of date and may not even be reinforced internally. To a large degree, what was done in terms of enterprise architectures has been influenced by the Zachman Enterprise Architecture Model[7] and several similar reference architectures[8-12] that targeted general issues of distributed computing and enterprise IT. As a practical matter, there have been only a few new introductions of formalized architectures specifically targeting e-business transformation. Only one of them, the IBM Application Framework for e-Business,[13] could be viewed as comprehensive reference architecture. Moreover, direct mapping (for example, implementation) of reference architectures to a particular company is a tenuous proposition at best. Existing architectures typically focus on different aspects of macrolevel issues of enterprise IT (for example, mainframe computing versus client-server, thin-client computing versus client-server, and so on) and naturally have different capabilities.

As a result, the topic of EBSTA is a relatively new area for many companies. Consequently, when faced with the challenges of e-business, many companies manage IT from a predominantly tactical viewpoint. Too often, after much study, important architectural constructs and the formal architectural structure become lost in the details of deployment. IT organizations are constantly under pressure to embrace deployment-driven approaches as "enterprise architecture," even when they may not fit the enterprise or be able to align technology with business goals and practices.

While EBSTA-type architecture developed by a company should absorb many of the elements of reference architectures, it is the systematic combination of all the insights that can lead to potentially effective enterprise architecture. The challenge of the EBSTA planning process is to establish a complex, yet structured and formalized, association of procedures, processes and technologies, creating a consistent, valuable technological context for enterprisewide e-business strategy. In order to successfully address this challenge, the focus must be more on the capabilities of architecture than on technological details. By abstracting notions of capability, we can at least match the capabilities of a particular technology to the architecture requirements.

The concept of EBSTA presents a promise of rigor, power, and the ability to guide e-business transformation. But the promise comes at a price: careful planning and implementation. It demands that IT organizations have a clear vision of their goals and set reasonable expectations—not only for the short term, but also for the future. It also requires that they translate those goals and expectations into intelligent decisions about the theoretical concepts they use, the tools they select to implement these concepts, and the management of the overall environment. Figure 2.5 illustrates the major activities of the EBSTA planning process and their milestones:

Step 1: Development and articulation of the EBSTA philosophy and set of architectural principles—Developing a definition of critical capabilities of the architecture, and defining the major architecture components and services that these components must provide.

Step 2: Development of architectural reference models—Developing a set of blueprints that describe the structure and interconnection of major architecture components.

Step 3: Development of the enterprisewide architecture model—Synthesizing an overall blueprint for e-business by assembling and consolidating the various models defined in the previous step.

Step 4: Implementation of a comprehensive systems development methodology—Defining a collection of activities, procedures, and techniques for guiding projects through all phases of the development life cycle (for example, planning, analysis, design, construction, and implementation), as well as focusing on ensuring compliance with the architecture.

Step 5: Development of engineering specifications for critical infrastructure services—Transforming the overall blueprint into detailed specifications by getting down to concrete technologies (for example, application development tools, Web site hardware and software, database software, and so on). Focusing on accurately addressing the requirements of architecture components and outlining specific technology investigations that must be undertaken to finalize and implement the architecture definition.

Step 6: Validation of the architecture—Instituting a three-step validation process. The first step is architecture reviews, during which a small, focused steering committee attempts to understand the overall system requirements and acceptable risk levels, and to review the architecture with respect to business alignment, technology readiness, adherence to standards, and costs. The second step is prototyping to identify and evaluate the technologies and design solutions that are critical to the success of the architecture, with a focus on assessing the technical and cost feasibility of using a particular design solution. The final step is building a pilot application to validate the implementation of the overall architecture and its technical solutions on a small scale.

Step 7: Development and articulation of the architecture transition strategy—Defining the appropriate transition paths for moving from the current computing environment to the target architecture specified by the models. Creating an information infrastructure roadmap is very important because not every company is capable of a fresh start (i.e., replacing the entire existing IT infrastructure).

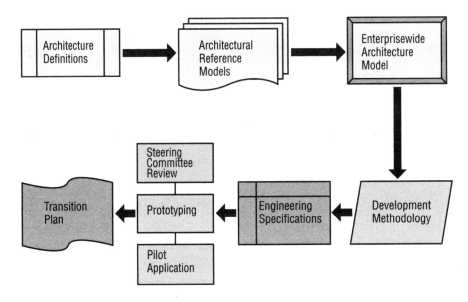

Figure 2.5: EBSTA Planning Process

One area of reference architectures, reflective of open systems implementations, that has received considerable attention in e-business technologies is object orientation (OO). From the architectural perspective, any enterprisewide architecture must embrace fully OO, and in particular, EBSTA-type architectures. Following OO principles enables you to meet many EBSTA requirements (cited in the following list in the form of key infrastructure capabilities), not the least important of which are scalability and platform/tool neutrality. However, the most profound reason for embracing OO is to facilitate reusability. Given the scope of e-business initiatives, reusability is an issue of paramount importance.

The key capabilities of EBSTA-type architectures (Figure 2.6) include the following:

- User Flexibility
- Thin-Client Application Structuring
- Multitiered Application Layering
- Component-Based Application View
- Openness
- Industrial-Strength Capabilities

- Security
- Manageability
- E-Service Enabling

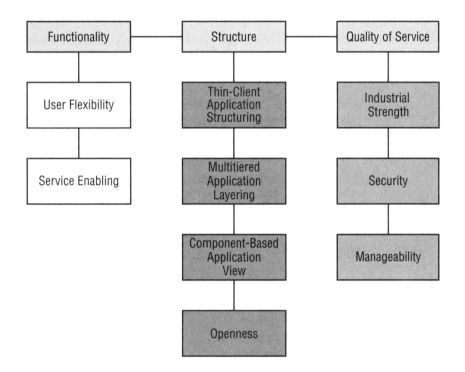

Figure 2.6: EBSTA Characteristics

Each capability is described briefly in the following paragraphs.

User Flexibility

This is a multifactor, interrelated set of characteristics describing the available user connectivity options and productivity features of the user interface. Support for a wide range of connectivity options (for example, enabling users to get access when they need it, regardless of their location or the location of the information) and of virtually any device type (for example, portable and desktop computers, network computers, cellular telephones and hand-held digital devices, and so on) is critical for an effective architecture. Productivity features of the user interface include ease of use (for example, maximizing self-teaching and self-guiding aspects of user interactions) and richness and completeness of the presented content.

Thin-Client Application Structuring

Thin-client application structuring refers to the level of adherence to the principles of thin-client application architecture. E-business systems must be built to adhere 100 percent to the principles of thin-client application architecture. This requirement means full adoption of a browser-only policy toward the user interface's operating environment for accessing e-business application services, and a server-only policy toward the application services' operating environment. It is hard to overestimate the importance of this factor.

Multitiered Application Layering

This is the level of adherence to the principles of the multitiered distributed computing application architecture (MTDCAA). MTDCAA, which is the basis for client-server systems, is an approach of partitioning an application into any number of logical layers (tiers), in which each tier performs a delegated task or series of tasks for which it is best suited. These logical tiers may operate in multiple configurations, using any number of physical systems, thereby providing substantial flexibility and growth potential. As a result, in a multitier structure, the entire application is processed by several cooperative tasks. Until recently, the most popular application organization was based on a three-tier structure, in which the client typically interacts with the user (including the presentation of results), the application server handles the business logic processing, and the database server provides the database functionality. Now, *n*-tier organizations, in which one or more intermediate tiers are used to manage and execute the business logic, have become the *de facto* standard for building robust, high-performance, large-scale distributed systems. Multitiered application layering facilitates the separation of concerns within a business domain, making it possible for application developers to focus on multiple tasks (for example, connectivity, distribution, security, database management, and so on) simultaneously. It also facilitates separation of the intricacies of user interfaces, such as dialog management, details of presentation devices, and so on, from the implementation of core business functions. Multitiered application layering is extremely important for achieving high performance and scalability of both traditional client-server systems and Internet-based applications. It needs to be pointed out that MTDCAA is a totally logical concept, in which each tier may or may not use separate computers for presentations, running business logic, and database accesses.

Component-Based Application View

To be successful, EBSTA-type architectures must facilitate a component-based approach to systems development. Component-based development is the process of designing, assembling, and deploying systems from a variety of independent, functionally discrete pieces (components). The component approach concentrates development efforts on defining the best partitioning scheme for an application, decomposing the conceptual and physical designs of the application into a set of collaborative yet independent "building blocks" according to that scheme, and defining (publishing) interfaces between blocks—for example, formalizing an application programming interface (API). The end result is clear—the components can be provisioned independently, using a variety of technologies, according to the existing standards, such as Microsoft's COM/DCOM, Sun/IBM's Enterprise Java Beans (EJB) specification, and the Object Management Group (OMG) CORBA. The components could be constructed from a newly developed code by wrapping some existing legacy code or data (for example, using new code as an "envelope") or by using an API of a purchased package.

Component-based design is closely aligned and, to a large degree, based upon OO concepts that facilitate the development of isolated reusable functions. Following OO concepts, object-oriented design integrates the data relationships and processing requirements into objects that are fundamental constructs for componentization.

Openness

This refers to the level of compliance with open standards across all of the architecture's interface specifications to ensure portability and platform/tool neutrality. The Internet is based on a wide range of worldwide standards, such as TCP/IP; Internet messaging access protocol (IMAP); hypertext transport protocol (HTTP); hypertext markup language (HTML); extensible markup language (XML), which has evolved from HTML and standard generalized markup language (SGML); and so on. Broad-based utilization of object technologies, Java development tools, CORBA and EJB services, and many other open standard elements and technologies is critical for enabling portability. Portability and platform/tool neutrality are defined here in terms of the ability of critical architecture components to operate without modifications on multiple computing platforms (for example, all major flavors of UNIX, Windows/NT, Linux, and so on) and multiple database servers (for example, DB2, Oracle, Informix, Sybase, Microsoft SQL Server, and so on) and, more importantly, the ability to interoperate with software components from multiple vendors. Full compliance with standard networking protocols is mandatory in order to ensure unlimited connectivity to the Internet economy and the ability to leverage the external outsourced network services (for example, outsourced e-mail or security and network system management services) easily and economically.

Industrial-Strength Capabilities

There is no question that e-business technology solutions must be industrial strength. The business success of many companies depends on this. Given the highly dynamic nature of e-business, technical infrastructure has to be able to constantly keep up with needs, especially in terms of performance and high availability.

Consequently, first and foremost, the architecture has to ensure scalability in terms of the ability of the infrastructure to cope with the increased transaction rate by effectively utilizing additional processing capacities. E-business interactions can grow quickly, both from the transaction rate and the type of processing standpoint (for example, switching suddenly from look-ups and inquiries to updating transactions). Scalability is important for supporting such dynamic processing changes.

Another critical issue for e-business systems is high availability. The nature of the Internet is "to be always on-line, any day, any second." No one can afford downtime. The architecture must ensure that the technology infrastructure is robust and highly reliable.

Security

With the increased role of the Internet as one of the primary means for sharing information and supporting commercial transactions, the need for security has increased significantly. The enterprise network can easily be compromised if appropriate security methods and procedures are not built into the entire technology infrastructure.

The multidimensional heterogeneity, complexity, and highly distributed nature of Internet resources have compounded the problems faced by IT organizations in the security area. To be effective in dealing with the problems, e-business applications must be deployed using architectures that support comprehensive security capabilities. At a minimum, EBSTA-type architectures must address the following four key security requirements:

- Enabling flexible capabilities for user authentication (for example, verifying that users are who they claim to be).

- Ensuring confidentiality and privacy of data, and the impossibility of alteration, whether inadvertent or malicious, when data is stored and when data is traveling across networks.

- Enabling full system accountability in terms of providing the ability to tell who did what and when, involving all elements of applications, systems, platforms, and networks.

- Providing strong attack deterrence capabilities (for example, to protect the physical infrastructure and application resources from malicious and unauthorized accesses or attempts to cause disruptions in service).

Different kinds of security technology are now available from a variety of vendors that can effectively support the cited architecture requirements. These technologies include securing electronic processes based on the secure sockets layer (SSL), encryption protocols and keys, user and resource authentication based on digital certificates and interoperable public key infrastructure (PKI), virtual private networks (VPNs), and more. Nevertheless, it is important to make sure that the primary focus of a company's architectural efforts is not on specifying a particular security implementation or security policy (for example, the use of encryption), but rather on providing design guides as to where security should be applied, and specifically on defining main points where security in the form of authentication and access control should be inserted.

Manageability

In the e-business model, a typical IT environment will consist of multiple heterogeneous computing systems, hardware devices, communication networks, operating system services, and applications. The unavailability, incorrect operation, or inefficient operation of mission-critical components, services, and applications will mean real business losses. Special attention must be paid to organizing computer operations, network operations, and service desk areas for effective operation and management. As a result, the architecture must ensure that network and systems management processes will be structured within a standard network and resource management infrastructure. This is one of the most difficult characteristics to achieve because it requires changing the current approach toward network management used by many companies, particularly larger ones. Currently, in order to manage large computer networks, companies are relying on multiple, tied-together network and systems management consoles, each with a different underlying control model and user interface which results in a complex and costly network and systems management. A standard management infrastructure will dramatically simplify the entire network and systems management processes and reduce associated costs. The key attributes of a standard management infrastructure are a lightweight directory access protocol (LDAP)-based network directory system integrated with other elements of the infrastructure, one console, one access control model, one messaging platform, and the tools to support these standard facilities.

E-Service Enabling

The architecture should support the highest possible level of e-service enabling. One of the primary characteristics of e-service enabling is the ability of any type of device or computer system, or any business process, to act as a server. This enables businesses to leverage their existing information systems and data assets as e-services accessible from the Internet.

What follows it is not a description of a specific EBSTA-type architecture. Rather, it is a presentation of artifacts that can be used to describe a particular architecture.

Practical experiences with enterprisewide architectures have suggested that, conceptually, there are certain benefits (positive outcomes) in describing this type of architecture in terms of architectural domains and reference models. An architectural domain is a set of related principles, architectural interpretations of concepts, and underlying technologies that can be considered a unit for determining standards and best practices in order to satisfy a corresponding set of related system requirements.

In the case of EBSTA-type architectures, domains represent the definition of critical capabilities of the architecture, its major architecture components, and services that these components must provide.

In general, a specific EBSTA-type architecture could be described using at least three types of domains, where each type represents a particular view of the architecture:

- Functional domains
- Infrastructure domains
- Integration domains

Figure 2.7 depicts an example of EBSTA-type architectures described in terms of domains.

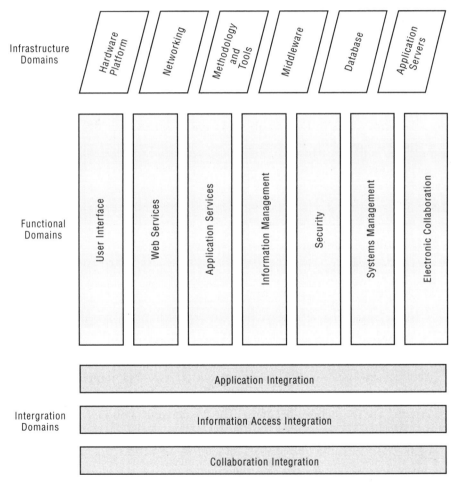

Figure 2.7: EBSTA Domains

As you can see, the example has seven major functional domains representing the functional view of the architecture:

- User interface domain
- Web services domain
- Application services domain
- Information management domain
- Security domain
- Systems management domain
- Electronic collaboration domain

Functional domains are tied together by two "dimensional views": the integration view and the infrastructure view. Three major domains represent the integration view of the architecture: the application integration domain, the information access integration domain, and the collaboration integration domain.

In terms of the infrastructure view, the architecture is described using six major infrastructure domains:

- Platform domain
- Network domain
- Methodology and tools domain
- Middleware domain
- Database domain
- Application server domain

For methodological reasons, it is convenient to assume that domains can be separated, but in reality they are deeply intertwined. Such separation is necessary in order to map industrywide and enterprise-specific aspects to a detailed specification of the domain. Of course, this mapping can be done only in approximation. The larger the set of applications, the more imprecise the approximation becomes. The challenge in building the architecture is to strike a balance between generalization and specifics: representations of the domains must be general enough to be valid for a wide range of e-business applications, but specific enough so that the effort of designing a particular application is limited. Therefore, in case of EBSTA-type efforts, domains should be viewed as frameworks for requirement definitions, design specifications, and implementation guidelines for systems development and integration. However, a certain amount of detailization (e.g., customization) will always be required. This is the role a systems developer has to play in the architecture.

Regrettably, this book cannot identify characteristics for each architectural domain to help the reader create appropriate e-business architecture in the appropriate style for his or her company. But what it can do is provide sufficient details about two of the most critical domains: the information access integration and collaboration integration domains.

Other important artifacts that could be used for the development of EBSTA-type architectures are architectural reference models. A reference model is a set of blueprints that describe the structure and interconnection of architecture components within a particular domain. A reference model is a "semicomplete" high-level system design, representing a specific subsystem of the overall e-business application. Developers can form complete designs by "inheriting" pieces of the models. Several related models might be selected.

Often, for practical reasons, a number of domains are "collapsed" into one reference model. The primary reason for such consolidation is the similarity of domains derived from the applicability of overreaching concepts like data warehousing or corporate portals.

Any strategic architecture for supporting the development, deployment, and management of mission-critical business applications will have to deal with real-world constraints. EBSTA-type architectures will be no different. There are a number of important constraints that will shape the overall architecture:

- **Performance and Cost**—Issues of performance and cost will be extremely important. Often, compromises and trade-offs among different sets of tools and services will be necessary. Much work will be necessary on an on-going basis to understand fully the nature of these compromises and trade-offs as well as to understand how the underlying infrastructure components and services should be integrated and distributed.

- **Accommodation of Legacy Applications**—The majority of companies are unable to rewrite or replace existing legacy applications with commercial off-the-shelf packages all at once. Consequently, legacy applications will have to be integrated with emerging e-business applications into a fully EBSTA-based environment. Technically, the integration involves encapsulating legacy applications (for example, "wrap-around") as server processes using application integration technologies, which are a substantial resource-consuming undertaking.

No company today, especially large enterprises, can envision that these capabilities will be instantly adopted or deployed. In most cases, it takes years to achieve a full EBSTA model throughout an enterprise. However, these capabilities represent a "future state standard" of e-business architecture against which you can measure your IT strategy and technology infrastructure and define the appropriate steps to develop it in conformity with the architecture.

The Role of the Portal

Our discussion of the e-business architectural blueprint has arrived at a point where it is no longer possible to continue without touching on the main subject of the book—the portal. Although the term *portal* has appeared already multiple times in the text, it has so far been treated casually, in broad strokes, without explanation or definition.

Since the early days of the Internet, there has been a common attitude that a Web browser is the most important technical component of the digital world. Because the whole concept of the Internet is based around the notion of exploiting common Web protocols, such as HTTP, to access information and information dissemination services with ease, the concept of a common Web browser is fairly important. And, yes, there is definitely a basis for the bloody war between Microsoft and Netscape for dominance in the browser market, a war that has resulted in the landmark antitrust proceedings against Microsoft.

The current importance of the Web browser is analogous to the early days of space exploration, when access devices such as rockets and all-purpose space vehicles (for example, space shuttles) occupied our imagination. But what has happened since these early days? Are we still glorifying access devices? Not really. We are now into space stations and the possibilities that they can offer. This is similar to what is happening with the evolution of our thinking about Internet technology.

The widespread diffusion of the Internet and all kinds of related "e"-technologies and information facilities has given rise to the concept of the *portal*, or, more broadly, the "cyberspace station." Initially, this concept was structured around the information searching and dissemination possibilities presented by the World Wide Web. Hence, the term *portal* meant *an entry point or originating Web site for combining a fusion of content and information dissemination services, and attempting to provide a personalized "home base" for its users, from which they will be able to launch broad-based exploration "expeditions" into cyberspace.* Features such as customizable start pages to guide users easily through the Web, filterable e-mail, a wide variety of chat rooms and message boards, personalized news and sports headlines options, gaming channels, shopping capabilities, advanced search engines and personal home page construction kits, and many others have become common characteristics of portals.

More recently, the convergence of general information searching and information dissemination technologies with a wide array of business-oriented features, such as business intelligence tools (e.g., OLAP), data warehousing, collaborative and workflow systems, EAI tools, Web publishing and personalization tools, and so on, has opened an entirely new set of possibilities and, more importantly, responsibilities for portals. The convergence of these (from the standpoint of information dissemination) functionally related technologies offers a substantiality and massiveness of information exchange on the Internet at such high levels that it has given rise to a new conceptual theme of "cyberspace technical landlords" or "e-business docking stations," referred to variously as "enterprise information portals," "corporate portals," "B2B portals," and "Web portals," to name a few. This has generated momentous changes in the nature and operation of information technologies and business processes both in virtuality (cyberspace) and in reality (traditional business).

These "docking stations" defined by the flow of information and power of integration have raised all kinds of highly important questions about the Internet, in general, and e-business, in particular. The most important questions are about what really constitutes "presence on the Internet," making it perfectly clear that a traditional Web site, such as the electronic storefront, only partially defines the space under consideration. What kind of e-business technology architecture emerges if indeed these stations render a view of the Internet as a physical, global network of interconnected access points to all denominations of "information spaces" and electronic communities?

By whatever name, Web sites that provide nothing but multifaceted access points to Internet resources and give the user a single place to communicate with others—for example, AOL, Excite, InfoSeek, LookSmart, Alta Vista, and Yahoo!—have become big businesses themselves. And such trends will continue. Many leading industry observers, for example, Gartner Group, predict that as many as 10,000 portal sites will exist within the next several years.

E-business extends the notion of an Internet access point (portal) to one that deals with both information dissemination and business-oriented services. As a user moves around from portal to portal, the services that are available can and will change. Therefore, *an e-business portal is a mechanism (or a physical device) that provides access to a changing set of business services while providing access to specific information dissemination services that can be used to communicate or deliver information to a user*. It is also a logical unification point for security mechanisms within the network environment (e.g., SSL, digital signatures) because it mediates access to an information space or community.

Architecturally, what is an e-business portal? An e-business portal is a complex information "bridge" or component layer that supports two separate architectural technology domains. (See Figure 2.8.)

A front-end, or access, domain is used to access the portal and the content published on its "premises," and a back-end, or service, domain is used by the portal to access Web resources and services. Conceptually, such a layer provides two other architectural elements ("constituents") that make it a very different concept from a Web server, and, topologywise, place it directly and transparently beneath the Web server:

- The first element is a portal manager, a service that maintains and controls the published content and access views to services available through the portal (for example, it provides the user interface to access the services). The portal manager also implements security policies for accessing the services by providing a customized view to a set of resources and services that is dynamically created based on the user identity (user rights) and portal policies.

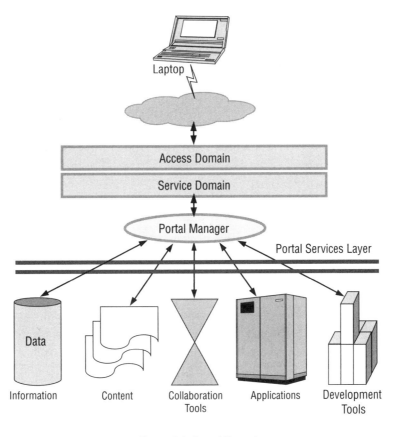

Figure 2.8: Portal Domains

■ The second element is a technology unification mechanism provided by a portal as an integration service. Basically, the portal provides a direct framework (methodology and, optionally, tools) for integrating information resources and services represented by the portal.

The subjects of the implementation and detailed scope of portals will occupy the majority of the discussion in the following chapters. Nevertheless, one critical question should be addressed here. Which architectural elements are most important to the technical infrastructure to have in place prior to pursuing e-business in a big way (such as network infrastructure, Web servers, Web-enabled applications, and so on)? It is unlikely that there is a simple, one-size-fits-all answer. Certainly, initial e-business infrastructure planning is all about the Web enabling of existing applications, bringing new customer-focused applications, server capacity, redundancy, failure, and bandwidth to the Internet. That is all well and good, but the portal is the key infrastructure that will wrap all the applications and services provided into a single, powerful delivery package for e-business. I see the portal as a part of initial e-business issues along with enabling information sharing and access from the Internet to key service infrastructures.

With that said, the more that companies start to fully realize the importance of portals in enabling e-business and how to really engineer a comprehensive portal solution, the more successful and viable their e-business offerings will become.

Portal strategies of many leading companies, such as Intel and SAP, are clear evidence of exactly that point. For example, SAP's e-business solution mySAP.com is the foundation of the entire SAP strategy for delivering customercentric, open, personalized, and collaborative interenterprise solutions to the company's customers. The philosophy of mySAP.com reflects the modern view of e-business as a business landscape, in which each customer's needs must be met immediately. In order to deliver such optimal service, it is necessary to provide integrated, open marketplaces on the Internet, within which companies of all sizes and industries will be able to leverage their suppliers, partners, and customers.

All software marketed by SAP and deliverable to customers through mySAP.com is accessible through a comprehensive, flexible, role-based business portal called the mySAP.com Workplace. This portal organizes business processes and related software functionality according to user roles and their responsibilities to provide a unified access to a wide range of applications, such as CRM, supply chain management, product lifecycle management, and business intelligence. Moreover, architecturally, the mySAP.com Workplace is the key element of the SAP Internet platform, which offers a comprehensive and seamless integration of back-office and front-office applications, providing users with a unified view of the data integral to supporting the cited applications. The real strength in SAP technology is that it delegates to the portal the responsibility to facilitate interenterprise collaboration and interoperability through an adaptable portal design and a flexible component-based architecture of the whole platform.

Developing
e-Business
Functions

Chapter 3 continues the presentation, begun in Chapters 1 and 2, of a business-driven framework for building an effective e-business transformation strategy. This chapter will focus on finalizing the discussion of topics directly related to the theme of "setting the stage for corporate portals."

This chapter draws attention to recent and continuing changes in IT strategies in regard to information access and delivery, and the increasing demand for universal information access capabilities required for entering the new economy.

As was emphasized in Chapters 1 and 2, developing e-business functions can mean a lot of things. It includes forging unconventional thinking, reengineering IT and business organizations, cultivating corporate cultures that openly embrace change, transforming all elements of the processes by which enterprises manage customer relationships—and above all, understanding that e-business is not only a new way to sell or buy products and services, but also a fundamental form of information exchange and a way to gain the economic value from it.

The assertion that the value of knowledge obtained from information exchange is the "centerfold" criteria of e-business transformation efforts is putting many companies into a rather challenging position. If there is sufficient understanding of information exchange needs, and if all that we have to do is provide unlimited access to information ("any time, any place"), the question becomes, how do we do it?

The discussion in Chapter 2 started to outline the main message of the book, which is that the solution lies in delivering unified information dissemination and integration support services using the corporate portal concept. In order to explore the power of this message further, however, a better understanding of critical information exchange and access needs is required. As a result, the main goal of Chapter 3 is to help the reader forge such an understanding.

Today's Biggest Challenges of e-Business Development

You cannot pick up a trade magazine or a book about e-business these days without reading about how much hard effort, planning, and execution goes into a successful e-business initiative, and about the most significant challenge facing companies everywhere around the world today: Gather all the means and start transitioning to e-business, fast.

Clearly, e-business transformation is not a simple endeavor. There is a growing awareness (a disturbing realization, if you will) that there are plenty of challenges, from both business and technology perspectives, facing companies on the road to success. Also, there is a realization that, because of time constraints and enormous competition, many challenges need to be addressed in different sequences or often in parallel, depending upon specific business goals and limitations of the current business environment.

But what are the biggest challenges? Or more precisely, what are the core challenges that must be addressed as an absolute requirement while "e-enabling" a company?

From a business perspective, undoubtedly, they are as follows:

- Ensuring strong management from the initial stages of the effort to avoid drawn-out development cycles and to maintain direction that is not achievable without evangelical support of the program from top executives, characterized by projecting the urgency, authority, and high profile needed to surmount obstacles along the way.

- Ensuring an enterprisewide view by crossing organizational boundaries and creating a working environment in which different organizations (for example, sales, marketing, logistics, IT, and so on) are pulled together to create the e-business solution.

- Thoroughly realizing the significance of merging the existing business into a whole e-business initiative and adapting business practices and processes to e-business requirements (for example, avoiding stapling e-business functions on top of existing processes).

- Extending development efforts beyond corporate walls, ensuring broad collaboration with customers and partners.

- Ensuring that the IT organization plays a crucial role as a business enabler and strategic partner in e-business transformation.

- Among the core technology challenges that IT organizations are facing, the following two are the biggest:
  - Enabling enterprisewide integration of systems, data, information, front-end and back-end applications, and business processes that find new solutions from combinations of technology assets. Not only must a company deliver integration capabilities within the enterprise, it must also extend these capabilities to business partners, suppliers, and anyone else who needs or desires to interact with a company. Companies that can offer significant ability to integrate systems and business processes across the entire value chain will be well positioned for growth and profitability because of strengthened partnerships.

  - Enabling easy, fast access to all information, as well as streamlining information and content delivery. The ultimate goal must be to turn Web-based systems into a business intelligence service for a company's staff, customers, suppliers, and all other partners. Today, more and more, success in e-business is determined by the ability of a company to provide customers and partners with the technology and information they need—first and foremost, to do business with the company, and second, to help them run their businesses more effectively and efficiently. In a nutshell, one of the biggest technological challenges faced by a company today in the race to e-business glory is that the company must offer electronic self-service for the entire value chain.

A comprehensive IT management strategy for e-business incorporates both enterprisewide systems integration and information and content delivery aspects. Because these aspects are, to a large degree, "opposite sides of the same coin," their management has much in common. This point is communicated in much detail throughout the rest of the book.

Also, the cited view offers one important consideration: The focus of IT organizations cannot be limited to technical aspects of enterprisewide integration. This limitation may well mask the value that streamlining information access and content delivery brings to the enterprise. Therefore, a strategy that balances the focus of IT organizations from technical aspects of integration to issues of information and content delivery is more effective from the standpoint of the value of IT initiatives.

The following sections of this chapter discuss the business drivers for streamlining information and content delivery and information access. The scope of the discussion does two things: First, it reflects the elements of business value that could be strategically the most important to the enterprise, such as enabling e-service capabilities. Second, it highlights ongoing business requirements in information access and delivery areas that are strategically and tactically important from the e-business perspective.

Build Your Company's Vision of e-Service Ideas Tailored to Your Customer's Specific Needs

In Chapter 2, the e-services concept was introduced as the new emerging trend in e-business over the Internet. This concept envisions transforming the Internet into a global ecosystem with the mass proliferation of highly autonomous and intelligent services of all kinds, supporting commercial transactions, information gathering and dissemination, and many other forms of B2B–B2C activities.

Furthermore, this concept formulated a vision of the state of enterprise computing in which the majority of functions and capabilities provided by IT organizations are "packaged" and managed as corporate assets, and made available commercially via the Internet. For example, Hewlett-Packard's description of the concept provides the following definition of types of e-services that companies could be offering commercially[1]:

"What is an asset in an Internet context? . . . It can be a software application that you make available as an app on tap (rental software on the Net). It can be a real world service that you make available on the Net. It can also be a proprietary process. Data. An IT resource. Your know-how. Any company that has an asset can make money in an e-services world by turning that asset into a service made available via the Net. . . . From your company's perspective, it means you'll have more ways to reach your customers, more ways to turn your assets into revenue streams, and more ways to conduct business. In addition, by adopting a modular architecture that's strategically important in an e-services world, you'll also gain more flexibility in how the IT resources in your company are managed. You'll continue to build your most strategic applications, but you'll 'rent' virtually everything else as e-services on the Net."

The provisioning of applications and delivering a task-specific capability of a high-level service are not discrete types of e-services, but rather more like two tightly coupled stages of the concept's evolution. This implies that a highly focused effort in areas of both understanding of specific user objectives and integration of underlying business processes and information sources is a constantly progressive strategy. Such a strategy requires a company to identify the areas where additional value can be realized in, and possibly throughout, an e-service. This formulates a "shell" for the scope of competitive advantage.

Clearly, looking forward to the new, potentially successful world of e-services requires an understanding of how a company can get ready and what it has to do to speed up the transition. Again, in this case, the need to develop the company's own EBSTA strategy (i.e., incorporate into it the various experiences, views, and criteria popularized by industry leaders and frontier-minded IT vendors such as Hewlett-Packard that are most relevant to the company situation) is vital. Hence, let's take one more look at the Hewlett-Packard recommendation.[2] According to Hewlett-Packard:

> To participate in this e-service economy, you can do many things. What follows are three trends you can capitalize on today . . . .
>
> 1. Take your own assets and offer them as an application available via the Net. Drive your own IT costs down by tapping into other apps on tap.
>
> 2. Build your own e-services portal by transforming your current Web site into a collection of e-services, or by creating an e-services portal for specific types of customers. Or create an e-service that you can syndicate across other portals.
>
> 3. Begin preparing for a world where dynamic brokering will be the most efficient way to conduct business. The first step is to ensure that your IT infrastructure is modular.

The emphasis on portals and modular, component-based infrastructure is very significant from the technology perspective. Equally significant, however, is the fit of the e-services strategy with the expectations of the customer. An e-service offering should focus on what target customers will need most from the offering. For example, they might need efficiency in performing the kinds of day-to-day tasks for which they will use the offering (for example, an e-service for updating software automatically), adequacy of the types of information they will be looking for (for example, an e-service for distance learning), or adaptability and ease of incorporating the offering into their work processes (for example, an e-service that automates procurement).

By focusing e-services on customer expectations, two main effects could be obtained. First, the competitive position of the supplier of the e-service could be more fully differentiated. Second, and most important, commoditization of e-service could be avoided. Commoditization of e-service offerings is the most negative side of e-business experiences that companies have to deal with.

Start with Your Key Information Access Requirements

What are the requirements for an IT solution that optimizes information access and content delivery? There has been much dialogue in the industry about information accessibility, the need for universal access and utilization of information about all aspects of the enterprise, and how such access must change the way the enterprise's staff plan, make decisions, and perform work. In short, the notion that any company must transform itself into an e-enabled organization in which information is viewed as an asset and used to create the strategic competitive advantage is widely accepted nowadays. Nevertheless, there are still only a few examples of companies in which such a vision has fully materialized.

Creating an environment with universal access to information is a highly complex and resource-intensive task, requiring sophisticated data and information processing technologies. Yet the marketplace is beginning to understand that by embracing portal-based solutions with careful attention to Web-based systems and infrastructure design, substantial success in the area of universal access is economically and technologically feasible.

Achieving universal data access hinges on articulating and maintaining an appropriate suite of information access requirements. As an initial step in this effort, it is necessary to define a set of core requirements that focus on instituting an orderly approach to the implementation of future application functions as consolidated and integrated systems within the e-enabling IT infrastructure. For this purpose, the initial set of information access requirements is, basically, a consolidated, standardized, global corporate view of the strategic information contained within the many operational and decision-support systems in the enterprise. As depicted in Figure 3.1, some of the key decisive factors that can be used as guidance during the definition of the core requirements are as follows:

- Obtaining a common view of key business subject areas across the organization based on critical success factors (CSFs) established by decision makers on the "front lines" of the enterprise.

- Improving information service definitions.

- Enabling enhanced trend analysis and ad hoc reporting capability for key business subject areas (for example, customer relationships).

- Decreasing the time spent reconciling data for financial reporting.

- Enabling application interoperability (integration) for mission-critical operational systems (for example, ERP systems).

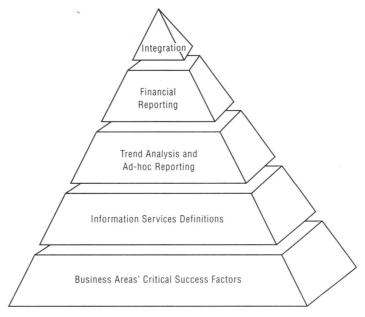

Figure 3.1: Defining Information Access Requirements

Consider the example of enabling a customer-focused strategy in a manufacturing company. Defining a common view of customer–client interactions will help the company determine what type of information is critical to the implementation of the strategy. Specifically, it may emphasize the need for combining certain information from existing operational systems, such as inventory information to speed up customer service responses to inquiries and accounting information to enable faster approvals on large orders, and for providing an easy and flexible access to that information.

In understanding the cited approach it is useful to make the following distinction: Business organizations should be responsible for defining and managing their information requirements and IT organizations should be responsible for providing technological solutions to satisfy those requirements, especially in terms of accessibility. However, the advent of the Internet and the rush to e-business have blurred this distinction. Too often, IT organizations are trying to set up all kinds of Web sites following an approach that is best described by the phrase "Let's build it first, and then they will come." It is good practice to avoid such situations. The important decisions regarding technology choices and implementation solutions should be based on the real information needs of business organizations and analyses of their potential business value.

Understanding the Process of Information Dissemination over the Internet and the Problem of "Information Overload"

As companies are turning to the Internet and Web technologies to maximize business opportunities and position themselves as e-service providers, new electronic forms of information delivery become extremely relevant. One of the manifestations of this is that the Web has grown from a communication medium for a small user group (mostly the scientific community) to a worldwide broadcasting capability, a primary mechanism for information dissemination, and a "mass medium" for collaboration and interaction between individuals and their computers. In terms of information dissemination, it is estimated that, in the United States alone, about 150,000 public and private entities, newspapers, interest groups, educational institutions, and so on offer information over the Web.

On the other side, this new mechanism of information delivery has contributed significantly to today's state of industrial evolution, termed "the age of information overload." What has happened is the following. As the Internet pervades more of our lives, we find numerous indications that decision makers are starving for information in a glut of constantly growing amounts of messy data. You may know the situation by the name "cyberspace data smog." User evaluations clearly show that the most requested feature of Internet services is a simple and fast way of finding useful information. Overall, users want, first, to be able to find information of a high quality without having to spend lots of time browsing, and, second, to have access to platform-independent services that are capable of reducing massive quantities of information into an organized, summarized, and customized (from the content interpretation standpoint) set of information. In other words, "Just enough, just in time."

As a result, companies that are transitioning to e-business must start to develop a strategy for information dissemination in the space of their e-business initiatives, whether it be for internal networks (for example, intranets) or external networks (for example, extranets or the Internet). Much consideration should be given to the critical issues of disseminating information and how the organization of information within the enterprise can affect the way it is utilized by internal and external end users.

Before addressing the various issues associated with the subject of information dissemination, it is worth revisiting the reasons for disseminating information within a company and beyond its borders. In this way, the overall vision and purpose can be validated. At the same time, criteria can be established to measure the success at various stages of implementation of required services and system capabilities to support dissemination.

There are multiple pressing reasons why companies have to disseminate information. To a large degree, the reasons are associated with the need to increase the value of one or more of the following attributes of the enterprise stakeholders[3]:

- **Decision Support and Knowledge-Base Expansion**—Information has to be disseminated to order to create an environment in which individuals and entities in an organization will have an opportunity to improve their knowledge base and subsequently make better decisions in future situations. For example, dissemination of statistics on sales of particular items to decision makers may ensure better purchasing and inventory management decisions.

■ **Customer, Partner, and Staff Education and Awareness**—Information has to be disseminated in order to educate customers, partners, and staff about a concept, process, or principle. For example, technical specifications explaining product capabilities, instructions on how to perform certain functions, guidelines for recommended procedures, and so on are all ways in which information is disseminated for educational and compliance purposes.

■ **Response Facilitation**—Information has to be disseminated to ensure communication and feedback from customers, partners, and staff that might require additional information to be generated and disseminated. Examples include advertising, catalogs, questionnaires, market surveys, frequently asked questions lists, case study testimonials, and so on.

■ **Collaboration Support**—Information has to be disseminated in order for a group of individuals to share knowledge and establish a framework of communication. Examples include message exchange within mail, workflow, control systems, minutes of meetings or workshops, and so on.

■ **Technology Transfer Support**—Information has to be disseminated to ensure that applicable technology can be transferred to a wide audience. Examples include presentation slides, benchmark results, and so on.

Traditionally, organizations responsible for organizing and managing information content on corporate Web sites have dealt with issues such as these:

■ **Content Scope**—Who are their users, and what type of information and related services should be provided for them?

■ **Content Quality**—What should be included in the content collections?

■ **Content Organization**—How should the content be organized and described in order to be easily found?

■ **Content Management**—What is still useful, and what should be weeded out?

These issues take on a much more expanded meaning in the light of each aforementioned reason for information dissemination and the challenge to adapt to the explosively growing volumes of information on computer networks (internal, external, or public). It is clear that because a large supply of and demand for information exist, new markets in information services are rapidly emerging, spurring development of strategic applications with intelligent information dissemination features. These applications are evolving within the concept of corporate portals, using such emerging dissemination technologies as push-and-pull media (for example, content notification, filters, automated pull and automated push, channel changers, and so on), intelligent agents, mediators and facilitators, and so on.

Advanced information dissemination and access infrastructure services are necessary prerequisites to the development of the mentioned applications. As a simple example, a monolithic Web site does not suffice for content navigation anymore, because users require customized searching capabilities that are sensitive to factors such as specific business requirements and personalized service needs. Instead of being forced to rely on general-purpose, broad-based content, users require customized content and analysis that emphasize information relevant to the user's objectives. Agent-oriented navigation tools with capabilities to take into account an individual's special interests and actively search for the best content have become a necessity. Therefore, the real challenge for infrastructure developers is to provide efficient and effective search methods that can navigate the network, handling a vast variety of interfaces to heterogeneous and geographically dispersed content sources and interpreting and collating the obtained results.[4]

Figure 3.2 illustrates three of the most critical types of required infrastructure services for information dissemination:

- Data access services that allow users to quickly locate relevant facts and software resources from a huge mass of heterogeneous, distributed data.

- Integration and translation or mediation services that convert information from one format to another subject to semantic constraints.

- Knowledge discovery services that process information in order to produce summaries, discover new patterns and relationships between facts, and check consistency.

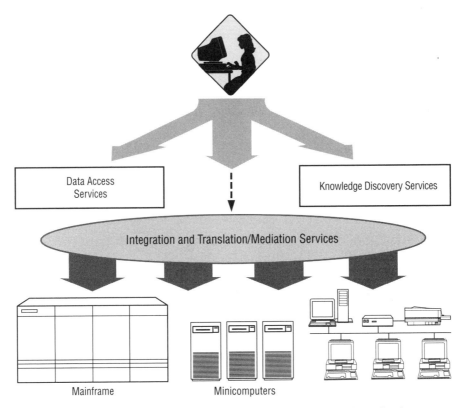

Figure 3.2: Critical Infrastructure Services for Information Dissemination

While you are enabling the above services, the issue of formats in which information is managed and disseminated by companies and accessed by users must also be addressed in parallel. The main problem here is that, currently, the majority of Web-based content is organized and disseminated as static unstructured data which significantly limits the availability of the various tools and approaches for enabling universal data access. Companies need to start moving to structured content based on the concept of "information objects" (the term *information object* is used here to refer to an information entity that comprises some related data and associated processing software—for example, active documents and Web page components). Broad-based implementations of structured content using new emerging standards and related technologies, such as DOM (Document Object Model) and XML (eXtensible Markup Language), will greatly enhance the whole area of information dissemination, enabling the transition toward adaptive information systems based on meta-data exchange and customized information objects.

Providing Mission-Critical Information When and Where It Is Needed Most

Let's continue the discussion of information objects started in the previous section, but from a specific angle: the dissemination of mission-critical information. One of the main challenges facing companies, from the standpoint of streamlining information dissemination and information accessibility, is ensuring that mission-critical information is made readily and easily available to those in the enterprise who need it most. As an example, consider these issues that companies have to deal with:

- The existence of a variety of database systems for storing and organizing enterprise data that use disparate, often conflicting, data models and access mechanisms.

- The necessity of including large numbers of information sources outside of the enterprise that are also important to the operation of the enterprise and make use of nontraditional data such as images, video, and sound.

Throughout business and the IT industry, increasing interest in Web-based information dissemination systems has focused on integrated software solutions that promise quick mastery of an organization's mission-critical information. Specifically, such solutions should do two things: They should deal directly with the heterogeneity and autonomy of information sources, and they should give the user the ability to move easily between tools that aid in the execution of specific tasks and those that help locate and analyze information to support these tasks. Thus, given the disparate nature of the emerging information sources, the need to maintain access to legacy sources, the heterogeneity of the software and hardware systems used to host the sources, and the need to provide users with transparent, universal access to the massive underlying information space, many experts repeatedly emphasize the importance of proper organization of information to enable the delivery of mission-critical information when and where it's needed most. Therefore, there is an urgent need to develop new paradigms for information search and retrieval that can form the basis of these future information systems. This should be viewed as a first-class competence for any successful e-business organization.[5]

The area of mission-critical information, especially in the context of what exactly "mission critical" means, is a subject in its own right. But in terms of the main subject, corporate portals, we have to consider only one particular issue—the preliminary planning a company has to undertake in this area before it implements a portal-type software.

The following two tasks are necessary in order to help prepare a company for both the implementation of portal-type software and doing a better job of information management on an enterprisewide basis:

- Information object mapping
- Establishing an information object repository

Each is discussed in the sections that follow.

Information Object Mapping

This is the process of identifying data items. It is critical for decision-making processes from strategic and tactical perspectives. Groups of related data items are combined into objects built around the information needs of a specific business objective.

The emphasis here should be on e-business facilitation, which involves reviewing back-end systems and databases that store and maintain critical data, such as catalog databases, product information databases, inventory databases, order information, shipping information, customer information systems, corporate financial databases, messaging systems for approval and notification, and so on.

In most cases, it is a step-by-step process, starting with one particular business area or organization and identifying its core, mission-critical information requirements and related data items (patterns in the information), the valuable data items that are inaccessible to the entire enterprise, and then going to the next business area. Attention needs to be given to the identification of data access requirements and the types of data that must be made readily accessible by the people who have the skills and knowledge with which to transform the data from the objects into solutions that will benefit the enterprise. Also, it is necessary to capture details that are helpful to ensure information sharing at the information objects' level among disparate systems. Finally, it is necessary to capture important information delivery characteristics in order to enable customized delivery to users who need the information most—in particular, workflow trigger specifications that are responsible for initiating a wide variety of information delivery actions (for example, notifications), event specifications and their sequencing, and timing.

Information Object Repository

This is the process of establishing a capability to store information regarding the managed objects. Ideally, this repository is object-oriented in nature, to enable a comprehensive representation of information objects' compositions, data items included with each object and their relationships, and relationships between objects and external elements (for example, data sources, presentation formats, users, when and how often the information is delivered to them, and so on). But, if necessary, any tool could be used to develop whatever repository an organization prefers (for example, Excel spreadsheets). As the information base of mission-critical information objects grows within the e-business environment, the repository will become one of the most critical components of the overall infrastructure.

Information Intermediation, Knowledge Resource Centers, and "On-Line Librarians"

Providing mission-critical information to a company's decision makers is a knowledge-intensive work process. How can a company be in a better position to create new automation capabilities to facilitate this process, in light of the continuous growth of volumes of data available over the Internet, as well as redefine the scope of traditional information dissemination functions?

The experiences of many leading e-enabled companies, such as Federal Express, Bank of America, IBM, Cisco Systems, Intel, and Dell Computers, have demonstrated the critical importance of recognizing the need to establish an Internet-based electronic information intermediation (EII) strategy in order to enhance the strategic use of information in management and organization at the top decision-making levels of companies. As a concept, this particular view toward the use of information is leading to the conclusion that a specific and integrated approach addressing the nature and value of EII is needed. Moreover, as a business approach, it has to enable a more focused management of information resources and information flows, resulting in improving both efficiency of the whole value chain and quality of information exchange. In many industries, EII has emerged as the new criteria of competitiveness.

In terms of the value of EII, it can be defined as the extent to which certain characteristics exhibited by an information intermediary, such as self-service information processing activities, scope and depth of coverage, and interaction dynamics, speed up the circulation of information and enhance its overall quality, both within companies and between companies and their partners.

Analyses of projects that deal with the standardization of ways to enable EII, especially with regard to the information disseminated by companies to potential and current customers and partners, have indicated the predominance of two forms of information intermediation:

1. The establishment of knowledge resource centers (KRCs) as facilitators between the supply and demand of information within and outside of the enterprise. A knowledge resource center is defined as an ongoing system of exchanges of information, knowledge, and consulting services in a particular area between enterprise and employees of the enterprise. Their central function is to provide access to information resources and the means for the implementation of a continuous process of transformation of generic knowledge and information into operating tools and processes for decision makers. Companies that have created KRCs have conceived a significant and systematic opportunity for improving their competitive strength.

2. The implementation of so-called on-line librarians as a service to users to assist them in locating information from the Internet. Techniques and tools that make it possible to carry out information exchanges, and all the interlinks that they entail, characterize the on-line librarian function. For example, a company can establish a simple service through e-mail boxes for collecting messages from users in which requests for information are specified. Or it can introduce a much more powerful solution through the use of specialized software with broad-based functions of searching, interpreting, and formulating answers to user requests. Commonly, this function is organized around three sets of activities: giving access to relevant knowledge and information, orienting users to par-

ticular tools and techniques that enable the resolution of specific problems with which a user is confronted, and providing references.

Some companies have become involved with both forms of intermediation, targeting not only the mere dissemination of decision-support information, but also the transfer of "know-how" (for example, transfer of experience, best practice, specialized production and technology knowledge, emergency assistance-type knowledge, and so on). The main idea here is to ensure that information intermediation as a service and a function within the enterprise delivers much more of a benefit than just the "gatekeeping" of the information—most of all, provides services of creating knowledge and effective education capabilities as value added to the basics of information control. This results in a number of improvements in multiple business areas, such as the identification of new market opportunities, the reduction of deficiencies in production, financial, and business administration, the efficiency of logistical processes, and many others.

Enabling Business Efficiencies Quickly through New Forms of Collaboration

E-business is a dynamic and turbulent environment that requires flexible and fast responses to changing business needs. Many companies have addressed these requirements by adopting decentralized, team-based, and distributed structures variously described in the literature as virtual, network, and cluster organizations.[6,7] Advances in Web-based information dissemination and workgroup technologies have enabled these companies to obtain and retain such distributed structures by supporting a high degree of coordination among people working from different locations.

A key feature of ensuring coordination among distributed organizations is providing a comprehensive platform for collaboration and informal communication. In distributed organizations, the main challenges in regard to coordination are a lack of formal rules, procedures, clear reporting relationships, and coordinated business practices. Therefore, more extensive collaboration and informal, personal communications are required.

The Internet is undoubtedly the main driving force in enabling collaboration by supporting interactive communications. Even as it links millions of people around the globe with networks of computers and telecommunications devices, it makes possible the management and manipulation of messages of various kinds (for example, text, sound, graphics, video, and so on) in a digital form. This allows the enrichment of communication by combining all digital forms of communication into a single message. Technically, this is often referred to as "computer-mediated communications."

But enabling electronic collaboration means much more. First and foremost, it means providing an environment in which engaged participants can be inspired to collaborate and exchange ideas, rather than being passive listeners or viewers. How can such a concept be accomplished? By empowering every participant to be a publisher or producer of information, as well as a consumer, using an electronic bulletin board and "interactive chat rooms" tools. There are many examples that validate this point—for instance, the enormous success of commercial services like America Online.

Second, it requires electronically enabling a so-called "cooperative work-oriented design" approach. This is an approach to organizing work processes within a team or between teams when multiple participants must cooperate in order to perform a task—for example, cooperative problem solving or product design—and this in turn requires the use of communication. In terms of functional requirements, it involves decomposition of the global task between participants, distribution of the description of subtasks to them, planning of the jobs among them (including possible formats and communication language of interactions), and specifying mechanisms to handle possible conflicts. Some examples of applications based on the cooperative work-oriented design approach are synchronous and asynchronous product designs by engineers, joint work on papers or reports, project management, and so on. Also, this approach envisions the electronic availability of certain extended functions, such as a mechanism for creating, managing, and selectively activating different sets of work-related knowledge (e.g., in the case of design knowledge, critics, spatial relations, domain distinctions, common tool box items, and argumentation) so that alternative ideas can be deliberated and either adopted, rejected, or modified. Several substantial benefits are achievable with this approach, including productivity, product quality, skill enlargement, innovation, and so forth.

From the technology standpoint, electronic collaboration applications have to offer a high degree of technical flexibility. This entails the ability to construct an application as a set of interleaved generic and application-specific tools providing the functionality of various application aspects.[8]

Examples of such tools are chat and editing tools, bulletin boards, "computer whiteboards," audio and video conferencing, groupware tools, integration tools, and so on. These tools should be integrated into a common framework that enables the entire collaboration process.

Effective information dissemination capabilities are central to electronic collaborative environments. The success of collaborative efforts in an Internet-based environment depends on the ability to share information that requires all the features discussed in the previous section, focusing on the organization (classification and systematization) of knowledge and expertise and providing an intelligent support in the searching and browsing of various information sources.

Collaboration is one of the key characteristics of the aspects of the buyer–seller or partner trading relationships in e-business.[9] It represents the form and the essence of such relationships, which are based on the exchange of information jointly developed by buyers and sellers (for example, product design, promotion design, demand forecasting and planning, store layout and shelf-space planning, and so on). As was stated in a 1999 report from AMR Research, Inc.,[10] "In a sense, collaboration is the highest form of e-commerce as it involves joint planning and plan execution."

4

E-Business
and Application
Integration

We have now come to the point in our discussion where it is most appropriate to describe the issue of application integration (AI), which is crucial to successful technology management in order to realize e-business solutions. As was mentioned in Chapter 3, AI is one of the biggest challenges that IT organizations are facing in e-enabling their companies.

Historically, AI has been viewed as a "cut and dry" requirement—the need to build point-to-point interfaces between existing systems to make it possible for them to share data. In the eyes of many observers, it has been perceived as a negative outcome (like some sort of "punishment") that resulted from inadequate application development practices, specifically because the common database approach was not embraced. Questions like "Why don't developers use a single file or database so they would not need to build all these nasty interfaces later and the AI problem will disappear?" have often been raised.

Although there were many reasons in the past to view the problem that way, today AI involves a lot more than just sharing data. As a system implementation requirement, AI cannot be avoided. It has become a significant part of the evolution of application delivery. This evolution was fueled by the introduction and popularization of software componentization, the increasing shift from monolithic development methods to "assembly-from-stock" approaches, and, more significantly, the widespread adoption of packaged applications as a way to reduce the IT budget. As a result, the key defining characteristics of AI have expanded in scope to encompass, in addition to data sharing, devising a coherence of functional behavior and business rules of disparate systems or their components. In other words, AI has been chartered to provide the integration of business events that are crossing between these components or systems. This is where the concept of enterprise application integration (EAI) enters the picture. An excellent discussion of the concept is given in the paper "Enterprise Application Integration: Making the Right Connections," authored by Katy Ring and Neil Ward-Dutton of Ovum Consulting,[1] which describes EAI as "the combination of technologies and processes that enable custom-built or packaged business applications to exchange business-level information in formats and contexts that each understands."

E-business has added additional requirements for EAI. In its nature, e-business is a complex distributed process that involves carrying out a wide range of services, such as performing multiple phases of work (transactions), accommodating various interacting partners, and providing access to heterogeneous information resources (e.g., unstructured information, video, and sound). Hence, EAI has to enable synthesis of all these services by various diverse internal and external systems. But the dynamics of e-business require that it be possible for companies to develop and refine rules for synthesis at an unprecedented rate. In this context, the field of EAI is challenged to provide a flexible composition of services (for example, the trading of services across boundaries of extended enterprises, interception and adoption of services at boundaries, and so on) and the coordination of their interactions and interoperability. More to the point, from an e-business perspective, the most pressing requirements for EAI are as follows:

- **Internal Integration**—Extending the major customer–client interactions (for example, registration, marketing, payment, and so on) and management of customer transactions (for example, accommodating requests from the Web for products and services and integrating the vast amounts of customer information). This type of integration includes the back-end processes required for complete fulfillment of customer requests.

- **External Integration**—Combining services from multiple providers (for example, partners of the supply chain) to support extended transaction management and, more importantly, information exchange, coordination, and collaboration across the extended value chain.

In response to these pressing requirements, numerous software vendors have "jumped" aboard the EAI bandwagon, offering a bewildering variety of EAI solutions to integration problems. EAI is now a huge market, with more than 7,000 vendors worldwide.

The drive toward EAI has spawned a full set of technology concepts, many of which have such significantly distinct characteristics that they have facilitated the definition of multiple new markets, such as the following:

- Application servers (for example, application brokers, message brokers, or information brokers)

- Middleware and messaging tools (for example, transaction monitors)

- Wrapper and adapter development tools (for example, COM and CORBA development tools)

- Database gateways and data access tools (for example, ODBC- and JDBC-based tools)

In any case, as I have emphasized previously, many of the technology topics in this book (such as enterprise architecture, component-based development, and definitely EAI) require too much coverage in order to address all their underpinnings, especially the associated technical details, and forge a reasonable level of understanding. Each of these topics is worth at least one entire book on its own.

Therefore, as much as I would like to, I cannot give to EAI the kind of treatment it deserves. But perhaps it is not necessary. Why is that so? Because numerous excellent articles and white papers (for example, the previously mentioned paper by Ring and Ward-Dutton and the Butler Group's paper "Application Integration: A Management Guide"[2]) have been written on the details of EAI in terms of the tools and technologies, such as middleware, and there is no need for repetition. Rather, we need to center here on why EAI is needed to help companies tie together applications both within their organizational boundaries and between their trading partners and suppliers.

For that reason, the information in this chapter is at an intentionally high level. The chapter focuses on describing the role EAI plays in enabling e-business transformation, how EAI technologies need to evolve to become a key component of extended enterprise application infrastructures, and, more importantly, how the integration requirements in terms of e-enabling that drive the pressing need for a unified integration platformare so diverse.

As you will see in the following chapters, the primary role of corporate portal technologies is to fulfill this need.

What Are Companies Facing in Today's Disparate Enterprise Application Environments?

To a large degree, enterprise-level integration challenges stem from the overwhelming condition of corporate IT today—the widespread use of older, "stove-piped" systems (for example, stand-alone applications that do not interface with, or share data or resources with, other applications) makes it difficult to exchange information within a single department or across departmental boundaries.

Over the last 20 years, corporations have been actively involved in automating linkages between dispersed business functions and organizational units. They have learned the hard way that engineering an integrated business environment requires consolidating and balancing the many islands of disparate information and systems scattered across an enterprise into a unified whole. They've also learned that it's a major undertaking: Complexity, integration lead time, and cost are major factors here.

Complexity derives from the number of applications, the number of data sources, and the interface functions needed to perform cross-departmental processes. Because, until recently, the most predominant method of application integration has been point to point, it is not uncommon for a large legacy application, such as an order processing or billing system, to have multiple interfaces to other systems, which have to be developed, managed, and maintained. The largest problem with this situation has been an expensive-to-maintain application environment. Changing business rules and process flows in such an environment becomes a horrendous, time-consuming task. A change in one application ripples throughout all the other applications it is interfaced with; thus, programmers are forever writing and rewriting special interface programs. Moreover, each new version of an application needs to be tested with existing applications, which adds even more time and effort.

Although the advent of multitiered client–server computing models, in which data access is separated from presentation and business logic, has simplified data sharing to a certain degree, it has increased the overall complexity of integrating multiple applications. Because, in most cases, application modules are implemented from different software developers or vendors, programmers face an astonishing conglomerate of programming languages, starting with Assembler and finishing with C/C++ application programming interfaces (APIs), as well as all kinds of other technologies that have to be integrated. Often the integration must occur at different structural levels (including the entire system, subsystems, and individual modules or components) involving multifaceted assembly from disparate sources (such as ERP packages, various stand-alone human resources and accounting applications, front-office packages, legacy systems built in-house, third-party services, such as credit authorization, and so on).

Consequently, EAI is largely an invasive process, requiring not only time-consuming source code modifications, but also extensive and disruptive reengineering of processes and systems that, in turn, introduces additional amounts of custom coding, and so the cycle continues. All in all, enterprisewide integration might add substantial cost, simultaneously restricting flexibility and scalability.

Certain e-business needs, such as multichannel integration, have complicated the integration problem even further. In order for companies to offer customers an identical level of professional service regardless of the communication channel utilized, enterprise applications have to be integrated with specialized technology solutions, such as interactive voice response (IVR), intelligent routing, and computer-telephony integration (CTI) platforms.

By and large, e-business elevates EAI challenges to new heights. Its absolute requirements for rapid deployment and flexibility have pushed companies to adopt packaged EAI solutions as a core element of enterprise IT strategies. Unfortunately, this has brought companies a significant dependency on specific technology platforms and proprietary vendor products (for example, creating a vendor "tie-in" situation) that, essentially, has created additional obstacles to enhancements within companies' IT infrastructure and the introduction of new applications. Currently, the costs associated with acquisition, implementation, and support of EAI packages are increasing faster than other IT budget items. In addition, as many companies have discovered, extensive vendor tie-ins make it extremely difficult, if not impossible, to integrate systems that exist outside an enterprise. The realization that it could be more complex and time consuming to develop and implement the integration than the actual systems it connects is not uncommon nowadays.

Deciding on the best EAI strategy and subsequently selecting EAI products that fulfill that strategy is a critical technology choice faced by many IT organizations. Neither decision is easily made. Companies need to be very cautious in how they approach the responsibility of making the choice. Special attention needs to be given to various business questions and related technology questions, such as these:

- Does the real need exist for application package integration (for example, using an EAI product) or would a custom solution be more appropriate?

- How important is it for a company to focus on tactical point-to-point solutions at the moment? How important is it to provide a long-term architecture for continual integration requirements? What is the proper balance between tactical and strategic solutions?

- What degree of integration with external systems is required? Could a company have just an internal focus at the moment?

- What are the major inflexibility factors of a particular integration solution? How much may it affect the next generation of requirements?

- How many additional layers of EAI software might need to be introduced? What are the performance implications?

- What is the best approach for encapsulating those company sources of information that need to be integrated (for example, isolating the sources so their physical implementation can change without triggering reintegration)?

The growth of e-business is transforming the relationship of software applications, especially specialized system software like EAI products, to the enterprise. Given this, EAI should not be seen as a problem. Rather, it should be addressed on a continual basis as an important part of e-business strategic technology architecture (EBSTA) efforts focused on making rapid integration business a usual activity as much as possible. This change in perspective is important due to the way in which it drives specific requirements for new e-business application solutions and infrastructure technologies that are needed to support these new applications. When I think about the biggest effect of achieving rapid integration capabilities (not only within an enterprise, but also across multiple enterprises), one class of e-business applications that comes to mind is customer relationship management (CRM) over the Internet, often referred to by its catchy acronym "eCRM." The topic of eCRM and how EAI relates to it is covered later.

Enterprise Application Integration: A Multistep Process

Being successful with EAI means, first and foremost, understanding that multiple integration mechanisms and associated technologies are used in EAI solutions (as depicted in Figure 4.1), which are executed on various levels and in different phases of the application environment.

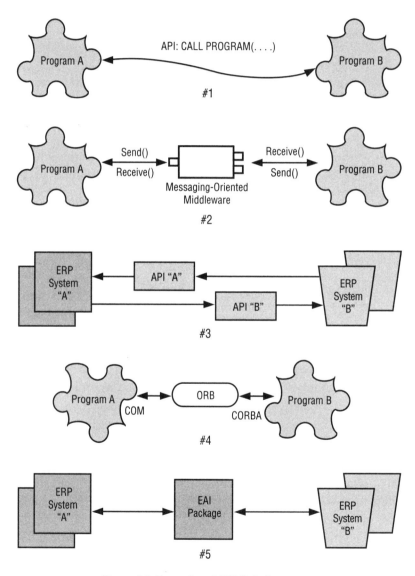

Figure 4.1: Examples of EAI Solutions

It is convenient to distinguish the following five categories of EAI solutions:

1. **Using the Application Programming Interface (API) Approach**— Applications provide specific, product-based (meaning "proprietary") APIs through which programmers create software routines (remote procedure and function calls) to enable communication and data exchange between disparate systems. The most popular development choices are:

   — Custom coding using all kinds of remote procedure call (RPC) libraries and middleware protocols, such as IP sockets or CORBA's IDL.

   — Using transaction monitor software products, such as IBM's Customer Information Control System (CICS) or Microsoft's Transaction Server.

2. **Using Messaging-Oriented Middleware**—Communication and data exchange between disparate systems are enabled by sending and receiving messages using some sort of queuing processing. Message exchange occurs synchronously or asynchronously depending on the communication requirements of the conversation (for example, flexibility, guaranteed message delivery, and so on). The most popular development choices in middleware products are multifunction message queuing software products such as IBM's MQSeries or Microsoft's MSMQ.

3. **Using Proprietary Integration Features of Application Packages**—The majority of packaged applications, especially ERP-type systems, provide interfaces and APIs for data exchange purposes; the SAP R/3 system, for example, has a so-called Application Linking and Embedding (ALE) API.

4. **Using Object-Oriented Protocols, Interfaces, and Related Middleware**— There are several open and proprietary object-oriented protocols that enable interoperability and data exchange—for example, CORBA, JavaBeans, and Microsoft's Common Object Model (COM). The most popular development choices are as follows:

   — Custom coding by using the interoperability features of these protocols.

   — Using software products, such as object request brokers (ORBs) and application servers, which themselves utilize interoperability features of object protocols.

5. **Using EAI-Packaged Tool Sets**—A wide range of EAI vendors, such as CrossWorlds, Software, Inc., Oberon Software, Inc., Vitria Technology,

Inc., Active Software, Inc. (recently purchased by webMethods, Inc.), and many others, provide packaged tool sets for the integration of many popular ERP and front-office packages (for example, SAP R/3, Peoplesoft, Oracle, Baan, J.D. Edwards, Siebel, Vantive, Clarify, and so on) and custom-built legacy applications.

All of the cited integration mechanisms deal explicitly or implicitly with a class of software that we commonly call *middleware*. Middleware is a set of common infrastructure services executing on top of operating system services that enable applications and their components (for example, presentation, business logic, database access, and so on) to interact with each other across a network. In other words, middleware acts as the "glue" that binds together the communication and data exchange between different software components and systems.

While middleware technologies provide the necessary communication and data-level integration capabilities, they do nothing to enable the integration of business processes—especially in cases such as enterprise-level systems involving ERP packages. In addition, if the development approach of coding directly to middleware APIs is chosen, code maintenance challenges and high support costs often result.

As the focus of application integration moves from just building a "data bridge" between applications A and B to multienterprise integration over the Internet, a process-centric application integration model emerges. (See Figure 4.2.)

New business processes are created by building new services at both the source and target application sides, which transparently integrate and customize existing processes. In order to enable the process-centric integration model, a higher level of abstraction than middleware APIs becomes necessary; what is needed is a solution that hides technology details and allows systems developers to work with constructs that represent the real business entities and processes. This level of abstraction is achieved using object-oriented (OO) concepts, and specifically, using objects that encapsulate data and related business process logic together (so-called business objects).[3]

Both packaged application and EAI vendors are working to make EAI possible at the level of business processes. Related activities are split into three areas:

1. Packaged application products are being rebuilt toward a more componentized OO structure.

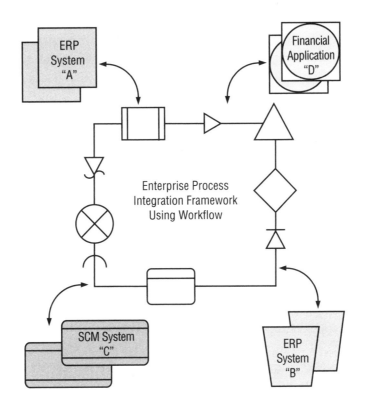

Figure 4.2: Process-Oriented EAI

2. These products are providing transparent programming interfaces to components and business objects (for example, SAP via its BAPI interface).

3. EAI products are becoming more object oriented, focusing on delivering prebuilt integration modules that encompass middleware and business-process APIs for various packaged applications.

De facto standards have also emerged. The Object Management Group has developed the business object component architecture (BOCA), which includes the business object facility (BOF) and common business object (CBO) frameworks. The BOF is a run-time object broker for business objects, with its component definition language (CDL) built on top of the interface definition language (IDL), and is a highly comprehensive infrastructure for enabling rapid integration of a diverse set of applications. At the same time, various consortia and standards groups are forging standards for industry-specific application integration frameworks. For example, RosettaNet is focusing on creating an electronic commerce framework to align processes in the IT supply chain, and the Supply Chain Council is covering logistics and supply chain management for manufacturing.

Until recently, from the standpoint of enabling Internet-based applications, the majority of EAI efforts have concentrated on bringing existing assets (for example, data and application access) to the Internet. Today, EAI requirements are encompassing not only integration of the Internet with existing assets, but the full spectrum of communications, business processes, and transactions occurring electronically. As illustrated in Figure 4.3, EAI is emerging as a multilevel domain-oriented field, with distinct but highly interrelated technology characteristics at each level:

- **Business Communications Integration (BCI)**—Includes all aspects of the delivery of information, such as establishing and supporting connections between the sources of information and its users, ensuring security and quality of service, and so on.

- **Business Asset Integration (BAI)**—Comprises all elements of enabling information dissemination, such as converting the information between the systems being integrated, providing access to application services from the Web, enabling real-time information sharing among employees, customers, partners, and suppliers, and so on.

- **Business Process Integration (BPI)**—Incorporates the integration of business rules that govern the execution of business functions and workflow processes across multiple systems. In particular, this includes services for automating and managing intra- and intercompany processes in terms of enabling such critical capabilities as immediate response to events (for example, just-in-time inventory management), auditing and tracking via a unified view of business processes across multiple systems, and so on.

- **Business Transaction Integration (BTI)**—Enables the deployment and execution of end-to-end business transactions over the Internet within the scope of e-commerce applications (for example, on-line procurement, bill presentment and payment, electronic fund transfer, loan processing, and so on).

- **Business Information Exchange and Collaboration Integration (BIXCI)**—Enables the timely exchange of information, such as product catalogs, pricing information, inventory information, order information, and so on. At the same time, it enables electronic collaboration applications by integrating various collaboration tools, such as chat and editing software, bulletin boards, "computer whiteboards," audio and video conferencing, groupware (especially e-mail), and so on, into a common, end-to-end collaboration process.

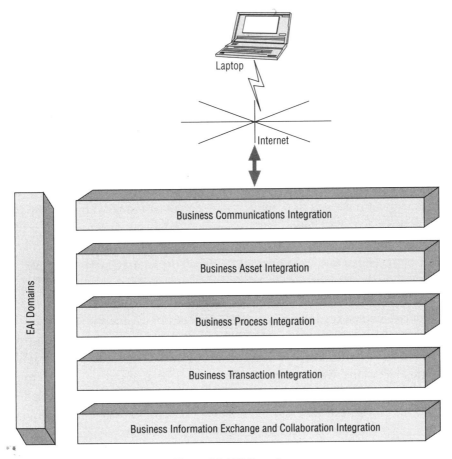

Figure 4.3: EAI Domains

eCRM and Forging a Single Vision of the Customer

More and more companies are beginning to fully realize that to thrive in this highly competitive economy, they need to go global to take a larger piece of the market and they need to enhance response time to the customer, regardless of where the customer is. Above all, they need speedy and responsive technology solutions to accomplish these goals. To enable such solutions, they need a reliable, secure, and flexible infrastructure that goes beyond anything they had before. eCRM is essentially a concept and a class of CRM applications that promise to fulfill the customer responsiveness part of the requirements cited in the previous section.

The main idea behind eCRM is to enhance customer satisfaction by managing the fulfillment of performance promises and the quality of the interaction with the customer on the Internet. The quality of the interaction with the customer is based on the understanding of what the customer really wants, which, in turn, leads to greater fulfillment. Many characteristics of eCRM were discussed in Chapter 1 (see "Striving for the Customer"). It makes sense to reiterate one point of that discussion—eCRM applications with a comprehensive set of "getting-to-know-the-customer" functions will play an essential role in the new digital economy.

But eCRM alone is not enough. A solution is required that brings together all customer data into a single resource in support of eCRM as well as other CRM initiatives. Forging a unified view of the customer within an enterprise and beyond—across supply chains or even virtual enterprises—means creating (out of disparate islands of data and events) a solution consisting of a coherent set of integrated business functions that yield the highest customer value.

The challenge is to integrate the whole set of enterprisewide applications into a single, integrated information network ("infostructure"). Such a network should be capable of imposing on all customer interfaces a single, complete view of every customer, allowing the optimization of all customer interactions with the enterprise. Moreover, this infostructure should be extended to the Web, so that customers can be engaged in self-care on the Internet. The benefits of such an approach are tremendous, especially for industries with extensive customer interactions, in particular, telecommunications and financial services. In these industries, the development of the cited infostructure presents an opportunity to bring all information related to customers to a single desktop. Consequently, this information can be used across the customer management value chain, through marketing, sales, and customer care, to radically improve "value" provided to the customer.

The impact of the need to achieve a unified view of the customer on requirements for EAI solutions is extensive. Therefore, there is a different mix of priorities from that associated with the most common EAI objectives, such as integrating a legacy system with an ERP package, or forging a "best-of-breed" environment (for example, integrating PeopleSoft's Human Resource module with SAP R/3).

As depicted in Figure 4.4, achieving a unified view of the customer involves linking (in real time) various software applications and business processes through standardized customer information models. All the customer information can then be delivered as a single, comprehensive view to customer touch points.

Figure 4.4: eCRM Integration Points

The key integration points are as follows:

- Front-office marketing and sales applications
- Web-based self-service applications
- Call-center applications
- Order-management applications
- Billing systems

- Distribution systems

- Partner gateways, especially ERP-to-ERP connections

The successful integration of customer information with customer touch points depends on three innermost processes (see Figure 4.5):

1. Integration of data from disparate sources, according to standardized customer information models and the creation of "storehouses" of information (for example, data stores that are formed to house unified customer views).

2. Construction of the infostructure that integrates the cited storehouses with Web-based customer interaction applications and delivers high performance, scalability, and presentation flexibility to address Internet-driven operational requirements.

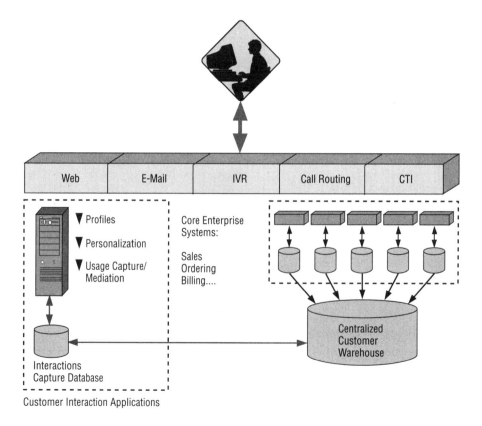

Figure 4.5: Customer Information Integration

3. Integration of disparate information delivery channels, such as e-mail, interactive voice response (IVR), intelligent call routing, and CTI platforms with the Web, to give a truly multichannel, unified view of the customer.

Although some characteristics of data integration for enabling e-business, in general, and eCRM, in particular, are similar to the characteristics evolved from business intelligence and decision-support activities such as data warehousing (for example, identifying, validating, and consolidating critical data about customers into a central repository), there are also significant differences. One difference is the need for real-time or near-real-time support of data integration. Another difference is the stringent requirements for data quality and the need for specialized data consolidation, transformation, and cleansing tools that can intelligently combine the customer data from multiple sources to create a single customer profile (for example, based on predetermined rules and conditions for converting data). Also, there is the need for update capabilities of data stores. Data stores that provide a common customer view must be updated at the customer record level, rather than completely refreshed or updated in increments as is typically done in non-customer-centric data warehouses.

Over the past several years, advances in data warehousing have led to the development and implementation of so-called operational data stores (ODSs), which are intended to integrate and synthesize data from multiple operational systems. There has been some confusion about ODSs and EAI, however, because there is some overlap in functionality. These concepts are quite distinct, and both are needed to forge a unified view of the customer.

To complete the subject of forging a single view of the customer, we need to expand on one important theme. In Chapter 3, during the discussion about information dissemination, it was stated that one of the most critical infrastructure services for enabling effective information dissemination is data integration services with translation or mediation capabilities for converting information from one format to another, subject to semantic constraints. (See Figure 3.2.) Such integration features have a specific meaning in the context of forging a unified view of the customer from a huge mass of heterogeneous, distributed data sources. In practice, it is very rare that all these sources will have the same customer identifier (for example, a data attribute that serves as the key for uniquely identifying a particular customer). Collecting customer records across all sources and merging them into a single record is therefore complex and difficult. Such a task requires data integration software with translation and mediation functions that use all kinds of algorithms (for example, fuzzy logic) to identify like or related records.

As you can see, the integration of disparate applications, operating systems, and business processes in terms of e-enabling unified customer views as a prerequisite of successful eCRM initiatives has some inherent complexity that many other types of integration tasks do not.

Integration Requirements to Support Internet-Based Customer Interactions

Clearly, the management of customer relationships is a major issue for e-business. To cope with these challenges, it is necessary to approach this issue from two perspectives: customer information and customer interaction. Consequently, the EAI concept has to take into consideration existing and adapted needs of CRM and eCRM, and also additional requirements that focus explicitly on customer interaction.[4]

What are the kinds of requirements that EAI has to deal with here? Essentially, supporting Internet-based customer interactions requires a complex combination of tightly integrated software technologies, such as advanced content management, personalized content syndication and broadcasting, and in-place data mining, on top of (or in addition to) well-defined EAI capabilities (for example, the availability of data integration modules that plug into ERP applications, transaction systems, and various legacy applications). Consequently, the cited requirements are intensifying the call for two critical integration capabilities (see Figure 4.6):

- Enabling the deployment of tools and services that ensure a high level of flexibility in operating systems, languages, database access, communication protocols, and distributed services such as CORBA or Enterprise JavaBeans (EJB).

- Enabling the deployment of tools and services that generate complex information "answers" from any customer information source within the enterprise.

Such robustness in application integration is necessary to allow for a rapid exchange of information among the many applications involved in managing the complex interconnections associated with customer interactions (for instance, communicating with the customer, taking and fulfilling

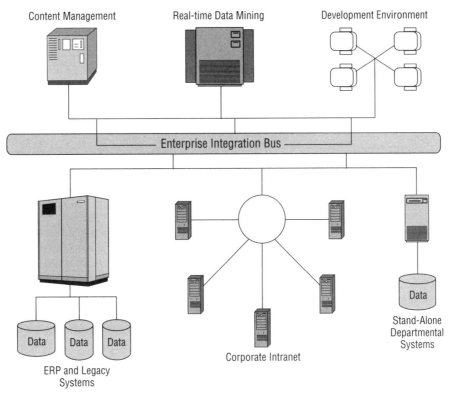

Content Management   Real-time Data Mining   Development Environment

Enterprise Integration Bus

Data   Data   Data

ERP and Legacy
Systems

Corporate Intranet

Data

Stand-Alone
Departmental
Systems

Figure 4.6: Enterprise Integration Challenges

orders as well as providing service-related information or tips on product usage, and so on). At a telecommunication company, for example, the enabling of cited levels of integration will allow, at the time of customer contact, the suggestion of new products or services for the customer, based on the results of a data mining application and the customer's up-to-the-minute call history. If a customer orders a new line via the Internet, the phone number and date of service can be provided immediately.[5]

For that reason, an EAI solution must provide a highly productive integrated development environment as well as a flexible component assembly platform. When deployed into such an environment, customer interaction applications should interoperate across CORBA, COM, JavaBeans, and EJB without custom coding, and access and exchange information with various internal and external enterprise systems. Detailed functional and integration requirements for the development environment are depicted in Table 4.1.

Table 4.1
Detailed Requirements for the Development Environment

Functional Area	Requirements
Integrated development environment (IDE)	Support for various programming models (HTML, XML, Java, ActiveX, HDML, DHTML, cascading style sheets, Java Script, VB Script, and so on) via a universal editor or best-of-breed tools.
Database access	Universal database access to major databases via native database drivers and ODBC/JDBC support.
Security	Integration of various security services supporting SSL, SHTTP, socket communication, Light-weight Directory Access Protocol (LDAP), auto message encryption, and an API for custom-built security features.
Application isolation	Accommodating stand-alone Java applications, servlets, JavaBeans, NSAPI, ISAPI, WAI & WAP, and traditional C/C++ options.
System management	SNMP integration of system management utilities via SNMP messaging.

At this point, let's discuss briefly the main characteristics of the customer interaction management tools that have to be tightly integrated.

Advanced Content Management (ACM) Tools

ACM tools provide an environment for team-based production and delivery of content. These tools allow IT organizations to manage information dissemination over the Internet collaboratively by automatically gathering, versioning, testing, and deploying vast amounts of Web content. All of this makes the process more reliable and efficient, which in turn enables companies to extract more value from their Internet investments.

Typically, content management is a custom-coded environment built on programming languages such as C/C++ or Java, various scripting languages, and template-based page layouts. In these environments, application developers spend significant time producing and maintaining content because everything is based on programming. In order to accommodate dynamic assembly of the content based on personalization, a simple HTML page, for example, has to be fully generated in "real time." Generating every page of the content on the fly is a challenging endeavor that requires not only complex programming for customer personalization, but also significant hardware investments to scale to acceptable performance levels.

Exploiting adaptive navigation, dynamic content assembly, and personalized content delivery, customer interaction applications that are based on ACM tools are capable of incorporating powerful content-component site management approaches. Specifically, such applications allow the definition of individual displayable components (a combination of content, format, and related application logic) without tying them to the specific pages on which these components might appear. Using such software, application pages are defined by specifying a series of nested content-component elements (or blocks) for building the page. This modular approach allows for an inherent, dynamic capability to separate content from presentation logic, letting users without programming expertise get involved in content production and maintenance. ACM tools become highly important for companies that have Web sites with a larger number of content-intensive dynamic pages that are updated frequently, and where, typically, more than 10 people are involved in content production, Web publishing, and support of those sites. Many leading companies, such as American Express, EMC Corporation, and Sharp Electronics, are already taking advantage of ACM technologies to shorten Web site management cycles and reduce costs.

Personalized Content Syndication and Broadcasting (PCSB) Tools

PCSB tools enable a company to better understand customer needs, behavior, and intentions by gathering profile information from each person's individual interaction history. This allows a more precise targeting of individuals and a segmentation of customers so that it is possible to offer highly tailored and personalized content, products, and services. Examples include the ability to provide a personalized Web page for each customer visiting the company's Web site, as well as automatically notifying customers of updates, new products, service requests, and so on, all of which tailors information and recommendations according to each individual customer's preferences.

PCSB tools simplify the creation and management of Web applications with syndicated content, and they push this content as personalized messages to the customer. In terms of message delivery, PCSB tools deliver personalized messages via multiple communications channels, such as the Web, pervasive devices (wireless), and voice recognition. As an example, take a Web site that likes to offer comprehensive travel-related content from different sources, such as destination information for cities, states, countries, and national parks and news, tips, maps, travel recommendations, and so on. Using a technology with powerful PCSB features, this site can provide such multisource content not only as a monolithic information set, but it also allows several interesting personalization features, such as personal travel pages and "chat rooms" to facilitate interaction between travelers.

In-Place Data Mining (IPDM) Tools

IPDM tools allow the execution of data mining functions directly against the customer-focused data sources located on the CRM servers, in contrast to traditional "sample and extract" data mining methods. These types of tools are a key variable in enhancing customer satisfaction and customer loyalty because they enable an integrated, "closed-loop" decision-support process.

The reality of today's business environment is that more and more face-to-face interactions with the customer are disappearing. As a result, companies must focus on the creation of tools and the capability to compensate for the absence of those interactions, and to gain a competitive advantage in customer-related areas of knowledge obtained from Internet-based interactions. Consequently, the ability to analyze customer interactions at the lowest level of detail (preferably, on a stroke-by-stroke basis) and in real time is becoming critical to enable the detailed identification of the key factors of successful (or unsuccessful) customer or prospect interactions and outcomes, and to ensure that marketing strategies and related messages are covering all the bases.

Controlling Business Process Integration: Being Virtual Rather Than Physical

Of all the integration levels described in the section entitled "Enterprise Application Integration," earlier in this chapter, BPI shows the broadest range of variations in integration solutions ranging from simple application-to-application (A2A) data exchange links to very complex arrangements (for example, transaction integrity support for complex purchases, work-flow routing for approval processes occurring at different systems, and so on). Taking into consideration the dynamics of today's economy, which result in constant reintegration requirements, it is almost obvious that the management of EAI development activities in the BPI area must be at the center of attention. In this area, the primary object of integration efforts should be achieving the flexibility or, more precisely, the reusability of integration components (application code, infrastructure components, and so on) and the extensibility of the integration system (for example, the ability to add a new capability to the same integration solution). Many companies do not pay enough attention to this fact. The integration components that served the first integration effort, especially the application code (for proper application integration logic), are often not reusable by the subsequent efforts. Moreover, architecture designs of these systems are done in ways that prevent extending the systems by adding additional components because of performance and high-availability concerns.

Many of the reasons for this state of affairs can be summed up in Figure 4.7.

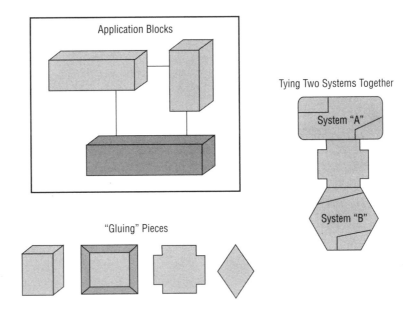

Figure 4.7: Monolithic Construction

As depicted in the top left of the figure, in the majority of cases, the application code that handles the business rules and proper application integration logic is built as large monolithic pieces of code with some internal structuring (or componentization) to encapsulate the pieces of infrastructure code such as API treatment. The boxes in the lower left reflect some pieces that are responsible for establishing interconnections between disparate applications (for example, "gluing" pieces). These pieces include, for example, the handling of legacy applications via file transfers, performing the actual message exchange between ERP systems, or interpreting the data retrieved according to some in-line mapping information in cases of electronic data interchange (EDI) operations. Enabling new requirements or enhancements to the existing functions often results in changes of the business rules that govern the application integration logic. Any such change requires many, if not all, of the "gluing" pieces to be changed, which is a risky mission because of performance, availability, and security concerns. The management of information about the business rules, such as the relationships between business rules and application code pieces, how pieces are maintained and assembled before compilation, and so on, is also cumbersome. This situation can get really messy over time, with the increasing amount of changes to the business rules that govern application integration.

In a nutshell, the traditional paradigm of application development in integration areas is largely based on fixed specifications of application integration components and their interactions. Therefore, these components are *process dependent* (for example, physically bonded). The execution model that supports such an application structure is commonly referred to as a tightly coupled integration (TCI) model. Today, TCI is the predominant model for EAI solutions at the BPI level.

In order to facilitate e-business relationships, a process-independent application structuring has to emerge. This structuring must support peer-to-peer interactions between loosely coupled integration components that offer different types of integration services through a common interface mechanism (for example, "wrapping" of the body of "gluing" pieces has occurred). In the process-independent structure, wrapped code becomes a property in its own right, and a new level of integration is established: the service-versus-process level. This new model, commonly referred to as service-oriented integration, contrasts with the previously discussed monolithic model. Consequently, the structure of integration systems changes to the structure depicted on the right in Figure 4.7. Appealing aspects of this structure include the fact that the current physical implementation of services is transparent to applications that require integration, and more complex services may be provided by combining multiple existing services.

Figure 4.8 illustrates the most common execution architecture to enable service-oriented integration (SOI).

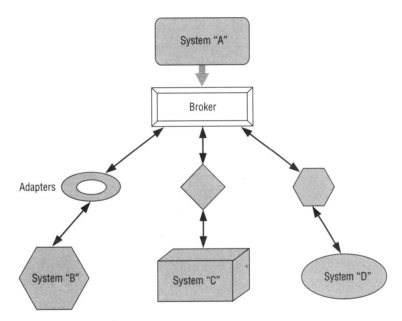

Figure 4.8: Broker-Adapter EAI Architecture

This architecture is based on the two-level programming approach that underlies the integration software, the so-called *broker-adapter integration* approach. The handling of all basic aspects of integration, such as the implementation details of BCI and BAI levels, is separated (into a "broker" component) from the specifics of the particular applications involved in each instance of integration activities. Those specifics are encapsulated into all kinds of adapters that are commonly available for popular packaged applications (for example, ERP and CRM packages), legacy databases, e-mail systems, and so on. In SOI implementations, a broker performs the duties of a proxy for various databases, applications, and infrastructure services, regardless of how they are physically constructed. This allows the application code, supporting the business rules of the integration process, to change without affecting the associated "glue" implementations. The two-level approach to integration software is the predominant reason why enterprises are investing in packaged EAI technology today.[6]

From the standpoint of connection architectures, there are two prevailing approaches for implementing SOI (as illustrated in Figure 4.9):

1. **Hub and Spoke**—Applications are connected to an all-purpose broker that can handle a variety of communication protocols and data formats, called the hub. The hub manages the business rules that govern the integration process and exchange of messages between the connected applications.

2. **Publish and Subscribe**—Integration is accomplished by following the rules of making information available via publishing (broadcasting) mechanisms. Many asynchronous message-oriented middleware products are based on this architecture.

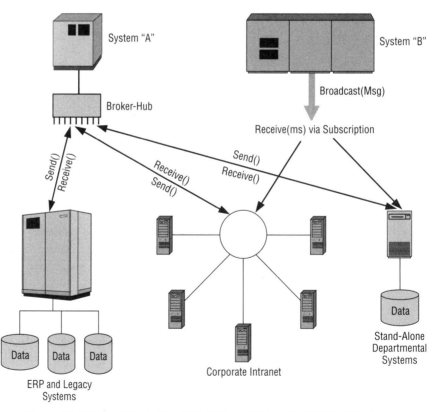

Figure 4.9: "Hub and Spoke" and "Publish and Subscribe" EAI Architectures

SOI holds great potential to streamline and improve business-to-business integration. However, not all adapter technologies are equally suited to supporting different business processes, especially across the extended enterprise. The most successful way to attempt to "knit" all these different systems, processes, and data sources into a cohesive whole, at this moment, is to use so-called *dynamic* (or *programmable*) *adapter technologies*. Currently, there are several commercially available dynamic adapter technologies with different flexibility-enabling features. The most powerful are solutions that are based on the new Dynamic Proxy API, introduced in Java 2 Standard Edition (J2SE) version 1.3, that make it simpler to dynamically create the necessary object classes. That, in turn, enables companies to quickly define, manage, and change their diverse enterprise and business-to-business integration requirements.[7]

This leads to a new state of integration, so-called *virtual integration processing* (VIP), one that does not affect (until explicitly made visible) operations outside the adapters. As a result, different integration models have been proposed to target the flexible composition (coupling) of services, the coordination of their interactions dynamically and in real time, and the maintenance of conversational state during business-to-business transactions that can span multiple systems across the extended enterprise. VIP will provide tremendous benefits from a cost and reengineering point of view in automating EAI tasks.

Enabling e-Marketplaces: ERP-to-ERP Integration Challenges

An e-marketplace is the place of exchange between buyer and seller on the Internet. It can involve two companies or thousands of companies. In many respects, the key defining characteristic of e-marketplaces is that they are *fluid* in nature. New e-marketplaces get established every day. A single company may directly participate in multiple e-marketplaces simultaneously, constantly redefining its relationships with a particular marketplace. Through the Internet, it can quickly and easily develop tight relationships with participants in the marketplace or get involved in supply value chains with companies outside its marketplace—establishing indirect ("virtual") participation in other marketplaces. It may cancel relationships just as easily.

The key to supporting this highly fluid environment is the meaningful sharing of information and business intent among all participants in the e-business relationship. This requirement takes the notion of EAI to the next level: enabling fast, easy, low-cost, dynamic electronic bonding between businesses and their customers, suppliers, and partners, spanning a diverse range of product and service providers across multiple industries.

Today, the prevailing models of e-marketplaces are as follows (see Figures 4.10, 4.11, and 4.12):

1. **Extended Trading Network**—An e-marketplace formed and owned by a single enterprise (usually a large one, for example, DaimlerChrysler or Boeing) to improve the efficiencies of its own supply chain.

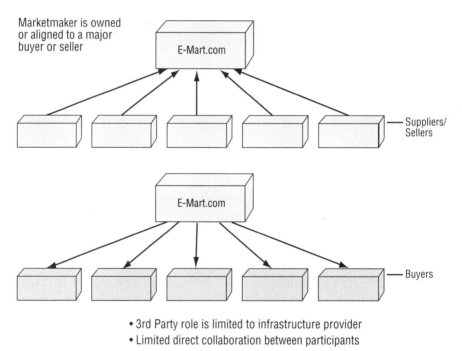

Figure 4.10: Extended Trading Network

2. **Governed Exchange**—An e-marketplace formed by a group of companies (consortium) or by an intermediary (for example, a direct beneficiary or a neutral facilitator) for the benefits of the market maker, yet fulfilling

the business objectives (for example, profitability requirements) of the participants. Various trading models exist, such as buy–sell trading (for example, trading exchanges where buyers and sellers can establish direct business arrangements via an e-marketplace hub), auction, reverse action, and so on. At the time of writing, there are many examples of such e-marketplaces in operation, including BigVine.com, VerticalNet, Inc., Chemdex.com, and so on.

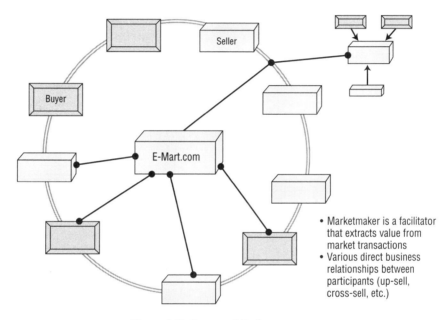

- Marketmaker is a facilitator that extracts value from market transactions
- Various direct business relationships between participants (up-sell, cross-sell, etc.)

Figure 4.11: Governed Exchange

3. **Virtual Collaborative Network**—An electronic community instituted by a group of semiautonomous or autonomous organizations under the premise that the group can achieve more as a group than the participants could do by themselves. Examples are collaborative design groups, buying or selling cooperatives, "pipelines," and so on, such as the European CONCUR Consortium.

E-marketplaces, especially governed exchanges, have a substantial impact on companies' computer systems, especially on mission-critical applications such as ERP and CRM. Current architectures of these systems depend upon precast distributed application models that focus on supporting preestablished interenterprise business relationships (for example, business process definitions configured in database tables). Those architectures are inadequate for supporting e-marketplaces. New architectures are required based on cooperative distributed application models, often referred to as *federated system architectures* (FSAs). FSAs are concerned with facilitating cooperation between autonomous systems for the purpose of sharing services and resources.[8] The realization of composite business process or service packages requires flexible management of the flow of integration services between systems that are owned by widely distributed autonomous providers. The processes or packages, in turn, require on-demand (dynamic) EAI capability.[9]

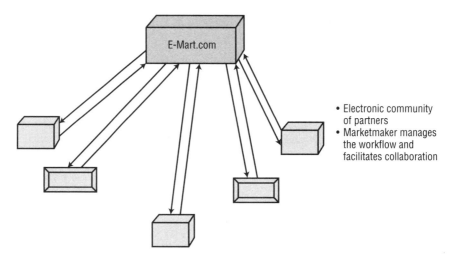

Figure 4.12: Virtual Collaborative Network

The notion of FSA adds a wide range of complex integration problems (and opportunities) to the "EAI plate," all of which must be addressed in a comprehensive and consistent manner. This requirement is driven by the rapidly evolving needs of companies that are actively pursuing the opportunity to participate in multiple trading communities, and, as a result, need to link their hubs to other hubs and marketplaces (possible topologies for such links are depicted in Figures 4.10, 4.11, and 4.12).

Four main FSA-related themes (objectives) could be defined in regard to enabling e-marketplaces:

1. **Heterogeneous Interchange**—Supporting the technological, naming or semantic, description, and binding aspects of federated interoperation between autonomous systems, and including detecting incompatibility and taking appropriate actions where possible to bridge it. There are two fundamental sets of problems that EAI vendors have to deal with in order to support federated interoperation. First, EAI vendors have to provide a comprehensive and highly effective approach for supporting dynamic composition of integration services (so-called plug-and-play integration features) within all kinds of hub-and-spoke configurations (for example, the configurations depicted in Figure 4.11). The subject of dynamic integration services and the related topic of avoiding the tight coupling of business rules that govern the integration and related application code with a particular application were introduced earlier in the previous section. Second, EAI vendors have to enable the seamless integration of very large numbers of individual items and semirelated information sets, each with its own mapping rules and translation conventions.

2. **Federated Process Management**—Supporting the overall management of processes across multiple hubs and spokes in a federated setting—in particular, managing policies for the interchange, monitoring, quality control (for example, nonfunctional aspects of dynamic integration services such as security, performance, dependability, and so on), accounting, and billing (for example, measuring transaction flows and billing and handling charges).

3. **Federated Authority Management**—Supporting functions that facilitate the identification of trading members and the products and services that EAI products offer.

4. **Federated Infrastructure Management**—Supporting mechanisms and protocols required for interoperation between multiple hubs and spokes that may be using different technologies.

Fulfilling these objectives requires comprehensive analysis of the technical challenges that arise from the perspective of the stated objectives—as well as techniques for dealing with them. This will lead to various development efforts by all kinds of parties (for example, companies that participate in e-marketplaces, EAI vendors, application providers, systems integrators, and so on).

One area that requires extensive analysis is ERP-to-ERP integration. The primary reason for this is twofold. On one side, there is a lot riding on the correct information exchange between such systems in terms of ensuring e-marketplace global efficiency—for example, in the areas of supply and demand management and timely delivery. On the other side, integrating autonomous ERP systems is a significant challenge because of numerous concerns, such as the tremendous complexity of issues related to heterogeneous interchange, especially information transfer; the need for EAI software to deeply understand the process logic of all interconnected systems; the fact that APIs vary in the degree of openness between different ERP systems; and the fact that there is no standardization across data and process models.

In order to support and manage the full range of ERP-to-ERP interfaces required for global exchanges, one must first understand the different kinds of EAI-based solutions currently being used for ERP-to-ERP integration. Let's conclude the discussion about this subject with a brief, high-level summary of the current state of the art in this area.

To support EAI-to-EAI integration, several different types of integration mechanisms are available. Examples of the most commonly used are as follows:

- **Proprietary APIs**—Examples include ERP package messaging, such as SAP's Application Linking and Embedding (ALE), and ERP application interfaces, such as SAP's Business API (BAPI). In order to provide wide levels of interoperability, these mechanisms have to be "wrapped" within adapters and made available in object interfaces such as COM or CORBA.

- **Message Queuing Products**—Examples include IBM's MQSeries, Microsoft's MSMQ, and New Era of Networks (NEON). The main advantage of these products is the fact that they enable asynchronous, loose coupling of distributed applications. To make them more attractive for companies with ERP-to-ERP needs, vendors are introducing additional products on top of the base products that will enhance their ability to link disparate ERP systems. IBM's MQIntegrator product is a good example. This product lets users interconnect ERP systems by using what is essentially a database-based rule engine that maintains business rules and templates as line items in a database. Nevertheless, generally speaking, message queuing products can require substantial effort to institute federated behavior. This factor is one of the major attractions of EAI packaged software, which makes use of such products.

■ **EAI Suites with ERP Adapters**—Examples include Crossroads 2000, an application integration suite from Extricity, Inc.; CrossWorld Product Suite from CrossWorlds Software, Inc.; Integration System from Active Software, Inc.; and ROMA Business Service Platform from Candle Corp. Most such products provide prebuilt adapters for leading ERP packages, including SAP R/3, Oracle, PeopleSoft, and so on. In addition, they often include so-called adapter development kits that significantly reduce the complexity of ERP integration.

To a large degree, the last category, EAI suites with ERP adapters, can be considered the "prime" approach for ERP-to-ERP integration, because solutions in that category exploit business objects as integration points and embrace the broker-adapter architecture and related hub-and-spoke connection structures. For example, Candle's ROMA represents an EAI suite that ties together, in a single package, the most commonly needed technologies for enabling e-business operations, such as connectivity, component-based application development, system management with message-queuing integration facilities, Light Directory Access Protocol (LDAP), and programmable adapters for connecting ERP systems. In ROMA, all of these technologies can be packaged as "business services" that can be invoked via a Java interface.

Although, increasingly, EAI suites will be able to solve many of the previously stated integration problems, at this moment, these products do not and cannot adequately address them in a comprehensive fashion. The main problem is that the traditional EAI frameworks exploited by those products do not adequately support the dynamics of ERP-to-hub-to-ERP connections (as depicted in Figure 4.13). This is because they assume that interfaces must be well structured, with the process logic functioning strictly according to given specifications and interactions between ERP systems occurring in predefined ways. As a result, from a practical, cost-effectiveness perspective, ERP-to-ERP interfaces can only be structured as static interconnections because of limited support for the dynamic configuration of such interfaces. Nevertheless, in a couple of years, we can expect to see significant advances in the EAI tool suite area, which is the subject of our discussion in the next section.

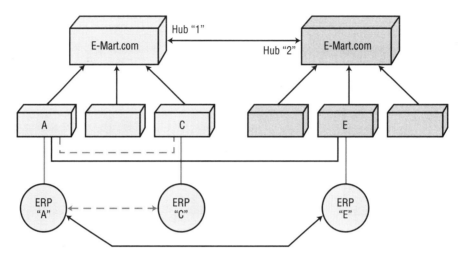

Figure 4.13: ERP-to-Hub-to-ERP Dynamic Networks

In the meantime, what can companies be using beyond the established EAI tools, which are still much preferable to building entirely custom solutions using APIs or message queuing, but provide only partial ERP-to-ERP capabilities? Recently, there has been an explosion in the number of announcements of so-called solution-oriented e-business platforms, attempts to address the most common functional and infrastructure requirements of all kinds of B2B models, including e-marketplaces, in a single, tightly integrated package (something like a "first aid" kit for B2B). One quite possible outcome of deployments of these technologies is that the integration of many common ("like-minded") ERP functions (for example, order management, billing, and so on) will be standardized, reducing the complexity of ERP-to-ERP tasks. Take, for example, the Ariba B2B Commerce Platform from Ariba Technologies, Inc. First, it performs the functions of an EAI suite. It sits on top of an ERP system and enables the exchange of information between the platform and the ERP system about orders circulating among buyers and sellers. Second, it automates many common business functions related to e-market making processes, including the assessment, design, creation, and management of transaction flows from requisition to payment; detailed pricing (as well as fixed-price mechanisms); and catalog management.

What makes all this a new approach to application integration? From the EAI standpoint, there is not much of a difference between this platform and the products highlighted previously under the EAI tool suite category. Architecturally, however, Ariba represents an approach with a much broader scope because of its "all-in-one" business service orientation that, ultimately, allows you to achieve a much more seamless level of integration between ERP systems.

Future Directions: Where Should EAI Be in a Couple of Years?

In the near future, EAI software is set to achieve significant advances in its capabilities; consequently, the market for such software is set to explode. I hope that the previous sections' discussion of business needs, issues, challenges, and opportunities is convincing enough to back up this statement.

Overall, we can expect leading EAI tool vendors to focus more on e-business integration, and in particular, to address common data and business rules integration requirements (for example, the transformation and mediation of disparate information) based on the exploitation of business objects as integration points and emerging standards, such as XML. But it is the wider adoption by businesses of dynamic organizational structures, such as virtual enterprises and e-marketplaces, that will ultimately bring answers to many critical integration questions posed by those structures. Componentization of EAI tools is also likely to occur shortly, allowing users to implement multifaceted "best-of-breed" EAI solutions. Basically, EAI will include a broad base of already-known EAI tools, bundled with sophisticated Internet tools and a number of innovative new technologies, such as intelligent agents, in-place data mining, wide-area workflow systems, and many more. In a nutshell: In the next couple of years, EAI will become a much broader concept than it is today.

Let's review some of the most critical upcoming advances in application integration.

Plug-and-Play Interoperability

As was stated previously, companies engaged in cross-enterprise schemas, such as e-marketplaces, require two (contradictory, to a large degree) forms of interoperability: first, tight integration with partners, and second, flexibility to drop or add potential partners. As a result, they require the capability to rapidly (almost "on the fly") reconfigure application-to-application links, basically to have such links functioning between partners only for the time required to complete specific arrangements.

Leading EAI tools will address the cited issues by incorporating into their core a mixture of concepts and technologies that enable the transition of the current application integration architectures. This transition will be characterized by removing the reliance upon preestablished business relationships and shared technical infrastructure. The next-generation architecture will support the construction of interfaces on the fly and on demand. By incorporating those concepts and technologies into the core of EAI tools, it will be possible to extend the base EAI functionality to include all the functions that users need for enabling many complex, intimate, many-to-many, concurrent interactions among departmental, enterprise, and productivity applications (such as context management, imaging, and workflow, as well as various business processes).

Over the next couple of years, a wide range of interoperability-related topics will receive considerable attention by EAI developers. Many of these topics have been already introduced along the way in this chapter. Nevertheless, because of the importance of the subject matter, it makes sense to summarize the key topics at this moment in our discussion:

- **Utilization of the Web for the Integration Infrastructure (for Example, Communications and Information Exchange)**—Using the Internet, extranets, intranets, and the corresponding standards, such as XML and the Simple Object Access Protocol (SOAP), improves Internet interoperability with an XML-based, platform-agnostic approach to programming the Web.

- **Introduction of New Standards for Plug-and-Play Interoperability and Convergence of Current Interoperability Standards**—At this time, there are no widely accepted standards for designing, implementing, documenting, and adapting plug-and-play capabilities. Moreover, existing industry interoperability standards such as CORBA, COM, and Java RMI are significantly differentiated with regard to supporting dynamic interoperability; they lack the necessary common semantics and features to be truly effective across multiple autonomous application domains. Therefore, it's essential for EAI vendors to work with standards organizations to introduce new standard specifications to support true plug-and-play interoperability and define features that meet needs of extended enterprises.

- **Utilization of OO Features That Are Capable of Enhancing the Extensibility of Cross-System Interfaces**—By employing additional levels of integration that utilize the OO concepts of "black box" frameworks and dynamic binding, it becomes possible to customize existing interfaces "on the fly." However, with dynamic binding, the resulting generality and flexibility often reduce efficiency. New options that have been recently introduced in Java to facilitate the use of dynamic binding (for instance, the Dynamic Proxy API) make the concept of dynamic binding practical for time-critical software.

- **Utilization of Component-Based Architectures within EAI Tools**—Only by fully embracing component-based approaches for structuring EAI interfaces, and especially by providing two distinct and fully independent component classes of "binders" and adapters that can be plugged together to form complete interfaces (a binder is a component that literally connects an adapter to the integration infrastructure), is it possible to support current EAI requirements, as well as to allow the flexibility to adopt new requirements and emerging technologies.

- **Utilization of Emerging Directory Services Standards**—By fully supporting a standard directory services approach based on Lightweight Directory Access Protocol (LDAP) to provide universal storage and management of user identities, network resource addresses, and security services (such as Microsoft's Active Directory or Novell's NDS), it becomes possible to enable the federated cross-systems integration capability.

- **Automation of Documentation Production**—Accurate and comprehensible documentation is critical to the success of large-scale EAI initiatives. However, documenting interfaces and integration details is a costly, highly time-consuming activity. Current EAI tools provide very little in regard to automation of documentation production, mostly focusing on visual aspects of capturing low-level details of transformation mapping. They fail to capture the strategic roles and collaborations among integration components. It can be expected that the advent of tools for reverse-engineering the structure of interfaces, data structures, and business objects of applications participating in complex interconnection arrangements will help to improve the accuracy and utility of EAI documentation. Likewise, we can expect to see a move by modeling tool vendors to explicitly support EAI development in their products to provide higher-level models of workflows and interface communications, and descriptions of business rules that govern integration.

Cross-Enterprise Collaboration

A key requirement for managing the work across multiple autonomous systems is to have a dominant interface that does not control systems behavior, but rather controls processes and access to information across systems (providing global workflow integration capability). More specifically, EAI should enable an application model in which cross-enterprise management of business processes is separate from the application interface. The National Industrial Information Infrastructure Protocols Consortium is addressing standardization activities necessary for the integration of workflow systems, but until recently, EAI tool vendors have been slow to develop this capability. Hence, we can expect to see an increase in the current trend of marrying EAI tools with advanced workflow technologies, such as wide-area workflow management (WAWM), to provide more dynamic workflow and process capabilities.

WAWM is a new workflow architecture that defines the technical and managerial aspects of the interaction of different workflow management systems in the interenterprise setting. WAWM will play an instrumental role within the scope of EAI. First, this emerging technology will provide universal access to individual workflow processes by separating the actual processes from the application protocol and by sharing data via electronic documents. Second, and most important, WAWM will enable organization of EAI processes entirely within the framework of loosely coupled collaborating systems. Such organization is key in simultaneously providing the mechanisms for flexibility and a relatively tight integration level. It allows the exhibition of both tight levels of integration (through coupling of processes) and flexibility (through looseness), and is characterized by the independence of process integration from application interfaces.

Integration of Decision Support and Business Intelligence Systems

Finally, currently, EAI tools are focused almost exclusively on issues of integrating transaction-oriented systems. But it is necessary to combine the decision-making capabilities of participating partners in order to monitor all the cross-enterprise elements. In other words, it is not enough to integrate operational processes and data. EAI tools must also enable the integration of interenterprise decisions. As a result, in the near future, as part of the evolution of corporate portals, we will see substantial emphasis on the integration of decision-making capabilities within federated settings of autonomous and semiautonomous organizations.

To conclude our discussion about the future for application integration, one very important point needs to be made here. Although the different technologies and concepts used to frame this new state of EAI will come from a variety of perspectives, there is only one ultimate goal for EAI in the future: higher integration between partners engaged in cross-enterprise processes, as well as the flexibility for them to respond to change quickly. More to the point, at a macrolevel, we have to view the future state of EAI as a bundle of multiple application integration capabilities and other types of technologies with distinctive, inimitable capabilities that enable collaboration and interoperability between operational systems, decision-support systems, and process-management systems in geographically distributed and legally separated organizations. Note that the concept of viewing EAI as a "bundle" should not be thought of as merely a way of representing technologies. Without a single platform to tie all those technologies into a cohesive whole, e-business integration will remain beyond an organization's grasp. This brings us to the next topic.

The Pressing Need for a Unifying Integration Platform

As the use of e-business technologies proliferates, it is becoming evident that substantial progress in the field of application integration cannot be achieved without defining a framework, an underlying backbone, that will tie together many tools and techniques used in association with integration projects. As a result, the unifying integration platform (UIP) concept has recently received much attention and popularity in industry and academia alike. UIP is aimed at delivering an increasing coherence between multiple technologies, potentially from different vendors, in an effort to best serve customer integration needs while keeping application development efficiency at a high level.

UIP is much more in terms of functional, technical, and physical views toward technology choices than just making sure that every tool you purchase was written to work on a "single executing platform." The reality is that, although tool vendors always claim platform adherence (to a specific platform), they have very few incentives to standardize and always seek out some form of "proprietary advantage."[10] More to the point, given the broad base of standards that are applicable to the field of application integration, pursuing a "best-of-breed" strategy based on the executing platform factor, as long as tools from more than one vendor are involved, is not economically feasible because of the amount of custom work required to overcome those "advantages." The UIP concept, in contrast with the platform-based approach, has a different mission: to synchronize development principles, models, business processes, execution coordination and cooperation, and infrastructures in which tools and integration technologies from any number of sources are running on multiple executing platforms. The main goal for the cited concept becomes one of outlining a comprehensive set of functional, architectural, and physical implementation characteristics (specifications) that define the fit of a technology in the integration processes that surround it.

To understand UIP, let's briefly summarize the main business strategies currently being pursued by EAI tool vendors to enable e-business transformation. For the most part, these strategies fall into the following key categories (a short description of vendor strategies is given in Table 4.2):

- Internet integration

- Process management

- Application management

- Data integration

- Infrastructure management

Table 4.2
Key EAI Tool Vendor Strategies for Enabling e-Business Transformation

Category	Strategy	Description
Internet application integration	Provide a framework for integrating Internet interactions	Support for information dissemination functions (for example, searching, access, publishing, and so on) and personalization. Integrated support for Internet application architectures based on applications servers that support Enterprise JavaBeans (EJB) and Microsoft's COM/DNA

Category	Strategy	Description
	Provide a framework for a collection of technologies that together enable time integration of multiple systems	B2B Integration: integration of middle- and back-office applications both within and across multiple enterprises in support of the full supply chain management business processes. Integrated support for combining new system functionality with ERP packages and client-server and legacy applications
Process management	Enable businesses to dynamically define, monitor, and change business processes	Integrated workflow and decision support both within and across multiple enterprises
Application management	Enable capabilities for IT personnel to size application environments, monitor user response times, and meet service-level agreement guarantees	Integrated support for performance monitoring and management, stress testing, and application infrastructure management
Data integration	Provide comprehensive data access, meta-data management, data cleansing, and data transformation capabilities	Integrated support for information repositories, database gateways; tools for extracting, mediating, transforming, moving and loading data; in-place data mining tools and information delivery tools (for example, OLAP tools). Integration of XML and related technologies
Infrastructure management	Provide connectivity among heterogeneous hardware, operating systems, and appli-cation development environments	Integrated support for hardware connectivity, middleware, communications protocols, programming languages, testing and debugging tools, and so on

Imagine how difficult and costly it might be if IT organizations were each embarking on their own way to make the "best of breed," formed out of products from all of these categories (because no single vendor has it or will have it all), to work effectively and efficiently? Preventing this problem by creating and managing a common functional, technical, and physical (executionwise) computing environment for the entire integration process is what the UIP concept is all about.

Conceptually, at a very high level, the vision of the UIP architecture is of a highly intelligent and collaborative federation. (See Figure 4.14.) The main question to be answered is "What is the most promising framework to realize such a federation?" The first wave of UIP-type solutions, in which software vendors took a "solution-oriented" (for example, turn-key) approach, has just arrived. Although there are just a few examples of fully functional offerings, analysis of the first wave allows us to answer this important question. The primary goal of the discussion that follows through the rest of the book is to elaborate in detail on the most promising UIP framework—the corporate portal.

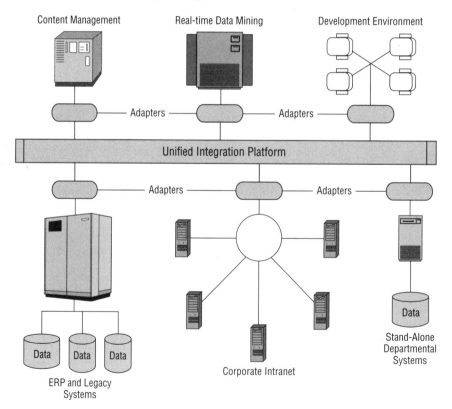

Figure 4.14: Unified Integration Platform

Soon We'll Have a Whole Virtual Enterprise: The Case of the European Construction Industry

In the conclusion of this chapter dedicated to the subject of application integration, we have to come back to the most imaginative, intriguing, and challenging theme of e-business transformation—the virtual enterprise (VE)—because of the role played by EAI technologies in enabling the VE. Shattering traditional organizational principles in manufacturing, construction, consumer goods, and other industries providing products or services, the VE paradigm will forever change the business landscape. Long-lasting business alliances, which make up the bulk of today's commercial world, will simply go away, to be replaced by all kinds of temporary partnerships of small- to medium-sized firms engaged in dynamic, project-oriented relationships.

Right now I think that a lot of companies are wondering whether this paradigm is a blueprint for revolution or merely hype. Clearly, implementing an extended enterprise solution does not offer a simple way to do business. But in spite of that, many reports of multiple extended enterprise initiatives (for example, the CONCUR experiment that is currently underway in Europe on a large scale) provide enough information to come to the conclusion that virtual enterprises are not hype, and if addressed properly, can produce extraordinary economic benefits.

One of the largest industries in Europe is the building and civil engineering (BCE) industry, with an annual expenditure of more than $300 billion. Besides being large, the BCE industry is also complex and fragmented. The majority of the companies are small- to medium-sized enterprises, located in different countries, which operate in a dispersed and concurrent business environment with project-centered, partnership-based characteristics. Until recently, the organization and execution of projects have followed very traditional process patterns, with corresponding traditional information sharing and exchange methods, such as drawings, meetings, faxes, and so on.

In the last decade, however, the business climate surrounding the industry has begun to change markedly. Competition has drastically increased because of globalization. All kinds of companies from the United States and Asia have entered the marketplace. Clients and facility operators have started to demand better quality, faster, and more cheaply built facilities, incorporating more complex technology. At the same time, European governments have considerably raised the regulatory constraints on safety, waste, and energy consumption.

The response of the BCE industry to these challenges is to improve its overall efficiency. Right now, the industry's focus is on facilitating the transition to integrated design and construction (IDC). IDC aims to capture and make available existing knowledge in the formative stages of a project and in the various stages of realization of the product. IDC requires the implementation of information and knowledge transfer mechanisms, such as the feedback of "constructability" knowledge to the design stage. Such information and knowledge mechanisms can only be practically implemented using integrated information systems and electronic data exchange and sharing within "virtual enterprise" environments.

In order to find the best possible solution for enabling IDC, the CONCUR Consortium, a group that comprises several large European contractors (Taylor Woodrow, IVO International, and Skanska), research and development institutions (VTT and TNO), systems house STABU, and universities (DUT and KTH), has started to develop, implement, and deploy integrated environments for commercial and industrial building projects (for example, power plants, incinerators, manufacturing plants, and so on). The primary focus of the CONCUR initiative is on managing the information at the interfaces between the different systems, thereby supporting concurrent design and engineering. The key underlying technology architecture used and elaborated in CONCUR is the so-called BCE Production Data Technology, which is based on a combination of EAI CORBA-compliant tool sets and formal knowledge management methodologies and processes that provide the vital data integration capability of the information to be managed in the entire spectrum of business processes characteristic to a construction project.

Europe has had the lead in information sharing standards for the past four years, notably in ISO/STEP AEC developments, with XML-based application protocols promoted by the United Kingdom, France, The Netherlands, and Sweden. This has now extended to leading technical and management roles for European organizations within the recently established International Alliance for Interoperability (IAI). However, both STEP and IAI are strictly focused on technology. In contrast, CONCUR picks up the evolving technologies and applies them to live BCE projects, providing know-how for European companies in the implementation of new methods, which will support concurrent design, engineering, and electronic tendering. This is strengthening the position of European companies on the worldwide markets.

In summary, the innovative contributions of CONCUR are as follows:

- The design and implementation of a multifaceted information exchange across the entire BCE supply chain (for example, between the client and contractor entities and everything in between), based on international standards such as ISO 10303-STEP, IAI-IFC, SGML, EDI, ISO 13584-Parts Library, and others.

- The enhancement of key industrial applications so that they can be hooked into the chain and applied in practice.

- The development, testing, and evaluation of downstream exchange of complete electronic tendering information and upstream exchange of information about alternative technical solutions.

CONCUR is a long-range initiative with multiple phases. The "prime" deliverable of each phase is defined in terms of industrial business objectives and expected achievements both in performance (time and cost) and in quality. Early results reported by several case studies (for example, for British Airports Authority) illustrate significant increases in performance; productivity increases of up to 50 percent have been reported. These increases are a result of the following:

- Savings in time and a reduction of errors from a leaner design process in which all information transformations between paper-based representations and computer-based representations are eliminated.

- Savings in time and a reduction of errors because a number of the current activities, like producing bills of quantities or producing specialized models (for instance, for structural analysis), have been done electronically.

- Improvements in quality and safety because the model-based backbone supports the reuse of successful earlier designs and of large amounts of knowledge (constructability knowledge, environmental knowledge, and so on).

- Improvements in time, costs, and quality because downstream processes have access to all the relevant upstream information, allowing alternative solutions to be proposed and communicated to clients.

■ Improvements in time, cost, and quality because it is easy to establish alternative project organizations with up-to-date information continuously available on-line.

The CONCUR initiative is also contributing to the development of a European construction e-marketplace. This would allow contractors to bid for projects that support neutral data exchange and sharing. Bidding systems and construction management and planning systems are being integrated within this marketplace. A lot of waste is thereby eliminated. Problems with national differences and language barriers are no longer a constraint. Other substantial savings will come from the increased speed and quality of the design and construction process of the entire multinational BCE supply chain. Fewer errors, greater consistency, improved communications, more care for the environment (by formalizing environment knowledge and applying that knowledge automatically during design and engineering), and more chances for adequate process reengineering will all lead to increased competitiveness of the European BCE industry in the global economy.

The Portal

The Chapter 2 introduction to the concept of portals revealed certain characteristics present in these significant constituents of cyberspace, attributes of a single entry point onto the Internet, and positioned portals within the frame of the e-business strategic technology architecture (EBSTA). This chapter presents a systematic description of the concept and its critical elements.

Portals are the hottest trend in e-business today, with virtually every company on the Web trying to capitalize on this phenomenon. The term *portal* is, however, one of the most misused terms in the marketing of software for e-business. It seems that most Web applications today—particularly those for Web-based business intelligence—claim some sort of "portal" functionality, in which the software performs information dissemination tasks for you automatically.

The concept of portals has evolved from the paradigm of the human intermediary (for example, the librarian). The goal is to provide a single entry point to the Internet by providing services most often used by Web users (for example, e-mail, search, personalized news, and other general information dissemination services), while keeping in mind the desires and preferences of the end-clients. This would describe our expectations of a good librarian. With the explosive growth of information available to us through the Internet, users have been attempting to carry out tasks for which we have traditionally hired this and other types of intermediaries to help us. But without the use of electronic intermediaries, the tasks become equally as daunting as in the conventional, physical world. Yet there is still faith that we can create a virtual world where electronic intermediaries with built-in intelligence act virtuously and virtually as our "librarians," making our professional and personal lives simpler. It is this vision that calls for an intelligent, overreaching intermediary (or, as it is generically known, an "intelligent portal"), as we grapple with how best to maneuver through the vast (and growing) sea of information that is now at our fingertips.

This chapter will focus on the architecture and practical aspects of the use of portal technologies by companies. Before we begin, however, it is important to at least relate these technologies to the two key areas within the scope of e-business transformation—technology and organization—in which they are playing a crucial role. With the business focus moved to the customer, and the decision-making power moved to the front-based end user, portals are the manifestation of companies' search for unconventional solutions in these areas:

- Technology—Recent key technology developments, such as interaction management and content personalization, have facilitated outward, customer-facing, real-time "killer applications," revolutionizing all aspects of the competition for the customer. Success is no longer gained by building Web site infrastructure, providing access, and publishing information; customers want new forms of business-customer interactions. When visiting a Web site, customers want to be able to establish a personal electronic space that works to make their interaction experience simpler, not more complex. They would like to be able to create a number of "personae," each with a specific profile of defined interfaces to communities of interest. Portals are becoming crucial technological elements of the Web architecture by allowing these new forms of business-customer interactions.

- **Business and Organizational Models That Make the Technology Successful**—The portal is not only a very important technological concept, but also one of the most intriguing organizational formats to come out of the latest Internet successes and hard-earned lessons. It does not resemble any known organizational models. This new model portrays the business role of a "digital broker" (or a "cybermediary") to add value to and mediate between a highly diverse and disparate universe of Internet users, such as information publishers and information consumers, buyers and sellers of goods and services, and all kinds of collaborative groups and "virtual" communities. It requires the business functionality of all known forms of information and service intermediaries (for example, libraries, on-line information services such as Lexis-Nexis, transaction clearing houses such as credit card companies, and so on) plus organizational structures for supporting sophisticated market processes for mediation between buyers and sellers.

The Portal: A Taxonomy

When it comes to obtaining a somewhat detailed understanding about a concept or a theory, trying to put together a descriptive taxonomy (basically, a "philosophical" interpretation) from the perspective of its evolution can be extremely helpful. This is especially true in the case of portals, because there is so much hype surrounding the concept nowadays. But there is indeed much substance beneath the hype!

Since the early days of the Internet, there have been major shifts in technology, providing users with the means to access on-line information and forms of on-line services over the Web—be it the Internet, intranet, or extranet. This has resulted in a mismatch between the availability of information, and the efficiency and effectiveness of information searching. The primary driving force behind portals was, and to a certain degree continues to be, the goal of eliminating this mismatch by improving search efficiency (for example, reducing the time it takes for an inquirer to locate relevant information about a specific subject, be it through a single Web site or through a network of distributed, heterogeneous information sources).

In general, a portal application (a portal, for short) is a single, Web-based interface into the world of heterogeneous and incompatible information sources distributed across the network. Portals originated from "search engines," sites that helped Web users locate relevant information on the Internet. In the early days of the Web, searching for information was a very frustrating and highly unproductive adventure, because users were required to navigate raw associative links between information sources using a complex command language. It soon became evident that navigating raw links to find even simple information, such as weather, travels, sports, and so on, was totally unacceptable.

As a result, new types of sites, termed "navigation sites," started to appear. In order to address user frustration and reduce the average "seek time" to find relevant information, these new sites provided the function of content categorization by prefiltering popular sites (and the documents they contain) into preconfigured categories according to content (for example, sports, news, and finance). As soon as navigation sites came up with reasonably attractive groups of content, these sites became, and continue to be, the starting points for many regular Web users. This was the commencement moment for portals.

Although the dictionary definition of the term is quite simple (a *portal* is an opening that objects must pass through on their way to someplace else), it has multiple meanings. The first meaning of the term portal is the following: a *portal is an originating Web site with search engine capabilities.*

Portals that began as search engines (Yahoo!, Lycos, Excite, AltaVista, and so on) have quickly evolved into central information location points for navigating the Internet, for gathering relevant information, and, most recently, for collaborative community activities. This was the moment in their evolution when portals became known as "Internet portals" or, simply, "Web portals."

From that moment, the concept of portals evolved (progressing and converging at the same time) along four key interrelated paths (see Figure 5.1):

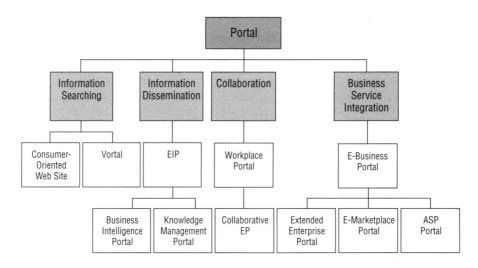

Figure 5.1: The Evolution of Portals

1. Information searching

2. Information dissemination

3. Collaboration (bringing people together)

4. Business service integration

Information Searching

The vast information resources of the Internet offer fascinating benefits to businesses, but only if they can be searched effectively. Because Internet users spend a considerable time searching (up to 50 percent of their time, according to recent reports), the Web portals, no matter how many other "bells and whistles" they have, require the best search engine technology possible in order to attract users. One of the most important objectives for Web portals is improving information search capabilities. Delivering timely, relevant, high-quality search results is, however, virtually impossible to accomplish within a single site because of the size of the Web. As a result, Web portals have evolved into two types of portals: consumer-oriented search sites, and "vortals" (vertical industry portals). A *vortal* is a Web site that provides a gateway to information (for example, unique editorial content, product reviews, and so on) related to a particular industry (for example, consumer goods manufacturing, health care, insurance, or finance) or to a group of people sharing an interest in buying, selling, or exchanging information about that particular industry. In other words, a vortal is a Web site with a tightly focused content area geared toward a particular audience. An example of a community that heavily depends of vortals is the medical community. Vortals such as Medcast and WebMD play a critical role in enabling the speediest broadcasting of groundbreaking medical news and providing information services to help with disease treatment, patient concerns, and practice management.

Until now, both consumer-oriented portals and vortals have employed mostly two types of search engines: keyword-driven engines (like the ones used in AltaVista and Excite), in which search results are resolved according to how well keywords match the content of Web pages, and directory-driven engines (like the ones used in Yahoo! and LookSmart), in which search results are resolved by traversing preconfigured directories. Recently, many consumer-oriented portals have started to provide more advanced searching capabilities based on capturing users' behavior, documenting popular results, and ranking retrieved documents based on that data. After search results are obtained, they are further filtered based on the rankings of popular results from previous searches (based, for example, on the number of previous users who have clicked on the sites matching an inquiry). Two terms are used to describe this type of search technology: *popularity measuring* and *collaborative filtering*. Collaborative filtering is a more advanced mechanism than popularity measuring because it is based on capturing the actual opinions of users about specific result set entries. The next step for both consumer-oriented portals and vortals is to combine these technologies with industry-specific catalogs. These catalogs classify the sources of information and provide automated information collection tools in order to customize the search experience for specific professions. Vortals will vastly improve the quality and effectiveness of information searching, fulfilling their precise goal of becoming search centers for their industries—basically, "feed lots" with all the relevant information available on the Internet.

An elaborate discussion on searching technologies would not fit within the scope of this book. One important aspect of such technologies needs to be mentioned here, however, because of its influence on the overall concept of portals. All search technologies rely on meta-data ("data about data") to satisfy a search request. In most cases, meta-data is created automatically using an application called a "Web crawler." A Web crawler retrieves Web pages for the use of a search engine by recursively scanning and extracting URLs from a starting Web page or a particular document on the page. Every page that is scanned is indexed, and sometimes ranked, summarized, and analyzed for its contents. This information is stored as meta-data. In most cases, meta-data is also "enriched" by an expert (a person or a system). Depending on the scope and coverage of a particular portal, Web crawling can be a serious challenge.

The next step in the portal evolution was triggered by the development of extensive intranets. As popular and powerful as they are, Web portals were not enough to satisfy the demand for applications that facilitate the management of information accessible over both forms of on-line services—public and private. Moreover, intranets have added an additional dimension to the issue of information searching: information sharing. Within intranets, in addition to providing access to text-based documents, Web servers provide a highly effective means of disseminating corporate information. Corporate databases (sales, financial, inventory, and so on) were connected to Web servers, allowing easy access to these databases from any desktop with a browser. A real need has emerged to provide a single point of navigation through the enterprise. This was the beginning for corporate portals, which are fueling many advances in IT, including information dissemination.

Information Dissemination

Chapter 3 addressed the topic of information dissemination, focusing on the fact that, as companies are turning to Internet and Web technologies to maximize business opportunities and position themselves as e-service providers, new electronic forms of information delivery have become extremely relevant. What are the most overpowering new forms of information delivery? Undoubtedly, these are corporate portals. As was articulated in Chapter 3, portals, in general, and, corporate portals, in particular, have allowed the Web to grow from a communication medium for a small user group (mostly, the scientific community) to a worldwide broadcasting capability, a primary mechanism for information dissemination, and a "mass medium" for collaboration and interaction between individuals and their computers.

In today's enterprises, no single process or even individual task involves a single information resource. Every business function involves coordinating multiple data sources, processes, and people, and sharing information among them. But in order to effectively share corporate data across the enterprise, some type of business intelligence or knowledge management application becomes necessary to synthesize the data (for example, to filter and refine internal and external data contained in heterogeneous and diverse data sources, and to address the problem of the sheer quantity of data). This requirement has brought us to a new and very exciting development in corporate portals, the enterprise portal (also known as the enterprise information portal, or EIP).

In the emerging corporate portal field, the main goal is to expose and deliver business-specific relevant information in the context of helping the modern employee to be highly productive and competitive. Being productive and competitive requires not only access to information, but also an ability to interact (communicate) with others using the obtained information as the base. This interaction is becoming especially important for knowledge workers, because they need to have a sense of a "bridge" to deal with the discontinuity of traditional forms of employment as a result of mergers, downsizing, and the popularity of employee "free agency" relationships with today's enterprises.

For that reason, corporate portals are focused on providing dynamic information dissemination capabilities that give today's employees a resourceful and aspiring role in the organization, allowing them to have a single gateway to the personalized information they need to make informed business decisions.[1] As Chapter 3 noted, corporate portals give today's employees two crucial capabilities. First, they are able to find information of a high quality without having to spend lots of time browsing; second, they have access to platform-independent services that are capable of reducing massive quantities of information into an organized, summarized, and customized set of information (from the content interpretation standpoint). More to the point, corporate portals allow the production of a corporate knowledge repository by capturing, archiving, indexing, managing, and distributing internal and business-related external information.

One of the most important things about the portal evolution is that both software users and corporations have adopted the idea of the corporate portal as the "window" into IT resources (for example, enterprise information, applications, and processes), and, as such, it has become the key scheme of their IT strategies. Corporate portals can be designed for different usage models, primarily to be used internally by a company's employees and contractors, or to be used internally and externally by its partners, suppliers, and customers. Although the complete set of requirements differs depending on the usage model, many of the features that are required of corporate portals are the same, especially in regard to information dissemination. Although these common requirements were articulated in Chapter 3, it makes sense to highlight the key characteristics in the context of this discussion. Many of the key characteristics can be grouped into the following two critical categories (see Figure 5.2):

1. Identification and categorization of corporate information resources, and production and delivery of relevant content:

   - Defining a comprehensive information aggregation level based on where the information is actually located, who the owner is, what the business processes affected by the portal are, and so on.

– Organizing unstructured and structured data into meaningful collections ("information objects") of business-related information that reflect all aspects of the enterprise.

– Target-based (personalized) identification and rendering of content sensitivity.

– Customized user access and interactive communications with information access tools based on user profiling, filtering, and categorized support.

2. Knowledge-driven information processing:

– Enabling knowledge discovery services that allow the identification of new patterns and relationships between facts, and helping to arrive at consistent business decisions.

– Enabling the transition toward adaptive information systems based on meta-data exchange and customized information objects.

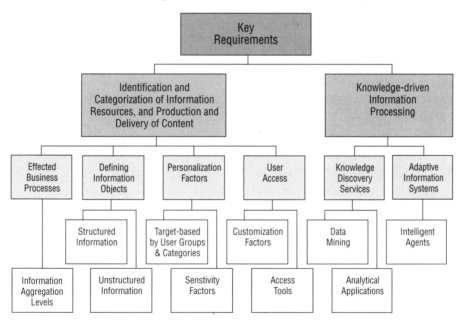

Figure 5.2: Corporate Portals: Information Dissemination Characteristics

Initially, the development of basic elements, mechanisms, and applications incorporated into corporate portals has followed a relatively narrowly focused vision designed to answer two questions: "What is wanted in terms of a common access to dispersed information?" and "What is technologically possible?" But as more rigid analysis of general requirements toward the concept has occurred, it has become clear that corporate portals have to evolve into multiple kinds of specialized portals. Currently, many technologies for portals have reached preliminary stabilization as the first multifaceted commercial products and are about to be widely implemented. But the problem is less a technical than a cultural one. Despite several years of experience with corporate portals, it is still difficult to formalize a comprehensive and radically successful corporate model for portals. Nevertheless, a couple of new models besides EIP are looking very attractive right now: a "workspace" portal with comprehensive collaboration capabilities, and an e-business portal as a unifying business service integration platform.

Collaboration: Bringing People Together

A workspace portal (often referred to as the enterprise collaborative portal or ECP, or collaborative EIP) is a corporate portal that connects users not only with every*thing* they need information deliverywise, but also with every*one* they need. Collaborative EIP consolidates a wide group of collaborative and office applications (for example, groupware, e-mail, workflow, and critical desktop applications) under the same gateway as information searching, access, and content production applications. Such an approach allows portals to focus on enabling collaboration among teams of users by providing generalized "virtual" project areas or communities along with tools and relevant information needed to work cooperatively within these communities.

The overall objective of such portals is to solve a problem in which a user has to work jointly with others in a task- or project-oriented setting by using a collaborative approach to organizing information. As a result, they are more appealing to business users, who have a collaborative style of working. Collaboration can be direct or indirect. The main form of direct collaboration is a community. Community features that are starting to be supported by collaborative EIPs include discussion groups (an electronic forum for participants to discuss topics on line), feedback gathering on activities of the visitors, "chat rooms" for support groups, personal ads, generic profession-related calendars, bulletin boards, mailing lists, and so on. Indirect collaboration occurs when others can reuse the results of one individual or a group without explicit coordination with the original problem solver. This requires not only information sharing, but also decision sharing. The integration of decision-making processes and results from such processes is becoming one of the top requirements for EAI technologies embedded into corporate portals. (See Chapters 3 and 4 for a commentary about collaboration requirements for portals and EAI.)

The e-Business Portal: Unifying Business Service Integration

The increased emphasis on e-business and the support for on-line transactions means that the integration of business services across the supply chain has become even more important in EIPs than information (content) dissemination within an enterprise. As corporate portals attempt to embrace e-business requirements, a new class of specialized B2B corporate portals is emerging. The new class differentiates itself from the EIP- or ECP-type portals by providing not only content, but also a breadth and utility of services for developing, deploying, and managing e-business applications.

As businesses and professionals start to get significantly involved in e-business relationships, B2B Web sites (or B2B portals) will be the place where business is conducted. Patterns of the development and implementation of corporate portals have begun to shift in response to this new environment. The idea of implementing a specialized supply chain management or procurement portal, in particular, has become increasingly popular as a means of involving the supply chain in gaining performance improvement through such portals. Hence, corporate portals are evolving along the following three key categories:

- **Extended Enterprise Portal (EEP)**—A B2B portal owned and managed by a single enterprise to support its supply chain management and procurement business processes, involving customers, partners, and suppliers. This type of portal focuses on aggregating product catalog information (for example, parts and pricing information) with real-time inventory information, potentially information from a large number of suppliers, and on supporting interaction and collaboration in order to help manage the end-to-end flow of related business processes.

- **E-Marketplace Portal (eMP)**—A B2B portal plays the role of a "trading hub," connecting buyers and sellers in virtual marketplaces. By this simple definition, any corporate portal that provides a unique combination of content and commerce (for example, where a user can get vendor information, third-party analysis, product comparisons, and the ability to transact–buy all from one place) is an eMP. The most compelling usage of such portals is when they are highly cross-enterprise in nature, catering to the specific trading needs of vertical industries, such as transportation, construction, steel, automotive, and so on. In addition to providing access to the breadth of information and products available across the industry, these portals enable specific services for e-marketplaces, such as bidding and auction–reverse action services.

- **ASP Portal (ASP)**—A B2B portal dedicated to providing support for the emerging business model of renting applications and services from so-called application service providers, or ASPs.

In this wider and more challenging business climate, what is the primary role envisioned for corporate portals?

Not surprisingly, we are beginning to see the IT organizations and software vendor community converge on the goal of improving competencies, processes, practices, and systems, focused through the concept of corporate portals as the single point of integration for the whole enterprise and its supply chain. The IBM Software Strategy White Paper, "Application Framework for e-business: Portals"[2] articulates it best: "A common theme of substance underlies portals—a theme of greater levels of integration. From a unifying technology perspective, a portal is a single integrated point of comprehensive, ubiquitous, and useful access to information (data), applications, and people. This definition encompasses all the different views of the purpose and functionality of portals. But more importantly, strong pursuit of satisfying this portal definition will help evolve the next generation of integrated services and business processes."

Corporate portals are driving many different requirements that extend and enhance almost every aspect of the Internet and information technology that surrounds it. The key emphasis of corporate portals is on improving the efficiency of Internet computing and achieving greater levels of application integration; this is accomplished largely through improved Web front-end definition (from the standpoint of a single entry for accessing corporate information and handling transactions), design, procurement, and implementation. Wrapping up the whole process, there is an emphasis on unifying all kinds of technologies and tools (for example, content management, application development, EAI, and so on) under a single platform to facilitate the development of integrated e-business applications and business processes.

The actual result of all of this activity will be a new state of computing, one that has come to be called "portal computing." In the near future, many e-business visionaries (for example, Scott McNealy, chairman of Sun Microsystems)[3] expect portal computing to become the "killer app" of the Internet era, extending its influence beyond business into everyone's daily life as portals are integrated more and more into devices of all shapes and sizes, including wireless phones, automobiles, appliances, and so on.

How Many Types of Portals Are There?

After the previous discussion, we can see that the concept of portals is bringing order to chaos on the Internet, and the set of services that it is targeting caters to many different types of usage scenarios, resulting in many (probably too many) different types of portals. The portal software industry is busy inventing itself, leaving many experienced IT industry observers wondering how to come up with a stable classification scheme for these technologies. Without such a scheme, the market definition for portals, especially corporate portals, is too broad and not clearly partitioned, which leads to more vendor hype and user confusion.

Figure 5.3 shows an attempt to provide such a classification, one that I've termed a "3 x 2 x 3 portal classification scheme." First of all, portals stand in three major categories:

- **Public Portals**—Portals that follow the "Yahoo! portal model" and define themselves as "new media" are focused on building large on-line audiences with compelling demographics or professional orientation (for example, having the inclination to "buy" what portal advertisers have to sell in terms of products and services). Public portals can be broken up into two subcategories: *general public portals* and *industrial portals (vortals)*.

- **Corporate (or Enterprise) Portals**—Syndicates of the new economy. The corporate portal market space is rapidly evolving. The key focus of portals is the integrated access to both information and application services, and greater levels of integration between the two. Corporate portals are extremely valuable to business users because they simplify complex information, provide context-specific and useful application services, and foster collaboration and community building across the extended enterprise. These characteristics represent the rapid evolution of corporate portals from mere corporate intranet sites to mission-critical business tools. Corporate portals can be broken up into two subcategories: *enterprise information portals* and *role portals.*

- **Personal Portals**—A future state of portals driven by the vision of ABC (appliance-based computing). This can be further broken up into two subcategories: *pervasive portals* [portals embedded in cellular phones, personal information devices (PIDs), and so on] and *appliance portals* (portals embedded in TVs, automobiles, major appliances, and so on).

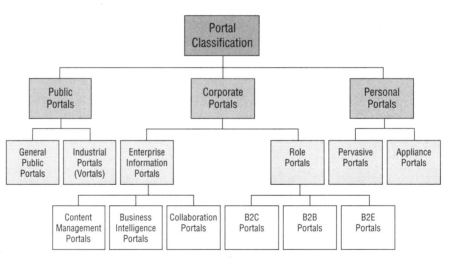

Figure 5.3: "3 x 2 x 3" Portal Classification Scheme

What's more, because of the proliferation of highly specialized corporate portals that provide a so-called digital expertise-oriented workplace, especially in B2B market space, it makes sense to further categorize the corporate portal category. What does it mean to have a "digital expertise-oriented workplace"? A typical example of such a portal is a site where a user team finds everything it needs to effectively manage mission-critical management activities. such as customer relationship management (for example, access to ERP/CRM applications, productivity tools, analysis tools, and relevant internal and external content), consolidated and made accessible via the Web. Another good example is an on-line employee-training site. Therefore, the corporate portal category could be broken up, perhaps, as follows:

- **Enterprise Information Portals** (EIPs)—Designed to improve information access and information processing and include content management portals, business intelligence portals, and collaboration portals.

- **Role Portals**—Designed to enable three key e-business models: B2C, B2B, and B2E. B2C portals are focused on attracting and keeping the attention of buyers; B2B portals (EEP, eMP, and ASP) are focused on everything from managing a global supply chain to setting up an information system on a rental basis; and B2E portals are focused on providing employee assistance (for example, training, best practice exchange, and so on).

Obviously, the above classification is not the only possibility. Other popular classifications exist. For example, Delphi Group's classification[4] represents the portal market as follows:

- Publishing portals
- Personal portals
- Commercial portals
- Corporate portals

In the future, the horizons of information technology used to support the concept of portals will be radically and quickly raised, resulting in many more types of portals, especially in the corporate space. Challenges abound, among them management of a combination of multiple corporate portals within a single enterprise, security and privacy concerns, performance requirements from demanding users, and constant technological change and innovation. These challenges necessitate a "conciliatory" approach toward portals, or more precisely, a truly federated architectural framework. Chapter 6 will cover this subject in much detail. However, it makes sense to pinpoint here one very important fact: To a large degree, the technologies needed to build such a framework, one through which the real advantages of portals can be realized, already exist.

EIP: Inside and Outside

As previously mentioned, EIP is probably the most widely referenced example of corporate portals. Although there are all kinds of observations in numerous books and articles defining EIP, I think the definition given by Christopher Shilakes and Julie Tylman in Merrill Lynch's research report "Enterprise Information Portals"[5] provides the most comprehensive description of this category of portals and its characteristics. This particular definition emphasizes both the basic functions of an EIP and the subsidiary applications that are converging to produce EIP applications. According to Shilakes and Tylman, "Enterprise Information Portals are applications that enable companies to unlock internally and externally stored information, and provide users a single gateway to personalized information needed to make informed business decisions." EIPs are also "an amalgamation of software applications that consolidate, manage, analyze and distribute information across and outside of an enterprise (including Business Intelligence, Content Management, Data Warehouse & Mart and Data Management applications)." These definitions highlight the fact that EIPs present a strong decision-support and content-management emphasis. In addition to those two types of emphasis, and as was previously mentioned, a new subclass of EIPs is emerging. Called *collaborative EIPs*, these portals support real-time collaboration so that it is easy for users to find colleagues, partners, customers, and suppliers on-line and communicate with them regardless of distance and differences in time zones.

The real value proposition for EIPs is:

- Improved productivity for an enterprise's employees based on providing integrated access to general corporate information, critical data from enterprise applications and business intelligence tools for processing that data, as well as universal communications between business constituents.

- Improved enterprise business processes resulting from better information flow between knowledge workers and enterprise applications, as well as from the collaborative environments that help reduce the time needed to transform raw information into knowledge and expertise that feed such processes.

- Shortened time to market resulting from the reduction in deployment and management overhead for information gathering and decision making in an enterprise.

- Improved customer, partner, and supplier relationships as a result of more valuable communications and information exchange, providing the basis for better profitability.

EIPs can be used in a variety of contexts, from very specific to very general, depending on the desired business value and tolerance for related costs. The most common EIP usage scenarios are as follows:

- **Group #1: Basic Information Dissemination**—Dissemination of general corporate information (internal company information, policies and procedures, human resource and benefits information, and so on) and miscellaneous content combined with news and Internet search and links.

- **Group #2: Knowledge-Targeted Information Dissemination**—Extension of the first group's features with support for more advanced information dissemination and "knowledge management" features: specialized directories and bulletin boards, comprehensive searching, identification of experts, consolidation of information about best practices and lessons learned, and so on.

- **Group #3: Basic Workplace Integration**—Collaboration and project support, access to data from disparate enterprise applications, and business process support (for example, customer support).

- **Group #4: Decision-Oriented Workplace Integration**—Extension of the third group's features with enabling access to and intelligent integration of business intelligence and customer-relationship management software, as well as support for role-based workflow integration.

Figure 5.4 depicts in broad strokes an empirical relationship between expected business value and the above usage scenarios. Although some skeptics are still expressing a lot of doubts in terms of realizing real business value based on the effects of EIP introductions,[6] there are many proven cases in which significant EIP benefits have already been achieved (for example, as described in IBM Global Services' White Paper on enterprise information portal strategy).[7] In this respect, looking at Figure 5.4, we can conclude that by combining different scenarios into a particular EIP implementation, a significantly more attractive business value could be realized (compared to implementing a very specific EIP). Obviously, the implementation cost of a more generalized, comprehensive EIP solution could be substantial; this should be taken into consideration when analyzing potential implementation strategies.

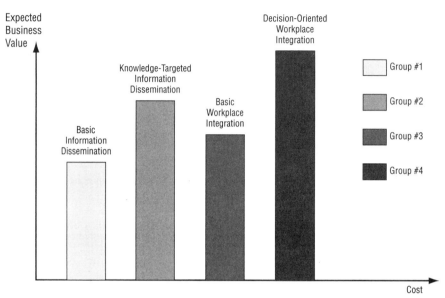

Figure 5.4: EIP Usage Scenarios: Expected Benefits

Having defined what EIP is and what it accomplishes in terms of the business value, we can gain a deeper understanding of this category of portals by examining key components that the EIP architecture includes and the application functions performed by these components in an EIP solution.

At a high level, EIP architecture is a cohesive blend or a tightly coupled combination of the following infrastructure and functional components (see Figure 5.5):

- **Information Assistant**—A component responsible for delivering presentation services in the form of a customized Web-based user interface (for example, a front page like Yahoo!'s) that works in conjunction with a search engine and provides access to other components.

- **Search Engine**—A component responsible for delivering the ability to search for and retrieve information objects (for example, Web documents, electronic word processor files, images, or audio and video clips).

- **Personalization Engine**—A component responsible for delivering the ability to present the relevant content to the user based on individual needs and preferences, as well as the necessary features to enable personalization (for example, user profiling, behavior analysis, content-based filtering, and so on).

- **Content Management Engine**—A component responsible for identifying, grouping, and consolidating the internal and external content according to categories of interest (for example, real-time news, stock quotes, weather, financial data, competition data, and so on) and also responsible for Web crawling (the automatic retrieval and indexing of Web pages).

- **Content Publishing Engine**—A component responsible for providing the ability to create and store content, such as documents, spreadsheets, images, video, audio, HTML and XML pages, and decision-support objects such as queries, reports, and analyses.

- **User Management Engine**—A component responsible for providing security (for example, user access authorization and authentication) and subscription (user registration) services. User registration is used to control how business information is disseminated through the portal (this might be based, for example, on an organization's content access policies, user interest in certain types of information, or on other types of business rules, such as a request to deliver a particular piece of information to a group of users). Another key feature is single sign-on, in which a user logs on once to gain access to all portal resources.

- **Application Services Engine**—A component that provides seamless links to all kinds of Web-enabled and legacy applications (for example, access to ERP-transaction processing, sales force automation, financial and customer support applications, and so on). Access to legacy applications is supported through the use of all kinds of connectors (adapters) provided by the EAI software incorporated into the portal.

- **Business Intelligence Engine**—A component that provides a cohesive decision-support environment and the ability to present a unified view of corporate information by integrating various internal databases and external data sources (for example, on-line information feeds, discussion forums, and so on). The key capability of this component is common access to multiple business intelligence applications, such as on-line analytical processing (OLAP) or data mining and analytical applications (for example, financial modeling).

- **Collaboration Services Engine**—A component that enables all kinds of community and groupware features, supporting collaboration between parties both within and outside the enterprise. The prime focus is enabling support for discussion groups (an electronic forum for participants to discuss topics on-line), feedback on activities of the users (for example, "the most used SAP application feature was..."), support groups, personal and generic profession-, function-, or role-related calendars, bulletin boards, mailing lists, and so on. Also, this component provides access to groupware (for example, workflow) and personal productivity tools (for example, Web-based training, a mortgage advisor, a selling contract advisor, and so on).

- **Infrastructure Support Engine**—A backbone component that enables communications (networking), system management (for example, logging services), site administration (for example, allocating and managing resources such as user workspace and disk quota), and application integration services. Because portals must support access from both inside and outside the firewall, this component has to provide the support for a comprehensive set of security and network access services, including virtual private networks, intrusion detection, secure sockets layer (SSL), public key infrastructure (PKI), and so on. Providing support for a variety of devices (for example, wireless phones, pagers, faxes, PIDs, laptops, and so on) is another one of the key responsibilities of this component.

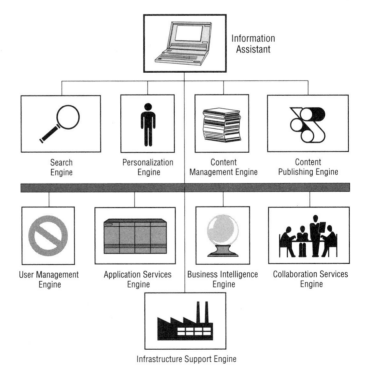

Figure 5.5: EIP Architecture

In general, this sort of architecture allows virtually any kind of EIP to be created. These may be horizontally focused EIPs, providing enterprise access to a wide variety of basic content management, business intelligence, and collaborative functions, or vertically focused EIPS, providing a comprehensive set of features in one or two categories.

Business Intelligence Portals

One type of vertically focused EIP that deserves to be examined further is the business intelligence portal (BIP). As compared to the other two main types on the EIP market (content management portals and collaboration portals), BIPs offer companies the bigger potential payback, since they help business users find and leverage corporate business information for reducing costs and increasing revenue. The target user of BIPs is the enterprise decision maker. A BIP helps executives, line managers, and knowledge workers access the set of systems that constitute decision-support applications and make prudent business decisions. It allows the leveraging of enterprise database sources across the enterprise, providing timely, accurate, and targeted information. BIPs reflect a fundamental transformation in the IT industry's view of enterprise information management from a series of isolated tasks to the coordinated integration of decision-enabling information.

As depicted in Figure 5.6, in terms of included decision-support technologies, a BIP is a compound environment comprising end-user query or reporting, multidimensional analysis/OLAP, packaged data marts, data mining, and visualization and analytical modeling software. Although these technologies are usually available as completely independent and stand-alone products, in the case of BIPs they are embedded (seamlessly linked) in the portal environment. With the influx of readily available, yet completely disconnected, decision-support products on the market, it has become clear that most organizations urgently require the means to navigate accesses between these products and link their results with related business processes. BIPs, then, have the potential for substantial impact.

End-user query or reporting and OLAP tools are used, to a large extent, to analyze operational transaction data to answer questions about regular day-to-day business operations and business performance. *Data marts* create an environment in which data is stored, managed, and optimized for analysis. Data marts, combined with analytical modeling applications, perform multiple tasks. First, these tools allow you to leverage historical transactional data to answer questions about business trends (for example, how business operations change over time and what the opportunities are to reduce costs or improve customer service). Second, they let business users factor in external events (macroeconomic conditions) and perform all kinds of "what if" analyses to forecast future business conditions, such as sales forecasting, budgeting and planning, customer churns, and so on.

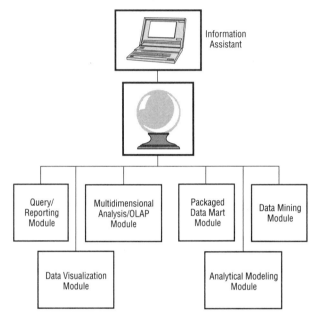

Figure 5.6: BIP Components

When data mining and visualization tools are integrated into the portal infrastructure, they provide a rich set of content analyzers capable of identifying hidden patterns and relationships in historical data (for example, logged "click-stream" data) about business transactions and user interactions. Based on uncovered patterns (something like "62 percent of consumers who buy toothpaste at the grocery store also purchase a toothbrush"), business users can make decisions about what actions (if any) are required to improve the efficiency and competitiveness of business operations.

The key benefits of BIPs come from two directions. First, these portal platforms provide information and decision-support aggregation services by giving business users a single point of access to multiple heterogeneous data sources (for example, legacy file systems and databases, relational databases, multidimensional databases, and so on) and analysis tools. Such capabilities help companies obtain greater precision and speed of analysis. Second, BIPs allow support for complex and enterprisewide decision-making processes. All kinds of query results, analyses and reports, and associated decisions and actions can be stored in documents managed by a BIP. As decisions are made and actions taken, the BIP can be used again to measure the impact on business operations, creating a closed-loop decision-making process. Using such decision-support processes, companies can make more prudent business decisions, leading to cost savings, increased revenue, reduced time to market of new products, and many other tangible and intangible benefits.

It is important to realize that, in general, there are some differences between BIP and traditional data warehousing/data mart (in short, data warehousing, or DW) systems. DW systems are, to a large degree, "suites" of all kinds of independent products that perform a multitude of functions: "extract, transform, and load" (ETL) tasks, data cleaning, schedule facilitation, administration and meta-data management for databases (which store the warehoused data), and supplying analysis tools to interrogate those databases. In contrast, BIP is a tightly integrated tool for developing decision-processing objects like reports and analyses, for organizing and running these objects, and for disseminating the results to business users.

The increased emphasis on integration and on sharing decisions among business users means that business process automation using workflow is even more important in BIPs than in DW systems. Although some DW implementations have included a workflow product, this practice is considered somewhat optional. A BIP implementation, in contrast, would totally ineffective without a systematic workflow and group collaboration capability assisted by portal infrastructure services.

Also, in BIPs, there is a specific emphasis (largely renewed) on data mining. In the DW systems context, data mining is, in general terms, an extension to the process of building data warehouses. The warehoused data is subjected to all kinds of additional messaging activities (extraction, transformation, and loading) based on the requirements of data-mining tools and the numerous mining techniques they use (such as sampling, profiling, clustering, predictive modeling, decision trees, and neural networks). Data thus prepared for mining is loaded into a data store, usually a series of flat data sets. In the late 1990s, however, many leading companies started to expose data warehouses with large amounts of detailed transactional data to off-line data mining, and business users encountered several serious problems with the overall process. In cases in which the data warehouse contains a limited volume of historical data (for example, only a few months' worth), it is difficult to arrive at really meaningful trends or patterns. Also, although historical trends and patterns discovered in the warehoused data are valuable information for long-term planning, tactical decision support (to which business users are exposed when using a BIP) requires the more timely use of transactional data. Furthermore, piecemeal, fragmented analyses using samples from the data warehouse may produce inconsistent results from the same data, depending on how you apply the data-mining techniques. Finally, because of the complexity of data-mining tools and techniques, business users often become dependent on help from so-called analyst intermediaries, which slows down the decision process even further. These deficiencies of the data-mining process, as an adjunct to the data warehouse, became clearly apparent with the introduction of intensive e-business models (specifically, e-marketplaces). Tactical decision-support capabilities are extremely important because they enable effective governing of the network of organizations involved through upstream and downstream links in production processes. Unfortunately, because of the vast amounts of detailed data that must be filtered and converted into valuable information within the extended enterprise, the task becomes almost impossible to tackle. As a result, there is a distinct trend toward enhancing BIP capabilities to combine data mining with real-time operational processing using the intelligent agents based on Java and enabling real-time or near-real-time data mining of operational databases.

Overall, BIPs are becoming the delivery platform for data warehousing and similar systems using publish-and-subscribe and broadcasting delivery mechanisms and customization, personalization, and collaborative features for information sharing. As a result, the dividing line between the three types of enterprise information portals is becoming more and more blurred.

Role Portals

While EIP applications certainly represent a big part of the excitement surrounding portals, there is already evidence that corporate portals are evolving into more vertically focused specialized *role portals*. This is not just a matter of semantics and labeling.

The idea of role portals directly ties into the concept of e-business. In e-business, there is more to the role of corporate portals than merely helping knowledge workers navigate the volume of information at hand. First, corporate portals have to significantly improve processing and management of the information in order to keep up with the pace of information overload. Second, in order to effectively transition to e-business, we have to put a "cap" on information growth by providing extremely targeted portal solutions capable of managing mission-critical tasks from end to end and maintaining the underlying connections between tasks' important information objects, which are the basis of corporate knowledge.

Role portals are emerging as the most dynamic segment of the corporate portal market. This segment combines all kinds of B2C, B2B, and B2E portals. Although there are substantial differences between a B2C and a B2E or B2B portal, the following key ingredients—known as the "Four Cs"—represent their common, essential characteristics (see Figure 5.7):

- **Content**—The key ingredient that attracts new users to a portal site. Instead of focusing on disseminating general corporate content to a wide audience, role portals are focusing on providing unique content that is solely available at a particular portal site, along with access to general information from across the enterprise and beyond. The ability to differentiate on content is key to the early success of a role portal. In order to accomplish this, a role portal has to have a highly sophisticated information aggregation and expertise-enriching set of capabilities. In e-business, the door is wide open for entirely new electronic content aggregation companies to act as information brokers for role portals. Information brokers combine specialized information access tools with domain expertise, providing a versatile way to access information based on users' requirements for highly relevant content.

- **Customization**—The ability to craft the experience to meet each group of business users' specific needs and interests (for example, detailed personal profiling). For example, when using a company Web site configured as a B2C portal, a consumer may identify interest in product information and product support, and so news in these content categories will gain prominence on the consumer's unique version of that site. Other customization features include the ability to save frequent searches and user requests.

- **Commerce**—All but the most employee-assistance-oriented B2E portals need to support transactions and increase Web-based business activities. Although any corporate portal provides a way for business users to obtain relevant information, it must not be forgotten that the ability to engage in business relationships and conduct business is a key appeal to visitors to a corporate portal site.

- **Collaboration**—Another key appeal to visitors to a corporate portal site is the ability to share information and ideas with colleagues, ask questions, and find answers. In other words, visitors want to be part of a "virtual community" created by the collaborative features of the portal. Ideally, role portals include techniques and methodologies to foster and promote the highest levels of cooperation possible and appropriate for the task at hand.

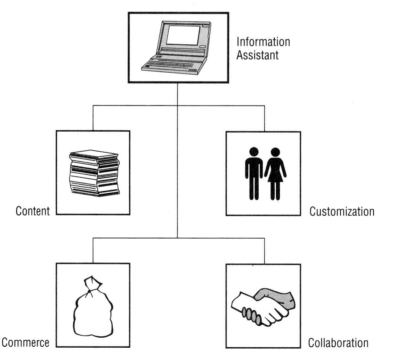

Figure 5.7: Role Portals—Essential Characteristics

As expressed previously, role portals are focused on how to efficiently reach e-business opportunities across all of their key players and destinations (consumers, businesses, and employees). The following sections will examine the most challenging opportunities—business-to-business and business-to-employee. B2C portals are targeted toward increasing e-commerce activities by giving consumers the information and tools they need to make buying decisions and to purchase goods and services. The most common uses of these types of corporate portals are[8]:

- Product information
- Product support
- Product ordering (configuration, ordering, payment)
- Customer service–customer relationship management initiatives
- Cross-selling initiatives

Business-to-Business Portals

B2B corporate portals are rapidly transforming supply and value chain relationships as enterprises of all sizes join the ever-expanding e-business economy. Once viewed by companies merely as a means to disseminate corporate information or to attract customers to a Web storefront, corporate portals have since demonstrated a genuine capacity to enable real-time, interactive exchange of business transaction information and integration of business processes among trading partners—buyers, sellers, brokers or intermediaries, and e-business service providers. Companies are turning to B2B portals to facilitate so-called trading partner networks, also known as "i-markets," in which each trading partner is using the portal as a central hub to transact business within the network. Consequently, the key focus of B2B portal technology vendors is to help companies overcome many of the challenges of i-markets (which are briefly summarized in Table 5.1), allowing the creation of open, dynamic e-business environments in which numerous partners can transact cost-effectively with each other.

Leading e-business companies view B2B portals as critical to participation in supply–value chain relationships, and they also see them as a vital technology for reaping the true benefits from such relationships. Why? Simply because the key question is not whether it makes sense to get involved in business-to-business e-commerce, but how to integrate a company's heterogeneous applications with so many other businesses in a manner that is advantageous to all parties. At the infrastructure heart of today's e-business integration strategies (see the EAI discussion in Chapter 4) is the fact that B2B portals are tools that are designed to build a flexible, self-sustained business-to-business model in which:

1. Every user inside and outside the enterprise is able to access every element of the corporate information base.

2. Every business-to-business interaction among partners is carried out in a comprehensive way that allows the seamless exchange of not only transactional data, but also business intent (for example, associated meta-data that describes business rules for interpreting that data).

For such a model to become a reality, companies must connect all their mission-critical systems and provide a unified access platform to the connected enterprise information backbone. This platform should encompass a coherent, yet loosely coupled combination of integration, navigation, and information dissemination components. Many envision significant opportunities for growth in e-business applications that tightly integrate these components under a B2B portal environment. By having a complete environment in "one place" (or, as I would say, "in orbit"), an integration platform could be designed to build any type or size of i-market required.

To accurately describe the features of B2B portals required for every type of e-business arrangement is pointless. Nevertheless, certain generic characteristics of B2B portals are important because of the particular functions they perform. The following characteristics are generic and architecturally driven; they require the evaluation and comparative analysis of specific, commercially available B2B portal solutions that you will find in the later chapters of this book.

Four key characteristics make corporate portals that focus on B2B interactions the right technological approach to drive a unified e-business platform (see Figure 5.8):

1. **Content Management and Integration**—Portals provide comprehensive content management services, such as content acquisition and content creation. In addition, portals can provide content integration tools to manage discrete content objects, which can be combined on the fly to create different target formats. By utilizing these tools, companies on the sell side of i-markets will be able to electronically publish their catalog con-

tent (products and services), providing high-quality, up-to-date content to all buying organizations in all trading networks.

2. **Meta-Data Services**—I-markets typically consist of hundreds, if not thousands, of trading partners (buyers and sellers) with a plethora of applications and data sources. The proliferation of different types of meta-data associated with different types of companies' resources, coupled with strong demands to support a variety of information exchange services, will make it necessary to manage the underlying meta-data used or created by each application in an integrated and cohesive manner. As a result, specialized meta-data authoring tools are required that support dynamic creation, editing, and rearrangement of meta-data and associated parameters. Portals can provide such tools.

3. **User Administration**—Portals provide a single log-in process and all kinds of user registration capabilities (for example, profiling and preferencing), which are necessary in order to enable B2B interaction among all trading partners.

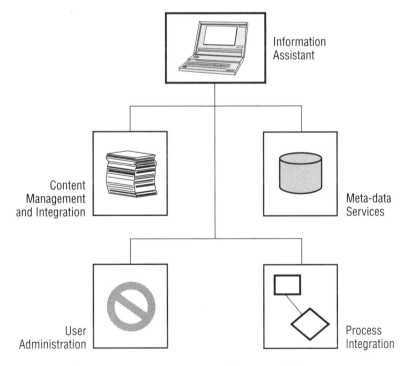

Figure 5.8: B2B Portals—Essential Characteristics

4. Process Integration—Portals provide the ability to build and participate in a workflow process in which cross-enterprise business processes can function in an integrated manner. Portals can play the role of a business integration server that performs two critical functions. First, it brokers information exchange across multiple, loosely coupled applications that need to work together. Second, it maintains workflow process definitions and routes business documents or messages via a robust messaging infrastructure. Portals can coordinate interactions from many different sources, including groupware/collaboration systems, mail servers, and so on.

Table 5.1
Key Challenges Facing Companies in the B2B Arena

Category	Challenge	Description
Information exchange	Availability of process-related information	In order to make purchasing decisions when dealing with multiple trading partners (sellers), buyers have to be able to obtain the necessary information on how to transact business (for example, internal company rules and procedures).
	Consolidation of catalog information	In order to provide buyers with automated order management capabilities, sellers require comprehensive catalog consolidation features to be able to introduce and manage a single on-line catalog.
	Real-time exchange of transactional information	Providing end-to-end order processing and purchasing capabilities requires real-time exchange of transactional information and the ability to fully automate "business process–to–business process" interactions.
Manageability	Flexibility of integration	Today's EAI solutions offer varying functionality enabling the integration of internal systems and business processes; too often, external integration capabilities are limited and useless when trying to integrate enterprise systems with outside applications.

Category	Challenge	Description
	Extensibility and scalability of infrastructure	Companies require a robust and scalable integration infrastructure so that additional services can be added and made immediately available to all trading partners without requiring them to install additional hardware or software as newly developed services emerge.
	Speed and ease of deployment	Companies want to interact with as many trading partners as possible by utilizing the most cost-effective and convenient methods; they need to have a speedy and easy process for joining markets.

Corporate Portals as a Virtual Employee Assistance Department

There are many potential uses of B2E portals, from providing access to general corporate information (for example, human resource policies) to providing the ability to build better employee relationships by turning the Web into a "virtual employee assistance department." Using a corporate portal as a "virtual assistant" creates an interesting and potentially highly beneficial scenario. Let's examine this point further.

Generally, employees regard the human resources (HR) department as a place to go to if they have problems. The exact nature of these "problems" is vague, although employees have a fairly accurate assessment of the HR functions in terms of personnel administration, recruitment, employee assistance, and internal communications. However, in many companies, employees do not utilize the HR department to its fullest extent. Worse yet, they sometimes only have a hazy conception of the "peripheral" services that could be derived from the HR practitioner. Deploying a portal that is specifically focused on providing detailed information about HR services and enabling personalized "employee-HR interaction spaces" is a powerful strategy to dealing with such issues.

Another important example of the use of B2E portals as "virtual assistants" is the use of portals to increase job knowledge. Nowadays, employees are often faced with problems that need immediate attention, and they perhaps discover that they may learn about the solutions only in future training programs. The current working environment and new technologies result in increasing demands on the work force and training needs that require interactive, effective on-the-job training (so-called just-in-time training). Again, a portal can assist here by focusing on helping employees find and access the needed training information (for example, a computer-based training course that is placed on a company's Web site). Furthermore, with a portal, they can selectively study only what is relevant and critical to them.

When a company uses a B2E portal for on-line training, the traditional role of the trainer changes. It evolves into someone who facilitates, mentors, and guides trainees on how to use the best and the most timely training available. Furthermore, the primary responsibility of the corporate trainer becomes to find, interpret, and assess a wide range of training information and product descriptions, and publish this information as content on the portal's site.

Advanced content management, personalization, collaboration, and workflow are the most critical services provided by such portals. For portal applications that focus on employee relationships, a key portal function is to enable fast and easy modification and distribution of training material as dynamically assembled personalized documents. As a result, portals require content integration tools capable of managing discrete content objects, which can be combined on the fly to create different target formats, including automated language translation of discrete content objects during the assembly of the target document. It is very useful to provide an expertise location feature, which maintains profiles that can be queried directly by users to locate experts by skill, experience, project, education, job type, and many other attributes.[9]

Why is using a portal oriented toward on-line training effective? To a large degree, today's view of the best instructional methodologies sees the underlying ability to interact as the main source of instructional effectiveness. These methodologies usually decompose the instructional message into compartmentalized elements of information and interaction and then form one or more rules for delivering the elements to the learner. Research shows that fragmenting the message and apportioning it out to the student does make a difference in learning. Portals provide to the trainer some very concrete training design tools that are easy and efficient to use.

The On-Line Virtual Workplace:
A Small but Growing Phenomenon

Let's continue to examine the subject of B2E portals, focusing on today's growing phenomenon of using such technology to facilitate the emergence of distributed teamwork environments.

During the last decade, the Internet and improvements in communications tools have encouraged many organizations to allocate tasks to groups of employees that are distributed rather than colocated, creating "virtual" teamwork environments. The main goal was to take advantage of the particular skills and expertise of workers without incurring substantial travel or relocation costs. Although a number of successful cases proving the approach's potential were publicized intensively, the attempts were, to a large degree, still an "experiment," largely because achieving effective coordinated activity in physically distributed groups has been shown to be a big challenge. When group members are located at great distances from each other, they are highly dependent on mediated interactions for coordination in order to avoid "deficits" in the important information they need to have about the day-to-day activities of their teammates.[10] Although many new forms of mediated communications exist to support distributed groups, simple access to communication media alone is insufficient to promote and support the intense collaborative activity that distributed teams often need to have.

With the introduction of collaborative B2E portals, it has become possible to construct fully functional, collaborative systems explicitly focused on addressing problems faced by distributed (or virtual) teams. That has spurred a wide rollout of these new organizational forms, especially in multinational corporations, which operate across time zones and work in different organizational and cultural contexts.

As depicted in Figure 5.9, collaborative B2E portals can effectively fulfill the following key requirements of virtual teams in terms of collaboration and information dissemination:

- Sharing information in a variety of forms, including documents, designs, and pictures of objects not only by delivering the information to each team member, but also through the establishment of a common place accessible by all members where digital representations of team artifacts can be stored and retrieved.

- Enabling real-time interactions by providing access to a host of interaction and coordination tools, such as chat or conferencing, electronic bulletin boards, discussion groups, e-mail, workflow, groupware, and so on.

- Maintaining awareness of the day-to-day project-related activities of team members through a wide range of calendaring/workflow mechanisms and delivery tools.

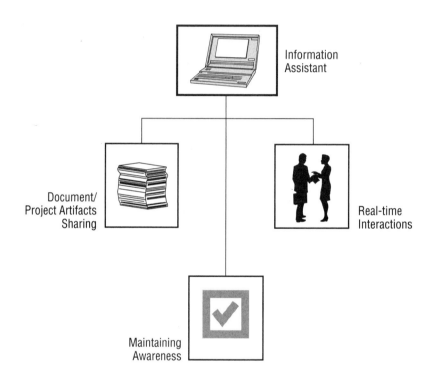

Figure 5.9: Collaborative B2E Portals—Essential Characteristics

Maintaining awareness is, perhaps, the most attractive feature of collaborative B2E portals. Table 5.2 summarizes the characteristics of that feature in terms of data collection and delivery of the information related to maintaining awareness.

To conclude the discussion about B2E portals, one important comment needs to be made here. First of all, it should be clear that portal technology is meant to enhance human contact and to supplement face-to-face communication, not to completely replace those forms. Regardless of how powerful portals will become, a long-term virtual team cannot be successful without personal contacts. Portal technology is a tool to assist the teams in reaching their goals; it does not have to be the main form of communication.

Table 5.2
Summary of the Awareness-Enabled Functions of Collaborative B2E Portals

Category	Function	Description
Action/process awareness	Activity tracking	Synchronous logging of ongoing group-related activities and asynchronous notification of events by making the log files available for group members
	Availability tracking	Monitoring up-to-the-moment availability of team members by instituting interactive "calendaring" features (for example, requiring responses to special messages/interaction requests)
	Process identification	Providing process monitoring via workflow, giving team members a sense of where their pieces fit into the whole picture, what the next step is, and what needs to be done to move the process along
	External event tracking	Capturing and broadcasting events occurring outside of the immediate workspace that may have implications for team activities
Delivering awareness information	Passive/active delivery	Scheduled and real-time (for time-sensitive awareness information) alert broadcasting
	Customized delivery	Providing the ability to customize the types of awareness information and the frequency of awareness delivery, for example, to select the pace and style in which awareness information is presented and to adjust the sensitivity of the monitoring function

Which Type of Portal Is Best for You?

As you can see, there are many different portal types and usage scenarios, and as a result, the obvious question arises, "Which type of portal is best for a particular company?" In order to answer this question, first and foremost, it needs to be reiterated that there are substantial differences between a general (Internet or Web) portal and a corporate portal. They serve two completely different types of audiences for completely different purposes.

Currently, in most cases, when applied to the corporate world, the term *portal* means an EIP-type portal. However, as e-business accelerates, there will be a proliferation of highly specialized role (B2B, B2C, and B2E) portals. A couple of years from now (or perhaps next week), the proliferation of highly specialized role portals will present a serious challenge to companies—how can a single portal strategy be established? The solution lies in creating federations of role portals that cover the spectrum of a company's interests and needs—corporate portal networks that pervasively service a user with the most comprehensive set of information and application services. Here, the term *federated* implies a union of independent portals working together to provide specific functions.

To create such networks, vendors will offer function-oriented tools that can be deployed on multiple role portals regardless of orientation. Moreover, vendors will combine the benefits offered by both EIP-type portals and role portals in a single product suite. In aggregate, the corporate portal will provide a comprehensive architecture framework, in which a specialized role portal can participate in a larger, networked implementation of a true enterprise portal to enable the better targeting of mission-critical processes within and beyond the enterprise.

Furthermore, because the greatest inefficiencies in today's large enterprises exist between systems, business processes, and user communities, the imperatives of implementing long-term corporate portal strategies based on the federated portal architecture are driven by major strategic business issues, such as competitive responsiveness, customer relationship management, and e-business integration. Thus, economic and competitive advantages will force a rapid evolution from portal "mania" to portal consolidation, in which the corporate portal truly becomes a source of aggregation, community, and business efficiency.

The Corporate Portal Framework

In their emerging role as the pivotal integration platform of e-business, portals will cause a paradigm shift in corporate computing that will totally transform our notions of data access, intranets and extranets, business intelligence, customer relationship management, and much more. But more importantly, their ability to integrate information flows and business processes across a given enterprise will well surpass today's integration solutions (e.g., enterprise resource planning), allowing the delivery of a seamless and both vertically and horizontally joined business environment as a one-stop information service for employees, customers, and all kinds of partners. Moreover, they will provide the necessary link for business interactions among all of these constituencies. In a nutshell, in today's "chaotic world" of e-business-related activity and change, the corporate portal concept will bring users and resources together in a systematic and productive way.[1]

Why will the corporate portal concept enable a much greater degree of integration than other, more well-known concepts, like enterprise resource planning (ERP)? First and foremost, because corporate portals shift the focus and perspective of integration—specifically, they are targeting integration challenges beyond the systems integration of back-end operational processes and focusing on the real-time unification and seamless integration of all aspects of information delivery and front-end Web-based user interactions (a critical paradigm shift in itself). Such a shift provides the necessary foundation for offering or taking advantage of two of the most promising e-business concepts: B2B e-services and application service provider (ASP) solutions.

Nevertheless, as has often happened in the past when a "hot" idea has caught on very quickly, in the race to deploy Web applications as soon as possible many companies are busy designing separate sites for their employees, customers, and partners. These sites, which they call "portals," are creating not only a growing management nightmare, but more importantly, highly limited, "stovepipe"-oriented environments from the e-business perspective.

How can a company manage the introduction of portal technologies in a consistent, enterprisewide manner? How can it set forward its e-business strategy, ensuring a broad-based implementation of portals as key enablers of all types of e-services along with the enterprisewide integration of information resources at the point of user interactions? How will these technologies align with existing investments in skills and IT infrastructures? How do you evaluate new products and all kinds of tools related to the corporate portal concept, taking into consideration the fact that, traditionally, IT organizations have paid weighty attention to the market position (market share), longevity, and support capabilities of a technology vendor, as well as the fact that the portal marketplace is so new and overcrowded with all kinds of start-up companies?

In order to answer these questions, it is necessary to answer some more generic but critical questions first, specifically:

- What is the common architectural and process-oriented (implementation and usage) theme in regard to portal technologies?

- Which strategic application development approaches are applied or emerging?

This chapter addresses these questions by providing a framework for the description of important architectural components of portals. (See Figure 6.1.)

This framework has been formulated through an analysis of the experiences of many successful Fortune 100 companies that have made a substantial commitment to portals and established strategic relationships with leading portal providers. It has also been influenced by the experimental work of many vendors (for example, Viador, Inc.)[2] that are transitioning from being technology suppliers for the Internet's big, generalized portal sites to being makers of products that enable "mass portalization," for example, products intended for turning ordinary companies into operators of personalized portal sites.

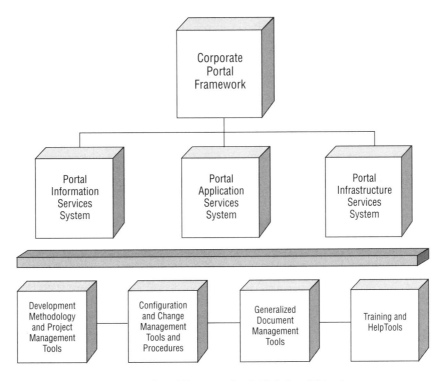

Figure 6.1: Corporate Portal Framework—A High-Level Structure

When it comes to describing new Internet technologies (for example, browsers, Web servers, and so on), the related literature is not consistent in the usage of the term *framework*, and, therefore, before launching a discussion about that subject, it makes sense to give a definition of what is meant here by a framework.

A framework is an all-encompassing specification for the collective set of products, components, and procedures necessary to create and deploy an enterprisewide technology solution. It represents a guiding source for collaborative, enterprise-based efforts, in which a comprehensive set of technology assets and business processes is developed, maintained, and integrated by involved organizations in order to enable strategic initiatives within a business area. Business and IT organizations use the framework as a "facilitator" to share resources, improve communications, and increase the efficiency of the design, development, and application of information technologies.

But how will the framework contribute to a realization of the business vision of a company embarking upon these initiatives? In order to answer this question, we need to consider a proper management strategy for governing the process of framework implementation.

The Corporate Portal Framework Defined

In general, the corporate portal framework (CPF) that is being described in this chapter is a comprehensive management tool for leveraging and extending companies' assets into the new digital economy through a unified set of technology and business processes. The CPF comprises key principles for the design, development, and application of the Web and other advanced information technologies, with the goal of creating both a widely available consolidated source of mission-critical information and a collaborative environment to support the use of this information. Following these principles, it becomes possible to construct a unified and integrated computing environment, potentially on multiple computer systems connected over the Internet, to forge the consolidated source of information.

The overall goal of the CPF is to enable the construction and implementation of highly efficient and flexible e-business integration solutions. Although it can be expected that the CPF will be a highly useful guide in a number of portal applications, including generalized, public portal scenarios, it is focused primarily on the corporate landscape and, more precisely, on the enterprise information portal (EIP) and role portal category (for example, B2B, B2C, and B2E portals). Thus, the primary target domain for the CPF is the integration of disparate corporate information sources and applications and closely related areas of development practices and infrastructure.

In these areas, due to a wide base of functional possibilities for portals, a focus on the key requirements is critical in order to successfully leverage and extend companies' assets. The CPF views corporate portals as comprised of a number of aspects, including information access and dissemination, collaboration, and application integration. In a general sense, these elements are likely to be addressed in one form or another in other, similar technical approaches and frameworks (for example, business intelligence and data warehousing). However, the CPF has certain unique properties and aspects that distinguish it from comparable approaches, among them shared support for many disparate and "unrelated" technologies, such as data access, content searching, workflow, groupware, and collaboration. In addition to sharing applications, interacting, and communicating, the CPF considers comprehensive facilities for data management and application integration as an integral aspect of corporate portal environments, thereby presenting a complete and coherent technology setting for many mission-critical Web applications. These facilities must provide not only traditional systems integration, but also (and more importantly) the unification of development and integration processes that allows you to move beyond systems integration to "plug-and-play" dynamic computing environments.

As outlined in Intraware, Inc.'s White Paper, "The e-Business Portal—Door to Internet-Scale Revenues and 21st Century Computing,"[3] "In the new world of e-business—where business relationships are constantly forming, developing, and dissolving, where new products, services, information, and offers are constantly being tested, deployed, modified, and swapped out—the traditional approach to developing and integrating systems produces a diminishing return. Too much is changing too fast; there's no time for hefty up-front investments to produce adequate payoffs." By embracing the CPF, companies will be able to evade such problems. Rather than focusing on tightly coupling different e-business technologies into a "solid" application, the approach formulated by the CPF is intended to provide a coherent and flexible environment in which content management, information dissemination, data/application access, computation, data management, communication, and a common workspace capability complement each other and operate cooperatively.

The principles embedded in the CPF allow you to deal comprehensively and effectively with the following key business objectives:

- Providing seamless "one-stop shopping" for a range of key information services across an enterprise and its value chain, available from a wider range of locations (including the home and workplace), using a range of different access methods.

- Enabling a distinct, "just-in-time" information dissemination capability, which is the ability for users to find and access the information they need, understand what is important, and "tie" important information pieces together for decision-making purposes, coupled with the facilities for content publishing and subscribing to such facilities.

- Enabling the capability to meet real user needs for collaboration, which is the ability for users to find resources that can help solve business problems and to get organized through "on-line" communities that connect people and enable collaborative work.

- Applying these capabilities to an enterprise in a manner that will allow for real-time integration of the enterprise's business processes, resulting in faster, more accurate business decisions, faster business cycle times, and reduced costs.

- Facilitating and encouraging users to take action when working within corporate intranet/extranet environments that can deliver rich information dissemination, collaboration, and integration value.

- Using continual feedback from users to refine the entire Internet computing environment.

From an architectural perspective, the CPF is an enterprisewide systems architecture focused on providing IT organizations with a comprehensive "blueprint" that will enable maximally flexible, scalable, and robust e-business applications. At the highest level, the CPF is an extensible collection of core services, tools, and applications that provide an appropriate (in accordance with the cited requirements) set of capabilities and infrastructure components that are needed for the construction of EIP and role-focused corporate portals. This collection is organized into three broad categories of integrated services and run-time procedures, collectively referred to as "systems": information services, application services, and infrastructure systems.

On top of the systems included in the CPF, there are a number of management tools that will add significant value to the actual implementations. These include the following:

- Life-cycle methodology and project management

- Change management tools

- Generalized document management tools

- Training tools

As enterprisewide systems architecture, the CPF possesses the following fundamental characteristics in addition to attributes typical to enterprisewide architectures (see the section in Chapter 2 entitled "E-Business Strategic Technology Architecture"):

- It is able to address the access requirements of a variety of channels (for example, LAN, WAN, wireless, and so on).

- Its composition accommodates different portal requirements (for example, EIP, B2B, B2C, and B2E).

- It has a highly scalable structure that accommodates growing and changing usage requirements with cost-effective incremental increases in infrastructure.

- It is focused on stringent security requirements (for example, digital authorization).

- It is centered around principles of application integration and interoperability focusing on the means to seamlessly interconnect all kinds of applications, components, and services; to add new services without major changes to the existing service set; and to encapsulate existing legacy applications and data without modifications.

- It embraces an object-orientated software development approach that allows the suppression of the specifics of directories, searching, "tunneling," and the "front ending" of numerous applications (ERP, groupware, on-line analytical processing, and so on) and many other underlying portal technologies, and it provides a clear component structure.

Because there will be a vast diversity in corporate portal implementations (in which each implementation will probably differ in terms of the combination of features of the cited systems it employs), features within each system category are separated into basic and advanced services. This implies that a basic service and an advanced service are not discrete types of functions provided by the portal, but more like two points on a continuum. In making a basic service into an advanced one, two main things happen. First, the user becomes proficient in working with the portal and he or she can clearly identify the overall functional focus of a particular category of services. Second, the relevance of the portal to user needs is greatly enhanced.

The CPF is a component-based architecture that represents the underlying set of interrelated software constructs (components), which can be used independently or assembled with other components to achieve specific portal capabilities or services. This architecture consists of four principal types of components:

- **Web-Based Portal Assistants**—A portal assistant provides a connection between users and common information and services. It is a starting point Web site where users enter to find and access information, and where they can collaborate using the various presentation service artifacts.

- **Portal Engines**—A portal engine is a self-contained, autonomous executable (subsystem) that is responsible for providing a complete set of functions (for example, searching, categorization, content management, meta-data management, e-mail, and so on). Portal engines interface with the portal assistant, with each other, and with other portal components (and particularly with application objects).

- **Portal Application Objects (also known as "portlets")**—A portlet is an object assembled according to the principles of agent technologies that operates as a stand-alone miniapplication under the control of an often large, multifaceted portal engine that acts as a portlet server. With portlets, an application can be divided into components that interact via interportlet messaging. Depending on their functions, portlets can be quite large in scope, each participating in the portal environment as a well-behaved, complete application. Every portlet is registered with the portal's management service.

- **Portal Adapters (also known as "gadgets")**—A gadget is an interface object (or more precisely, an application programming interface) that provides "bridging" (a gateway) between portlets, portals, and their servers, as well as connections from portal assistants to stand-alone applications (for example, legacy systems) and tools. Gadgets insulate the presentation and application service components from the complexity of back-end systems and the underlying infrastructure, enabling extensibility of portal services.

Structurally, the CPF is an open, multitiered (*n*-tiered) architecture focused on maximizing the flexibility and opportunities for infrastructure provider competition. It requires that every major interface in the portal architecture have an interface specification defined for it. This will allow architectural components, services, and supplier technologies and products to be replaced easily and a "plug-and-play" approach to be taken to architecture components, services, and infrastructure. Examples of the required level of specification include the adoption of numerous Internet standards that are of key importance to portals, such as HTTP, SSL, XML, LDAP, TCP/IP, EJB, XML, and so on.

Key architectural characteristics of the CPF multitiered approach are as follows:

- Flexible and cost-effective acquisition/exchange of services across tiers through the use of wrappers and adapters (gadgets).

- Comprehensive management of quality of service (QoS) aimed at delivering guarantees (dependability, security, and performance) across tiers.

- Support of the design, development, and implementation of interoperating objects, potentially by different organizations.

- High scalability as a result of treating scalability as a property of componentware and requiring the ability to build larger systems from plug-in component object services.

- Confederated architecture, meaning the environments collaborating in the federation are autonomous and free to operate at various levels of abstraction, using whatever technologies are deemed appropriate to satisfy "customer" (for example, numerous portal services) requirements (a broader discussion of federated systems architectures is given in Chapter 4).

A schematic representation of the CPF structural composition is shown in Figure 6.2. As you can see, the CPF anticipates that a portal architecture will include (but not be limited to) the following main tiers (layers):

- Assistant layer (presentation services layer).

- Engine layer (in turn, this layer may have a multitiered structure, such as a central portal engine that governs other functional engines, which are connected to each other).

- Portlet layer (for example, built-in specialized applications, such as workflow, e-mail, groupware, and so on).

- Gadget layer (for example, API and middleware objects).

- Back-end systems layer (for example, packaged applications, database servers, data warehousing servers, legacy systems, and so on).

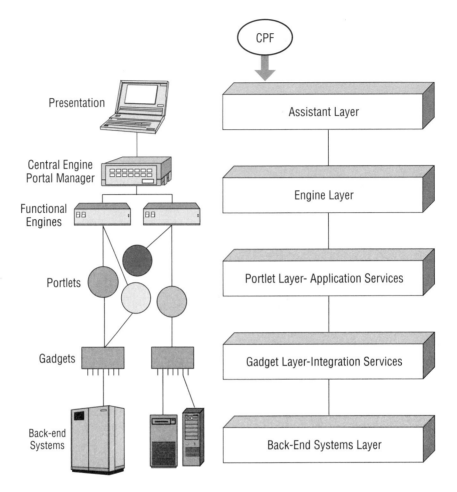

Figure 6.2: CPF Multitiered Structure

Let's reiterate the fundamental point about the CPF. The concept of the CPF contrasts sharply with that of traditional enterprise application integration (EAI) approaches, which are based on fixed specifications of software components and their interactions. The melding of multiple technologies into a unified approach to multitiered application development is truly a breakthrough.

Also, it is important to note that the CPF supercedes any particular product architecture. It is a reference architecture (or, better, a conceptual model) that serves as a guide for the design of commercial portal products and the evaluation of such products as well as for building corporate portal environments.

Corporate portals require a complex combination of software technologies that must interlock tightly and behave harmoniously to enable superior results. Companies have a host of options to consider in determining what their unique portal solution will encompass. Each step along the portal revolution presents a different set of processes and systems that a company can implement. This is why understanding the concept of the CPF is so important.

Generally speaking, at the strategic level, the CPF is a living (for example, extendable) application deployment architecture designed to provide the features and technical capabilities used to build e-business applications characterizing the corporate portal approach and its vision.

While many recently initiated e-business implementations call for numerous CPF elements, it is the systematic combination of all the CPF principles that can lead to a strategically powerful technological environment, potentially helping a company win against competitors. The challenge for companies is to use the framework to examine each area of the implementation and then assess how the areas work together to produce a stronger overall e-business environment.

Implementation of the CPF must be carefully done, since the provisioning of all kinds of tools and technologies called for by such a framework could add significant costs to the overall IT environment, reducing the benefits. Collecting user feedback and allowing users to define the scope and functionality of services within a particular category can also help to optimize efficiency. All in all, whatever the case may be, making portal services fit well with day-to-day tasks, cultural norms, and user working modes in their environment is key.

The previous paragraph brings us to a more generic point. In order for any such framework to be successful in the real world, what companies actually need is a mechanism to support their existing IT environments and their existing staff's expertise and at the same time engage in implementation of the CPF. Following CPF principles affects many critical underlying development processes, parts of the technical infrastructure, and operational capabilities of IT organizations. This makes it crucial for IT organizations to embrace an evolutionary model of the implementation of the CPF with the existing system's user interfaces being overlaid with the CPF's components, which handle data access as the first step.

The CPF community is developing momentum. Although the market promotion and technology push from such leading commercial vendors as IBM and Oracle has just begun, the CPF and an e-business development framework are becoming increasingly popular. Many developers are contributing to the concept and related materials.

Portal Information Services

As depicted in Figure 6.3, portal information services are represented by a set of various shared (integrated) procedures that enable "one-stop shopping" for structured/unstructured internal corporate and external information for users. They form an environment responsible for enabling the three essential characteristics of corporate portals:

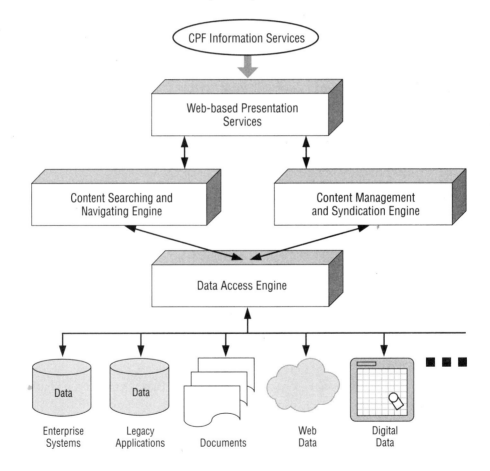

Figure 6.3: Portal Information Services

- A single (universal and seamlessly integrated) point of access to content, applications, business intelligence functions, and collaborative and community building functionality.

- Personalized views that enhance this sort of access with customization, basically "overlaying" generalized access capabilities with a tailored access in the context of an individual's preferences, access profile, and business rules (for example, an adjustment of form and content according to the environment of the users and their preferences).

- Flexible information navigation enabled by information structuring using categorization and traversing techniques (for example, file system metaphors), "site" maps (for example, a graphical representation of the flow and hierarchy of a portal), and information searching.

First, portal information services include presentation services delivered via portal assistants. Second, these services cover two critical information dissemination functions: content searching and navigating, and data access.

Presentation Services

The presentation services function is the Web interface for CPF-based portals that defines the "look and feel" of a portal and the environment for the user interaction with the portal. Under the CPF, it is anticipated that personalization of access within a portal will occur at various levels. At the presentation layer, personalization deals with tailoring the user interface, including the look of the Web browser home page.

In terms of the browser-based access, the user interface (UI) may be implemented in two ways: spawning a new browser window when a new application or portal function is launched, or partitioning the main browser window into frames and allocating each frame to a particular application. The second option is more advanced, requiring Web browsers to provide built-in task management functions for desktop and pervasive device environments. Virtually any kind of Web development environment may be used to construct the UI.

In addition to standard Web-browser presentation features, the presentation service function is concerned with the extensions for three-dimensional viewing, real-time sound, and video (from the perspective of enabling for data visualization).

The design of the best possible user interface layout and style is very important because the portal's main ("home") window influences what the Web interface will be accommodating from the functionality standpoint, as well as the type of elements that support access, and runs the portal. For example, the window may provide a reserved area, locating it after the browser navigation area, for purposes of notification and/or "advertising." Also, frequently, the window contains a so-called site control button bar that provides control buttons extended across the entire main window (horizontally or vertically), allowing the user to navigate among the set of activities related to the portal. In some cases, it makes sense to have a special area reserved for orientation—for example, the area located below the site control button bar.

As was mentioned earlier, presentation services are delivered to users via portal assistants (for example, portal clients). Users connect to a portal assistant from their Web browsers. In most cases, this can be implemented using Java servlet technology.

Content Searching and Navigating

This is a "family" name for the collective set of functions and capabilities necessary to support essential front-facing and information dissemination aspects of corporate portals, encompassing such key services as organizing content, searching and accessing multiple information repositories (for example, e-mail, corporate file systems and data stores, and external Web sites), and personalizing the presentation of information to users. These portal services include the following functions, performed by one or several portal engines (see Figure 6.4):

- Categorization
- Ranking
- Hyperlinking
- Searching
- Summarization
- Personalization

Categorization is a key background process that is used to organize content based on keywords or concepts found in complex document repositories. It provides users with a navigational directory (the so-called site map) that can be browsed to find specific information. Navigational directories can be organized alphabetically by subject, function, user group, or product.

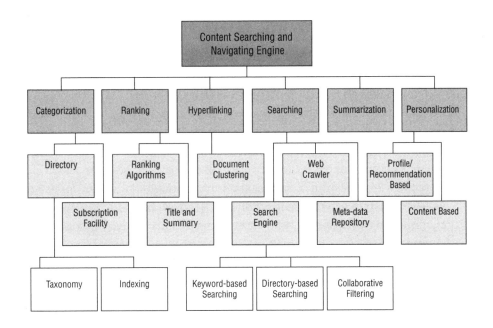

Figure 6.4: Content Searching and Navigating Engine Structure

The categorization process includes two applications (functions):

1. Identifying high-level categories under which content is organized within a directory. (This process is often referred to as "building a taxonomy.")

2. Indexing ("tagging") content and documents with appropriate attributes within the taxonomy to ensure quick and focused information delivery.

Having the ability to automatically analyze and categorize a large number of documents is very important to the success of a corporate portal. Automated categorization tools use algorithms that model human conceptual understanding of information. These algorithms are "trained" (configured) to identify high-quality Web pages and to categorize those pages according to either the prespecified classification scheme created by portal administrators or in accordance with user-defined custom categories. Once configured, these algorithms can be applied across large collections of documents.

The portal taxonomy can be created in two ways:

■ By integrating a general Web directory into a portal and customizing it according to particular needs—examining the content of the portal and adding, removing, or modifying categories or individual Web pages within categories.

- By creating custom directories from scratch.

The majority of automated categorization tools use "explicit categorization," which means examining every document in a collection. Recently, new categorization technologies have started to appear; these techniques employ "implicit categorization" methodologies that take advantage of implicit classification. As in the area of citation analysis, in which documents that cite a common source are a means to build a useful collection of documents, implicit categorization tools can build a directory based, for example, on the extracted sample set of documents, which functions as a set of categories.

Ranking is another background process responsible for organizing retrieved information based on scores ("ranks") according to a specific criterion (for example, relevance). As an example, for specialized and focused information searches, content may be returned to the user based not solely on the query terms, but on the overall significance of certain information found in a particular document.

Ranking tools use a variety of different algorithms and techniques, such as proximity, query completeness, number of hits, Boolean logic, and so on, as well as various combinations thereof. One algorithm can be used on a specific type of document and information source, and a different algorithm can be used to choose documents from another type of source.

Ranking is applied once all of the information is retrieved as a result of a search and before it is displayed to the user. Each piece of information is ranked for relevance, and usually, a title and brief summary are produced. A categorization tool may also get involved at this point to run across all information for purposes of tuning the taxonomy.

Hyperlinking is a portal service that enables users to discover relationships between documents and information within documents. It allows the creation of clusters of associated information within a collection of document sources.

Searching is one of the most important functions of a corporate portal. Because information is spread across multiple sources (for example, the Internet, e-mail, bulletin boards, databases, file systems, and applications), the CPF calls for a fully integrated search capability.

Searching is a multistep process involving different types of tools "bundled" as one or several engines: search engines, Web crawlers, and meta-data repositories, which have been discussed previously in the book (see Chapters 3 and 5). The CPF articulates two main aspects in regard to the searching process: collecting information to focus searches and executing the searches. As to the type of search engines to be used in corporate portals, the CPF anticipates the use of three main types: keyword-based, directory-based, and conceptual (collaborative filtering) searching. Keyword-based searching is the basic service and directory-based and collaborative filtering are advanced services.

For keyword-based and directory-based searching, the user enters one or more search words in combination with Boolean operators (AND or OR). For conceptual searching, the user enters one or more meta-data descriptors (specific keywords or queries highly relevant to information needs in a particular industry, for example, energy, transportation, finance, and so on) that are translated by the engine to the specific syntax of the underlying sources.

After the information for focusing searches is obtained from the user and search profiles are built, the next step is executing the searches. The CPF defines two ways of executing the searches: synchronously (instantaneously) or asynchronously (for example, in the background after several seconds to several minutes).

Also, the CPF defines a set of factors (criteria, features, and general issues) that can help with evaluating and selecting search engines for corporate portals, specifically:

- Speed (the length of time it takes to perform a search using a series of keywords).

- Flexibility and ease of use (the ability of the search engine to provide considerate little touches, such as suggested keywords or phrases for "related searches").

- Searching efficiency (for example, full-text search capabilities; the availability of power search capabilities for handling nontext items, such as MP3 files and images; the possibility of searching by attributes like date, domain, and so on; fuzzy and phonetical searches; and search refinement).

- Presentation of results (for example, allowing for content blending when consolidating information from multiple sources, including databases of breaking news stories, stock quotes, and users' own proprietary content, and seamlessly presenting it alongside directory search results).

■ Customization (taking into consideration user preferences via user profiles in real time).

■ Integration (especially with meta-data repository and categorization tools).

Summarization is a process of formulating summaries to present to the user. A summarization tool that intelligently parses the content and then constructs the proper summary information handles this process. If content has handcrafted summaries (for example, news feeds), the tool uses such summaries instead of automatically generated information.

Personalization is a broad-based set of functions that allows users to specify what they need or have the particular service proactively anticipate what the users' preferences and unique interests are, and to deliver content accordingly. The ability to deliver a personalized, highly targeted, and relevant set of information is critical to portal success. The CPF defines two basic services (profile-based and recommendation-based personalization) and one advanced service (content-based personalization).

Profile-based personalization tracks users' interests and creates a dynamic association between users' interests and content. Personal profiles are objects that contain user information and preferences. These profiles can be created in two ways: from information manually entered by users or by capturing search requests using automated profiling tools. The CPF requires the establishment of a central user profile shared across all portal services. Automated profiling tools use a number of advanced profiling features, such as behavior analysis and comparative metrics.

Recommendation-based personalization establishes user preferences through ranking and by observing the usage patterns of retrieved content.

Content-based personalization uses methods that are similar to those used by the recommendation-based scheme; specifically, it is based on automated personalization tools that are able to determine the suitability of a document by analyzing search keywords and selection criteria and their association with the ranking of results.

Data Access

The primary role of this service is to provide self-service, dynamic access (interface) to mission-critical business information sources—most importantly, to packaged ERP and customer relationship management (CRM) applications (for example, SAP R/3, PeopleSoft, Oracle, Siebel, and so on), legacy systems, and data warehousing and business intelligence applications.

Under the CPF, requirements for this service deal with issues of providing end-to-end solutions for analyzing enterprise business information. The CPF anticipates that corporate portals have to provide integrated access to key functional areas, such as reporting and ad hoc query processing, on-line analytical processing (OLAP) analysis, and data visualization, within the full scope of capabilities of the CPF's presentation services, which have been outlined previously, to deliver customized, relevant, and targeted information to the business user. Special attention should be given to enabling integrated access to business intelligence tools, especially tools with comprehensive data mining capabilities that provide a rich set of content analyzers, supported by visualization tools to identify patterns and relationships in data and interactions.

Portal Application Services

The CPF notion is that any process that presents information to a portal engine or a portal assistant (client) through an interface (API) is considered to be an application service. It follows, then, that every application service must have an interface (gadget) associated with it, whether that gadget is for an e-mail application or an ERP package. One very exciting benefit of the CPF is its emphasis on identifying and setting guidelines to aid in provisioning a rich, comprehensive set of APIs, which provides interfaces and management capabilities to incorporate all kinds of stand-alone applications and systems into the portal (for example, packaged applications, legacy systems, desktop applications, external applications, and so on).

At a high level, portal application services incorporate special features and technologies through a set of various APIs to accomplish corporate portals' purposes in multiple application-related areas. These services include the following:

- Workflow services to streamline business processes across different applications

- Collaborative services to facilitate communication and build community

- Transaction services to provide the necessary capabilities for commerce
- Legacy execution services to streamline operations of legacy systems, including creating and maintaining data in these systems
- Content management, subscription, and publishing services
- Proprietary applications
- Enterprise packaged applications, such ERP, CRM, and so on

The CPF identifies two ways to implement portal application services: via portlets and through stand-alone applications (those built outside the portal, including packaged and legacy systems). The following four major categories of portal features could be furnished very effectively through the use of portlets:

- **Content Management**—Content production and publishing, content syndication and broadcasting, content feeds, subscription services, and so on.

- **Collaborative and Productivity Services**—Global calendar, e-mail, workflow, chat, virtual conferencing, visual interaction and collaboration with customers and groups over the Web (for example, the exchange of graphics, diagrams, annotation tools, and screen shots), and so on.

- **Specialized Productivity and Analytical Tools**—Budgeting and planning, employee evaluation and training, churn analysis, and so on.

- **E-Assisting Business Services**—An environment in which to build and host transaction applications for commerce, such as the handling of buying–selling transactions, B2B document exchange, on-line catalogs and pricing, fund transfer, customer interaction management, and so on.

Therefore, applications can be installed within the portal in two ways: as base services by using portlets, or as applications that are not installed as base services within the portal but are built outside of the portal, and then registered with the portal and connected to it using "gadgets." It should be possible for any application (be it a portlet or a stand-alone system) to be designed and registered for horizontal service (used by many services, like an e-mail application) or vertical service (used only within the context of a particular service) within the portal.

As was stated previously, from an application point of view, a portlet is just a component. But it is a special type of component, and it plays one of two roles. First, the portlet can provide static and dynamic content for a specific content subject (for example, budgeting and planning) in the portal window's page. Second, the portlet can work cooperatively with other portlets, performing business logic processing on behalf of another portlet and providing results to that portlet.

The diagram shown in Figure 6.5 depicts an example of how portlets can be implemented within an Enterprise JavaBeans (EJB) development model. This example uses JavaBeans, EJBs, legacy data stores, and adapters (gadgets). Access to dynamic application data is done through EJBs and gadgets that play the role of legacy system interfaces. Once this data is retrieved, the portlet prepares the data and returns it to the requester.

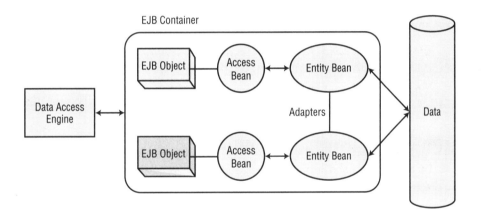

Figure 6.5: EJB Portlet Example

Portlets should be built in distributed, multithreaded fashion in order to allow application services to be distributed across multiple servers and machines for load-balancing purposes, if necessary, making the whole issue of providing a robust transaction run-time environment very important. Using application server technologies, it becomes possible to tie the entire suite of portal services together and to provide the common infrastructure to support appropriate distributed multithreaded characteristics across the range of services contained within the portal application service set.

The application server can play the role of a central portal management service with prime responsibility for managing communication between portlets and associated gadgets. The application server may also support access to stand-alone application services, integrating the services provided by that class of applications and especially, managing transactions across boundaries. Also, the central portal service can service requests or pass them to the other portal components, specifically infrastructure services such as the authentication portal service. Enterprise-level application servers, such as EJB servers, certainly fill an important need in many portal computing scenarios.

These comments bring us to a point in our discussion where it is necessary to reiterate the definition of a portal. *A portal is a doorway to the cyberworld of information. It is not a product sold by a vendor, but a goal to be achieved through the integration of multiple products from multiple vendors. It is a concept of a unification platform that allows for a collection of application services to work together to facilitate access to that world of information. The ability to aggregate these services and to provide the necessary platform for them to work cooperatively are the real values of this concept, in general, and of corporate portals, in particular.*

Portal Infrastructure Services

To provide all the services described in the previous sections, IT organizations face significant operational challenges from the technical infrastructure perspective:

- Incorporating simultaneously various multifaceted software components, tools, and product suites and ensuring their operational stability, potentially across multiple platforms (for example, cross-platform software availability).

- Providing unified authentication processes and single cross-platform/application log in.

- Providing a comprehensive unification and application integration platform capable of handling not only new tools and applications, but also all kinds of packaged, proprietary, and legacy systems.

- Enabling a highly multifaceted and integrated development environment (for example, component-based development, content publishing, metadata repository, EAI, and so on).

- Ensuring the kind of availability and performance characteristics that have long been associated with high-volume legacy transaction systems in the areas of information dissemination and e-business interaction management.

- Providing a centralized administrative tool model that enables administrative simplicity for the entire environment, ease of configuration, ongoing "health" monitoring, failure detection, and security administration within the extended enterprise support scheme for continuously changing and expanding portal-based services.

With those challenges in mind, the CPF notion is that key characteristics of portal infrastructure services are as follows:

- Insulation of presentation and application services so that they do not deal directly with system services, such as security, storage access, processor or server utilization and load balancing or distribution, messaging, networking implementations, and so on.

- Integration engines for tying presentation and application services together, including major communications and groupware and workflow systems, including enabling infrastructure components.

- Unified development facilities supporting various programming models (HTML, XML, Java, ActiveX, HDML, DHTML, cascading style sheets, Java Script, VB Script, and Java Messaging Service, which allows dynamic coupling between system components, and so on) via a universal editor or best-of-breed tools (referred to as the "portal builder" subsystem).

- Integrated data access facilities to major databases based on ODBC/JDBC support via native or third-party drivers.

- Unified content management facilities supporting personalized content syndication for enabling customizable colors, schemes, and other major publishing functions.

- Unified authentication processes supporting SSL, SHTTP, socket communication, LDAP, auto message encryption, and an API for custom-built security features.

- Unified state management facilities for fault tolerance and global interaction integrity with application, session, user, object, and string state management via independent state server processes to eliminate scalability problems.

- Integrated user interaction management facilities for gathering user information and categorizing profiles and for monitoring the status of interaction sessions with the user.

- Integrated administrative and systems management processes supporting Simple Network Management Protocol (SNMP) integration that incorporates system management utilities via SNMP messaging.

- Support for application portability by accommodating stand-alone Java applications, servlets, JavaBeans, NSAPI, ISAPI, WAI & WAP, and traditional C/C++ options.

- Common support for different communication protocols and interfaces, such as HTTP, SSL, FTP, RMI, IIOP, and so on.

Assembling such a comprehensive set of infrastructure services requires a careful, step-by-step approach. The first step is to address the issue of enterprise application integration (EAI) within the framework. Two requirements are important here. The first is deployment of tools and services that ensure highly flexible operating systems, languages, database access, communication protocols, and distributed services such as CORBA or Enterprise JavaBeans. The second is deployment of tools and services that generate complex "answers" from any customer information source within the enterprise.

A complete implementation of the CPF would give you a true, advanced-function EAI infrastructure that leverages extensible markup language (XML) to exchange information among disparate systems, including native data integration modules that plug into ERP applications (such as SAP, PeopleSoft, and Baan), transaction systems (such as CICS, MQSeries, and Microsoft Transaction Server), e-commerce environments, object systems, legacy applications, modeling tools, and security systems. Such robust integration is necessary for rapid information exchange between the many application services that manage the complex interconnections associated with user interactions with the portal (such as providing federated search capabilities across dispersed, heterogeneous data sources, handling commerce-related transactions, establishing collaborative workplaces, and so on).

For this reason, a corporate portal must provide a highly productive integrated development environment as well as a flexible component assembly platform. When deployed into the portal environment, applications should interoperate across CORBA, COM, JavaBeans, and EJBs without custom coding, and they should access and exchange information with diverse internal and external enterprise systems.

The second step is to establish a comprehensive environment for team-based production and delivery of content. Serving a fundamental need in establishing a successful portal infrastructure strategy, this environment lets your organization collaboratively distribute information over the Internet by automatically gathering, versioning, testing, and deploying vast amounts of Web content.

Typically, content management is a custom-coded environment built on programming languages such as C/C++ or Java, various scripting languages, and template-based page layouts. In these environments, application developers spend a lot of time producing and maintaining content through programming. In order to dynamically assemble personalized content, for example, a simple HTML page has to be fully generated in real time. Generating every page on the fly is a challenging endeavor that requires not only complex programming for personalization, but also significant hardware investments to scale to acceptable performance levels.

To exploit adaptive navigation, dynamic content assembly, and personalized content delivery, it is necessary to incorporate powerful content-component site management software that lets you define individual displayable components (a combination of content, format, and related application logic) without tying them to the specific pages on which these components might appear. Using such software, application pages are defined by specifying a series of nested content-component elements (or blocks) for building the page. This modular approach enables an inherent, dynamic ability to separate content from presentation logic, letting users without programming expertise get involved in content production and maintenance. These capabilities become highly important for companies that already have, or are planning to have in the near future, portal sites containing a large number of content-intensive, frequently updated pages, and that have more than 10 people involved in content production, Web publishing, and the support of those sites.[4]

Personalized content syndication can be done by employing a specialized software tool to simplify the creation and management of syndicated (highly personalized) content, and by pushing it to the user as personalized messages. This software should be capable of delivering these messages via any communications channel, including the Web, pervasive devices (wireless), and voice.

Consider a Web site that offers travel-related content—such as destination information, news, tips, maps, and travel recommendations—from different sources. Combining this sort of service with personalized content syndication features, the portal could not only provide multisource content as a monolithic information set, but also offer interesting personalization features, such as personal travel pages and chat rooms.

Security is the next challenge to tackle. The issue of security is extremely important because, in many cases, corporate portals host sensitive personal information and provide access to many confidential sources of business information. The integrity and confidentiality of this information must be protected. Resilience is also required, with resistance to so-called service attacks. In order to achieve those goals, infrastructure services should include such features as authentication, authorization, certification, firewalls, intrusion detection, and other security-related technology (for example, smart cards and public key infrastructure). The move to the single sign on is key.

Also, in order to enable robust security and manageability of user access, it is critical to incorporate directory services, such as Lightweight Directory Application Protocol (LDAP), which provide the ability to manage authentication or access control and user identity data. LDAP allows the passing of access rights and other user information from the presentation services layer to applications, enabling them to tailor their Web pages and interactions with the user appropriately.

Security management services are tightly coupled with systems management services. A systems administration tool should allow the system administrator to manage users, groups, and source rights. The same tool could help the system administrator examine how different users are using infrastructure resources. In the area of basic systems management services, all the functions typical of distributed environments are expected, including maintaining a complete log of all events that are processed by the portal and monitoring faults.

The main point is this: Portal infrastructure services are an integrated conglomeration of several distributed and client–server system environments positioned to solve the development and run-time challenges inherent in portal-based computing.

CPF Architecture for the Extended Enterprise: The Network of Portals

In order to complete the discussion about the CPF, it is necessary to mention the business and technical advantages of using the federated portal architecture to build a corporate portal, especially for large enterprises.

Structurally, the CPF is envisioned to be a confederated architecture, but so far we have described very little in this regard. Most of the discussions related to the topic of corporate portal solutions have been around approaches that can be accurately described as "centralized" (monolithic) portals.

The idea of the federated portal architecture is based on the stipulation that the benefits of the federated systems model (see Chapter 4 for details) can be applied to portal development. A federated architecture approach offers an attractive solution to the business problems inherent in large enterprises, especially in the cases of extending enterprise boundaries, such as planning, ownership, and budgeting, and technology issues, such as heterogeneity of infrastructure components, scalability, and growth.

A federated architecture for the CPF involves a network of connected role portals working together as a group of cooperative corporate portals. The word "federated" implies a union of independent entities working together to provide specific functions. This federated portal approach is exactly the solution needed to deal with the problems faced in building extended enterprises.

The primary advantage of the federated architecture model is its ability to include portals from a company's partners and suppliers as part of the federation. In effect, the portal network supports information sharing, collaboration, and decision making throughout a company's value chain.[5]

As depicted in Figure 6.6, at the highest level, federated portals require two architectural components that we have not yet discussed: a global shared user directory (GSUD) that describes every user in the network and a cooperative global meta-data repository (GMDR) that describes all information sources in the network. Each portal in the federation relies on these core components to determine which portal can best meet users' requests for information or assistance. Both the GSUD and the GMDR can be implemented as distributed components, in which each portal has local copies of these directories.

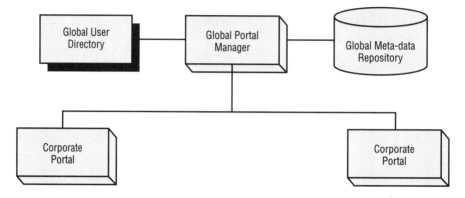

Figure 6.6: Federated Portal Architecture

From the application services standpoint, the federated architecture brings a high capacity for collaboration, using tools like workflow, chat, and expertise directory services that, in turn, lead to the possibility of inter-enterprise decision making, in which people from different organizations can participate in the decision-making process via collaboration.

The State of Corporate Portal Technology

Building a well-designed, powerful, and scalable corporate portal in accordance with CPF principles requires careful planning and a keen understanding of the current state of technology and its future trends. This is especially true when the portal will have to handle access to multiple, disparate data sources and applications, such as business intelligence, database query and reporting, dynamic content generation, and interactions with an exponentially increasing number of business users. There is a lot that could be said, and should be said, about the state of corporate portal technology—the ability to deliver on the vision of a single doorway into the world of information.

The concept of corporate portals is arguably the most critical component of the new e-business environment. Given the explosive potential growth of e-business, which is projected to do $3 trillion worth of business in 2003, according to many analysts, the market for e-business applications, especially the portal technology that enables these applications, will expand dramatically. As a result, huge numbers of software vendors are climbing aboard the corporate portal bandwagon. On one hand, this trend has been a key positive driver of technology-enhancing activity among software vendors that fuels technology progress and innovation. On the other hand, there appears to be a puzzling and incomprehensible diversity of products labeled as a "corporate portal" and marketed as a "full solution." Nowadays, almost every vendor of query/reporting, on-line analytical processing (OLAP), packaged datamarts and data mining, and enterprise application integration (EAI) software offers products promoted as portals. It has gotten to the point where vendors are trying to call almost any desktop product that has Web access and some type of reporting capability a "portal." Consequently, IT organizations must be very careful when selecting and evaluating such products because, in a lot of cases, they are nothing more than "relabeled" narrow-focused traditional decision-support solutions with Web-enabled front ends.

There are two key trends to watch in the field of corporate portals, and both relate in one way or another to the issue of market growth.

First, today's portal marketplace is undergoing a significant consolidation in terms of both corporations and products. Most portal software companies are small start-ups with limited investment backing. Therefore, rapid consolidation of the market will occur, particularly as some of the bigger software companies decide to establish a strong position in this highly lucrative area. Vendors such as IBM, Oracle, and Computer Associates, and others with a strong presence across information access, application integration, and Web applications markets, are likely to be major players in the portal space. These companies also have the infrastructure competency and ability to tackle the difficult architectural issues involved in reaching a broad, CPF-based solution. Nevertheless, the field of corporate portals is wide open at present, and this situation will continue for some time, which will bring more and more companies into the race.

Second, the marketplace is moving toward establishing more specific areas of specialization, which is changing the way portal companies deliver portal products and services to their customers. These areas include (but are not limited to) the following classes of products:

- Role-oriented generic and specialized portal suites (enterprise information portals; collaborative portals; B2B, B2C, and B2E portals; or a combination of these)

- Plug-in portal components and toolboxes (tools and components for software vendors and for corporate developers engaged in custom development of portal solutions)

- Portal platforms and frameworks (solution- and services-oriented products)

What follows is an overview of the portal technology marketplace. It is important to understand that this overview is a "snapshot" of the situation at the time of writing and, given the dynamics, may not necessarily be 100 percent correct at the time of your reading. However, it allows a view of the trends and, more importantly, of the key technology directions.

The State of Technology

In an effort to gain a realistic assessment of the state of the technology, it's important to go through a process that can be called a technology perception reality check (TPRC). The TPRC begins with solid customer research, which is much more than simply looking at market research and visiting a few customers of a particular technology or product. Most importantly, it means obtaining a "razor-sharp" understanding of exactly how that product is used by different customers and the "report card" in regard to the state of integration of those customers before the introduction of new portal technologies or products.

When applying the notion of the TPRC to the corporate portal market, some important actualities emerge. Two things are certain:

1. The present state of technology does not permit the achievement of a true CPF-based portal environment without a significant custom development. The next section reviews representative commercial products that can be considered effective components of a CPF strategy, but these currently fall short of a comprehensive "out-of-the-box" CPF-based solution. If a company is to leverage the sum of the parts described in the next section, it has to have an appropriate strategy in place. Key characteristics of such a strategy include solid architecture design, component-based development environment, cross-skill competency teams, and (more importantly) a culture of teamwork and sharing information. No one should be under any false impressions that technology alone can deliver a successful corporate portal environment, not to mention the necessary e-business computing environment, as a whole. Therefore, the real challenge of a successful CPF strategy is not so much in the technology, but in creating a culture in which the organization is able to really understand the value of integration and cooperation.

2. To a large degree, technical successes in the corporate portal world are inspired by the energy of development communities, fueled in part by the frustration inherent in the Web design process. As one of the developers

put it best in the CNET, Inc., commentary "Secrets of the Web Design Masters,"[1] "We all bemoan the state of technology, waiting with bated breath for the latest release of anything…. Once we use a tool, we know its limitations, and we want to upgrade. I love this medium. It is entirely frustrating and absolutely delightful."

Although there are many industry pundits that might argue differently, rapid and revolutionary advances in key Internet technologies (for example, Java, XML, application integration, and component-based development) are less likely during the next couple of years, because, unfortunately, many organizations still consider these emerging technologies to be "bleeding edge," which hinders their advancement. Enterprisewide deployment of these technologies is mandatory before anyone can consider initiating a large-scale portal implementation.

However, there are several current technologies that appear to be very important for the future potential of corporate portals. These technologies include pervasive computer networks, server platforms, e-business application servers, groupware and workflow systems, in-place data mining platforms and the developing technologies for convergence of different distributed computing (for example, Microsoft's COM/DCOM/DNA, OMG's CORBA, and Sun/IBM's EJB), and Web models. The following is an overview of the state of associated technologies, and these descriptions should be considered only a limited snapshot because technology in these areas is progressing at a very rapid pace.

Pervasive Computer Networks

More recently, e-mail, news groups, chat rooms, push technologies, pagers, cellular phones, personal digital assistants, and the Web have created a global telecommunications environment that has enabled a greatly expanded set of information exchange capabilities. Being able to disseminate information via pervasive computer networks is very nearly a necessity of every business in the modern economy. Pervasive network connectivity has changed the traditional computing model and made global systems feasible, including networks of corporate portals.

Server Platforms

The question of which platform the portal servers should run on is, to a large degree, answered for the foreseeable future. UNIX and Windows

NT/2000 are the two principal server operating systems, both with their strengths and weaknesses. UNIX systems have the potential for a larger number of processors on a single server. Windows NT/2000 systems are typically less expensive, so it is easier to aggregate a large number of machines in the service of a single portal system. In terms of performance, recent independent tests conducted by Mindcraft, *PC Magazine, PC Week,* and Hewlett-Packard all demonstrate that Windows NT/2000 systems perform as well as comparable UNIX platform settings, especially in serving the dynamic Web pages produced by corporate portals.

E-Business Application Servers

The application server market is well established, with products capable of meeting the needs of customers building corporate portal solutions. Examples include IBM's Websphere Application Server, Oracle's Internet Application Server (iAS) Services, BEA's WebLogic, and webMethods' B2B Server. These servers offer the following key characteristics:

- Time-tested capabilities of distributed computing architectures

- Accessibility using standard Internet protocols (HTTP and IIOP), as well as a component interface based on JavaBeans

- Support for clients that exploit just-in-time components

- A standard set of components that access network connectors to enable development teams to leverage enterprise legacy systems, such as CICS, IMS, and DB2

- Support for standards-compliant XML-based solutions to the problem of EAI for both Web and non-Web applications

- A unifying programming model (all development efforts, including access connectors that can take advantage of Java and the EJB standard)

Groupware and Workflow Systems

Groupware and workflow systems, previously viewed as "nice to have" technologies, are now seen as one of the foundational technologies for e-business applications. Current products allow companies to augment the human-centered processes in their enterprises with many rich collaborative features (for example, e-mail, discussions, chat capabilities, group scheduling, contact management, and so on) and information dissemination functions. This makes it easy for companies to add these functions to any portal-based solution. More importantly, workflow systems address the issue of complexity. When a company has implemented all of the CPF envisioned services and engines, adding rigor to its business processes will help make it possible to coordinate multiple types of business users and IT staff, including administrators, application developers, Web developers, and content providers. For this reason, this technology is crucial to many companies if they face the issues of implementing large-scale corporate portal initiatives. If they do, content management for them will be such a large space that it must be split in ways that make the problem manageable. Because of this split, however, several instances of the same content management system may need to be implemented to address specific subsets of content. The result is a distributive set of management processes, tools, and development groups that a company needs to manage as a whole. This situation makes workflow management an integral part of content management within large portal implementations.

In-Place Data-Mining Platforms

Automating and integrating real-time (or near-real-time) data mining of transactional data—in particular, data related to enterprise resource planning (ERP) and customer relationship management (CRM)—are gaining popularity among leading e-business companies, thanks to a number of promising new methods and technologies that have emerged recently. Examples of these methods and technologies include the following:

- Using EMC Corp.'s Time Finder software to capture near-real-time data so that the data can be mined by specialized data-mining products that are capable of enabling in-place (without extraction) mining of very large databases.

- Using message-oriented middleware, such as IBM's MQSeries, to capture transactions, take them off-line in batches, and mine these batches using a high-performance database manager with powerful memory-based data handling features, such as TimesTen Corp.'s TimesTen database server.

- Using a rule-based system that mines transaction streams by monitoring large volumes of transactions in real time, retrieving only those transactions that fit a particular predefined profile (exception rule) on materials availability, transportation, labor, machinery, and so on.

Although there are certain architectural and functional differences between these methods, all provide the ability to apply BI and data-mining techniques to business-to-business transactions in real time, and the applications and end results are the same: high-performance and high-productivity analysis of transactional data. This new approach for analyzing transactional data has been variously referred to as intelligent transaction mining (ITM), real-time transaction mining (RTTM), real-time data mining (RTDM), in-place data mining (IPDM), and zero-latency decision support (ZLDS). These technologies have much to offer when enabling e-marketplaces because they provide real-time responses to events occurring over large networks by monitoring transaction-level data. This, in turn, provides the ability to quickly design and modify cross-enterprise management procedures. This concept is especially powerful when tied to ERP systems because it lets companies use real-time transactional information for strategic, externally focused ERP solutions that are critical for managing all phases of time-dependent resources across the extended supply chain more effectively. Companies using real-time data-mining technologies can optimize their critical real-time resources in the context of the entire chain's needs.

Convergence of Different Distributed Computing and Web Models

As organizations have attempted to use the Web for increasingly sophisticated applications, such as corporate portals, these Web-based applications have begun to overlap in complexity with traditional, non-Web distributed systems. It was not envisioned, however, that the Web model would deal with issues attributed to complex distributed systems (for example, achieving high scalability and performance) for which distributed object architectures such as OMG's CORBA or Microsoft's COM/DCOM/DNA were originally developed. As a result, there are numerous technologies being developed that apply the known aspects of distributed object architectures to the problem of creating objects on the Web (combining state and behavior in the Web context). Examples include Dynamic HTML (DHTML) facilities implemented in popular Web browsers, DHTML's Document Object Model, JavaScript scripting language, CORBA Component Scripting, a response technology for defining interfaces between JavaScript and CORBA objects, XML Stylesheets (XSL), client-side object brokers for converging CORBA Interface Repository and the COM+ type information in the

Windows Registry, and, more recently, SOAP, which bridges Component Object Model (COM) and Distributed COM objects across the Web and runs natively in Windows' environments. A deeper integration of the Web and different object concepts into a unified Web object model would allow companies to use the concept of the corporate portal to fully integrate all computer-accessible data available internally or externally on the Internet.

The Corporate Portal Marketplace: An Overview

This section will cover two product categories: role-oriented generic and specialized portal suites, and plug-in portal components and toolboxes.

Role-Oriented Generic and Specialized Portal Suites

This section presents an overview of EIP, collaborative, B2B, B2C, and B2E portals, or a combination of such products.

Autonomy, Inc.

Autonomy's Portal-in-a-Box is a suite-type ("out-of-the-box") product positioned as an automated, turnkey solution for creating and maintaining a specialized EIP-type portal. The product offers features that address the processes of categorization and tagging, the hypertext linking of large amounts of information, and personalization. It provides capabilities for accessing and organizing information from hundreds of sources, including Web sites, news feeds, word-processing files, e-mail messages, spreadsheets, databases, Lotus Notes archives, and PowerPoint presentations. It also provides the up-to-date, personalized business information needed for decision-making processes.[2]

The strong points of Portal-in-a-Box are as follows:

- Aggregation of content from internal and external sources, focusing on issues related to the access of unstructured information.

- Personalization, including opening "splash pages" for each user (for example, enabling the so-called MyDot.com features) based on an analysis of text that they have previously accessed, user profiling, allowing users to create personalized newsletters using plain English to describe the topics they are interested in, and automatically alerting users whenever a subject of interest comes up in a chat room conversation or appears in a breaking news story.

- Collaboration, focusing on the ability to create virtual communities of interest or workgroups by putting users with related or mutual interests or areas of work in touch with each other.

The product's main shortcomings are as follows:

- Content management

- Integration with business intelligence tools such as OLAP and data mining

- Access to packaged enterprise applications

Brio Technology, Inc.

Brio's Brio.Portal Enterprise is a comprehensive EIP-type portal platform that is widely used for providing a broad-based integration of information residing in packaged enterprise applications, such as SAP R/3 and PeopleSoft. The main part of this portal platform is Brio.Portal, a combination of multiple service-oriented modules[3]:

- **Repository**—A centralized storage area for Brio.Portal objects that provides controlled, secure, and searchable access to these objects. Metadata that describes each information object is stored in a relational database.

- **Name**—A service that provides directory lookup, initialization, and configuration management capabilities for all Brio.Portal services.

- **Authentication**—A service that provides user authentication via native and external authentication systems.

- **Job Factory**—A service that automatically manages content creation, such as report updates, in real time, and inserts the resulting Brio.Portal objects from the reports into the repository. It communicates with the name service to direct jobs to be executed on specific servers or across multiple servers to balance the load.

- **Scheduling**—A service that provides the ability to schedule one-time and recurring scheduled events and dispatches scheduled tasks for execution in job factories.

- **Subscription**—A service that matches user preference profiles with new or updated information objects published to the repository in order to enable personalization.

- **Distribution**—A service that provides e-mail notification of subscription, scheduling, and job factory events.

- **Web Client**—A presentation services module that provides browser-based user interface capabilities for searching, viewing, and interacting with information objects.

- **QuickConnect**—An integration service (a set of APIs and scripting features) that connects Brio.Portal with popular ERP application environments.

Open Text Corporation

Open Text's Livelink platform is a fully functional product for enabling corporate portals, primarily in EIP and B2E categories. This platform is capable of handling many enterprise portal services, such as document management, virtual team collaboration, business process automation, workgroup scheduling, and information retrieval services, tightly integrated into a customizable and extendable portal solution.

Livelink's core functionality includes the following[4]:

- **Enterprise Workspace**—Provides users with access to corporate information (best practices, policies, procedures, business-critical news, and all projects throughout the enterprise).

- **Project Workspace**—Creates a focused collaborative environment in which team members can work together and share project-specific information.

- **Personal Workspace**—Provides a single point of access to real-time business intelligence information.

Architecturally, Livelink is a scalable three-tier system. The application server tier provides Livelink services that are extensible through an open backplane using JAVA, ActiveX, Visual Basic, C, and C++. The data server tier supports popular relational databases and systems, including Lotus Notes, Microsoft Exchange, SQL Server, SAP R/3, and Oracle, providing cross-enterprise and cross-Internet access to messaging systems and directories. Livelink's modular design allows users to extend and enhance its functionality and performance by seamlessly adding, removing, or upgrading optional modules. Livelink provides a set of adapters (termed "activators") and development tools for those purposes, including:

- **Livelink Activator for CORBA**—An adapter that allows the creation of applications that extend Livelink's functionality and integrate Livelink with external systems using Common Object Request Broker Architecture (CORBA) services.

- **Livelink Activator for Lotus Notes**—An adapter that allows the indexing and retrieval of information stored within Lotus Notes databases.

- **Livelink Activator for SAP R/3**—An adapter that provides seamless connectivity between the Livelink application server and the R/3 system.

- **Livelink Enterprise Activator**—A rapid application development tool to link to business-critical applications, making Livelink a single point of access.

- **Livelink Cataloged Library**—An application development tool to link Livelink to an external document management system.

- **Livelink Desktop**—An adapter to link to popular desktop applications, including Windows Explorer, Microsoft Word, PowerPoint, Excel, Outlook, Adobe Acrobat, and other ODMA-compliant applications.

- **Livelink Directory Services**—An administrative tool that synchronizes with a central directory service and provides single log-in access for users.

- **Livelink eLink**—An adapter that integrates Livelink with any standard e-mail application.

- **Livelink iRIMS**—A document management module that provides life cycle document management and enterprisewide record management functions.

- **Livelink Transit Central e-Publisher**—An administrative tool for organizing and publishing documents in Livelink.

- **Livelink Explorer**—A navigational tool that uses Microsoft's Windows Explorer-like drag-and-drop functions to cut, paste, copy, and move objects, including documents and compound documents.

- **Livelink SDK**—A built-in software development toolbox for customization.

- **Livelink Spider**—A plug-in Web crawler that automatically finds and indexes new or modified documents, enabling Livelink to maintain an up-to-date, searchable knowledge base.

Plumtree Software

Plumtree's Corporate Portal is a highly scalable and comprehensive suite of modules and components for enabling just about any kind of corporate portal (with the possible exception of B2B portals for large-scale e-marketplaces). Functionally, this product brings together tools for three major types of applications and content[5]:

- **Business Performance Analysis**—A set of reporting and analysis applications to monitor critical business activities (for example, revenue dynamics, customer activities, call center volumes, lead-generation volumes, and production and inventory characteristics).

- **Collaborative and Productivity Tools**—A set of embedded functions, such as calendars and mailboxes, and links to common groupware and office management systems.

- **E-Commerce Service Applications**—A set of e-procurement (for example, travel and office supplies procurement) and hosting [for example, 401(k) administration] applications.

The Plumtree portal also provides a set of embedded tools for enabling content management and information dissemination features. In particular, it provides plug-in agents termed "accessors" for scanning different data sources (for example, Web pages, groupware databases, and a wide array of database applications) for new information, indexing the text in a search engine, and creating a meta-data repository in an extensible, XML-based thesaurus. On the basis of the text and meta-data indexes, the Plumtree portal categorizes links to the content in a logical Web directory accessible by users.

The product has a well-defined personalization scheme, in which users log in to their personalized view of the portal, which is assembled based on user preferences from the available applications and content categories relevant to their work. Also, the product provides direct access to a wide variety of packaged solutions, such as OLAP, data warehousing, and CRM and ERP systems.

One of the strongest points of the Plumtree Corporate Portal product is its architecture, which enables sufficient levels of extendibility for building comprehensive portal solutions. The product provides distributed dynamic content processing using Plumtree Portal Gadgets, the content modules that interact with enterprise applications and Internet services. Using this concept, almost any external application can be brought into the main portal.

Portal Wave, Inc.

Portal Wave Enterprise Application Portals (EAPs) is a "family" name for a technology platform focused toward aggregating the functionality of multiple enterprise applications (ERP, CRM, and legacy systems) into a unified B2B portal interface. The platform provides enterprises and their supply chain partners and customers with bidirectional transaction capability, personalized workflow, integration with front- and back-office systems, and full Web accessibility.[6]

The main component of the Portal Wave platform is an application portal server (APS) that enables bidirectional transactional capabilities, role-based workflow across systems and applications within the portal scope, a single user sign on to all portal applications and systems, and a number of other user-specific features. In terms of personalization, the APS provides a so-called dynamic user interface (UI) generator that generates a user-specific, role-based interface including navigation bars, headers and footers, and any necessary alerts, all of which allows users to quickly access information pertaining only to them.

The APS's workflow engine manages user eligibility to perform specific activities based on your company's workflow rules and business processes. Activities are routed via electronic notifications and hyperlinks that get posted at the user's home page. Users act on the notification and e-mail is sent to the specified users with a hyperlink for the exact location needed to perform an action.

One of the strong points about Portal Wave's platform is the availability of a comprehensive tool kit; this allows customization of services for specific e-business processes, content management, form design, and so on.

SageMaker, Inc.

SageMaker's SageWave Portal is an EIP-type portal solution for integrating industry-specific content, real-time news, and common groupware and reporting applications. SageWave collects, integrates, and organizes information from more than 9,000 industry-specific publications, from sources such as Reuters, Standard & Poor's, the U.S. Department of State, and

McGraw-Hill, and combines it with internal enterprise information resources in an easy-to-use, personalizable browser window.[7]

TopTier Software

TopTier's eBusiness Integration Portal is an EIP-type product that offers tight integration of navigational features (for example, natural language searching, "Drag and Relate" information mapping, "bookmarking" and tagging content of interest, and so on) with embedded business intelligence and reporting services such as OLAP and query engines. One of the strong points about the TopTier product is its ability to extend other portal solutions, most importantly, SAP's mySAP.com portal. TopTier's Drag and Relate technology can be used to associate a workplace within TopTier's portal with mySAP.com.[8]

Verity, Inc.

Verity's Portal One is an EIP-type product that offers unified access to multiple information sources, intelligent classification of information (a highly powerful and unique feature based on patented fuzzy logic technology), personalization, integrated searching, navigation, and view capabilities. Verity Portal One provides extensive personalization features, allowing users to choose applications and information categories based on their relevance to users' jobs, and customize and personalize the layout and content delivered by the portal via interfaces called "connectors," which can be of three types: personal, role-based, or companywide.

Verity's product provides impressively precise and accurate searching and navigating capabilities using a rich set of query operators, advanced features such as free text natural language search, fuzzy operations (for example, typographical and sounds-like search), concept search, query by example and clustering, and user-definable business rules.

The product provides the capability to enable unified access to enterprise information via prebuilt interfaces (gateways) and an API that allows writing custom gateways to information repositories and applications.[9]

Viador, Inc.

Viador's E-Portal Suite is a comprehensive platform for creating B2B and B2E portals. The Viador E-Portal Suite includes the following major modules[10]:

- **Viador Portal**—A user portal interface that gives users the ability to access, analyze, and share personalized views of business information using browsers. It contains a user-friendly content and layout-editing tool called PageBuilder, push and pull document publishing, business alerts, and document searching by keyword and content capabilities. The Viador Portal Customization APIs allow portal administrators to further tailor the appearance and behavior of the user interface for specific users or workgroups or on a companywide basis, and to integrate applications and Web-based content.

- **Viador Information Center**—A server-based platform that provides a single point of integration and control for all portal information components and services. It supports Windows NT, UNIX, and mainframe systems.

- **Viador Gateway**—A set of drivers for enabling data access to a wide range of structured, unstructured, and event-based data. The Viador Gateway uses native drivers to provide efficient access to structured databases like Oracle, Sybase, Informix, DB2, Microsoft SQL Server, Hyperion Essbase, Oracle Express, and Microsoft OLAP Services. Unstructured data such as Microsoft Office documents, text files, Adobe Acrobat documents, and files created by third-party applications or proprietary systems can be registered, stored, published, and searched through the Gateway. Event-based data, like personal alerts, Web-based news, stock, and subscription services, can be integrated into the portal using the Gateway through personal folders, shared channels, or custom portal pages.

- **Viador Sentinel**—An extranet security module that enhances typical security configurations with an additional layer of security, providing secure Web-based portal access to remote employees, customers, and supply-chain partners. Sentinel operates in conjunction with existing enterprise security systems, like firewalls and proxy servers, to identify and authenticate users, process requests, and deliver encrypted results.

In addition to the above features, Viador's E-Portal Suite provides a powerful development tool kit that allows the construction of interfaces and services (portlets) for the purpose of accessing all kinds of systems (for example, packaged applications, legacy applications, popular office applications, and so on) and analytic applications in order to create a comprehensive portal solution that addresses a wide range of enterprises' business requirements.

The following group of vendor products is a representation of a very large collection of offerings that cover the plug-in portal components and toolboxes space, from products that offer prebuilt modules that can enable complete functional areas of portals to "small" plug-in components (portlets) that can deal with a single specific function.

Plug-In Portal Components and Toolboxes

This section presents an overview of the marketplace for tools and components for corporate developers engaged in custom development of portal solutions and for software vendors.

CoVia Technologies, Inc.

The CoVia Infoportal is a suite of prebuilt modules, primarily with CRM-type functionality, that can be used as a stand-alone portal with limited capabilities (for example, a departmental-type portal) or to extend a corporate portal with additional capabilities by integrating Infoportal's modules into the portal. The Infoportal suite includes the following modules[11]:

- **SalesOnline**—A CRM-oriented portal module that personalizes customer interaction management in order to accelerate the sales cycle, conduct commerce, and deliver products and propositions to customers on a personalized basis.

- **TeamOnline**—A collaborative portal module that creates virtual workplaces for managing creative processes and project organizations, including full document management and content management features as well as dialogue and discussions related to the job.

- **BizOnline**—A content management and personalization module to be used by small- and medium-sized companies to create Web sites with basic content publishing and searching features.

- **Intranet Included**—An intranet-networking module with a limited set of content management and information dissemination features.

Inxight Software, Inc.

Inxight offers an extensive set of numerous powerful plug-ins for application developers of corporate portals. This set includes[12]:

- **Inxight Tree Studio**—A plug-in component that allows developers to create very effective visual site maps called "Star Trees."

- **Hyperbolic Tree Server**—A software development kit (SDK) that enables corporate portal developers to integrate Inxight Tree Studio into their portal applications.

- **Table Lens**—A plug-in for importing, formatting, and publishing data to the portal.

- **Inxight Summary Server**—A plug-in for scanning large sets of documents and producing summarized content of hyperlinks.

- **Inxight Categorizer**—A plug-in tool that automates the process of assigning electronic documents to a taxonomy of categories.

- **Thing Finder Server**—A plug-in text analysis application that automatically identifies, tags, and indexes key content, allowing users to browse large amounts of unstructured text.

IBM's EIP Framework

This and the following section will present a new class of portal commercial technology, the so-called framework-oriented portal offerings. Instead of focusing on providing a complete "out-of-the-box" solution acceptable to many different companies, several leading software companies, including established vendors such as IBM and Oracle and newcomers such as Epicentric, Inc., have decided to focus on providing a framework-oriented solution, very much along the principles of the CPF. Such offerings are actually not specific products, but rather technology programs, containing in one package products and consulting services from the framework owner (for example, IBM or Oracle) complemented by products from the third-party vendors participating in the program.

The main strategy of framework-oriented offerings is capitalizing on key strengths of the framework owner, primarily its architectural know-how and the availability of successful technologies for integrating structured and unstructured data from multiple sources. These offerings also allow for the addition of front-end applications that provide personalization, collaboration, document management, and other important portal functions from multiple vendors. In a nutshell, the main goal of framework-oriented offerings is to establish a foundation upon which many vendors can build portal applications.

IBM's EIP Framework defines a comprehensive architectural blueprint for corporate portals. On the base of it, IBM offers an EIP product that provides federated searching of structured and unstructured data in IBM data sources (for example, DB2 and IMS), in non-IBM relational databases (for example, Oracle), and in Lotus Development Corp.'s systems (for example, Domino and Notes). On top of IBM's EIP, users can add front-end applications, including customization, personalization, and collaboration tools, as well as the user interface. At the time of writing, IBM has partnered with 33 vendors of such tools.[13] IBM's EIP enables rapid portal application development and deployment by providing a consolidated set of APIs to products of partnering vendors.

IBM has defined the portal framework within the scope of its strategy to help companies from all kinds of industries enter e-business and succeed in it, called the IBM Application Framework for e-Business. This strategy leverages the best technologies and support capabilities of IBM, but within an open architecture that accommodates custom solutions and third-party products with relative ease. Consequently, IBM's Portal Framework is geared toward providing the infrastructure and components to allow many kinds of portals to be created from a common EIP platform.

This sort of framework defines architectural implementation solutions for primary classic functions and for the capabilities of corporate portals:

- **Access and Federated Searching**—Providing a single point of access to relevant information dispersed among all kinds of structured and unstructured information sources, such as e-mail, fax, document imaging systems, OLAP applications, ERP systems, and so on.

- **Categorization**—Automatic construction of meta-data from various information sources, which enables users to identify relationships in the information.

- **Profiling**—Capturing and leveraging information about individuals and competencies, and providing profiles on the basis of that information to help the entire user community make effective use of the portal.

- **Personalization**—Customizing the portal to users' specific needs.

- **Collaboration**—Formation of teams and workspaces on the Web to leverage expertise, share insights, or implement policy and strategy changes, in real time or through shared databases.

- **Application Integration**—Enabling a single point of access to information and applications.

- **Security and Systems Management**—Ensuring security of information, and, at the same time, providing capabilities for simplifying the management aspects of authorized access (for example, single log on).

- **Unified Development Environment**—Common language and development tools set, common APIs, common change-move capabilities, and so on.

The framework's architecture is a multitiered architecture, in which each layer is responsible for enabling a correcting set of the above functions and capabilities. Technology specifications at each layer are:

- **Presentation Services**—An open architecture approach that allows many kinds of portal interfaces to be constructed using a variety of tools (for example, IBM's Websphere Studio and KnowledgeX, and third-party products from framework partners such as Brio and Plumtree).

- **Access and Integration Services**—A broad base of embedded IBM and third-party components (for example, directory/repository builders, search engines, Web crawlers, and so on) for supporting access/search, categorization/meta-data, personalization, and expertise/profiling; integration services are based on messaging (for example, IBM MQSeries).

- **Information Services**—A set of explicit connectors for accessing almost any kind of internal information sources and outside Web sources: structured data connectors for JDBC-accessible relational databases (for example, DB2, Oracle, Sybase, Informix, and MS SQL Server), unstructured data connectors for document management systems (for example, IBM's EDMSuite, Digital Library, Domino.Doc, and Documentum), Business Intelligence connectors (for example, for Business Objects), and an open API, with which specific additional connectors can be built).

- **Application Services**—Direct integration with ERP/CRM/SCM applications through IBM's CommonStore approach and partner-developed interfaces and with e-commerce applications through IBM's WebSphere and partner-developed interfaces.

- **Collaboration Services**—Direct integration with collaboration and groupware environments from Lotus Development Corp. (for example, Notes) and interfacing with other environments through partner-developed connectors.

- **Management Services**—Consolidated and unified support for all standard portal systems' management functions, particularly security, user administration and registration, logging, alerts, and performance/resource management.

- **Development Services**—A unified, comprehensive development environment that includes multiple levels of abstraction (visual and nonvisual components in an object-oriented development environment), a common set of portal functions, classes and APIs, pallets of parts for mass customization, dynamic binding constructs for Java, JavaBeans, C++, ActiveX, Dynamic Server Pages, LSX, and Domino ServerPages, and extensive XML support components.

To sum up, IBM's Portal Framework is an example of a vendor taking a reference architecture, such as the CPF, and building an integrated portal platform with APIs, tools, and services to allow customers and its framework partners to develop highly targeted portal solutions.

Oracle's Portal Framework

The Oracle Portal Framework is similar to the IBM effort, which is focused on stopping the growth of inconsistent, out-of-date Web sites and speeding up the creation of single-view corporate portals.[14]

At the heart of Oracle's framework is the concept of reusable corporate or external information components called "portlets." As in the CPF, portlets are reusable service-oriented components used to package commonly requested corporate information (such as budget updates, employee head counts, or directories) and external information (for example, stock quotes, weather, or news) together with the appropriate applications. Assembled portlets are stored in corporate libraries for users to "pick and choose" when building their custom portal sites.[15] From a technology perspective, a portlet is a set of "wrapped" objects created using standard Java API information sources or applications.

Portlets leverage the infrastructure provided by the framework, such as single log on using any LDAP-compliant directory, personalized views, mobile device support, business process management using built-in workflow processing, or collaborative services (for example, discussion/project group support, calendars, event scheduling, and so on). They run within an application server (in the case of the Oracle, the Oracle WebDB server) and deliver "live" content (HTML streams) to the client interface. Portlets are developed using a specialized software development kit (Oracle Portlet SDK).

Oracle's application server, WebDB, which is a part of Oracle's Internet Application Server (iAS) Services built around the Oracle 8i-database product, plays the central role in the framework. It provides critical technology services, such as enabling the integration of enterprise information and applications through portlets and incorporating interfaces with core portal services (for example, customization and personalization capabilities, workflow, search capabilities, security, single log on, and application development environment).[16]

Within the framework, application integration services are structured around the popular hub-adapter architecture (see Chapter 4 for additional information in regard to this subject), using XML to extract information from legacy and ERP applications such as SAP. Portlets render that information on the desired Web site. Information dissemination and analysis features are enabled through Oracle's business intelligence and data warehousing tools, such as Oracle Reports, Discoverer, and Oracle Express, which are tightly integrated into the framework.

As does IBM, Oracle gives a lot of attention to building support and third-party participation in the framework. The Oracle E-Business Portals Partner Initiative (OPPI) is dedicated to fostering a community of leading system integrators, content providers and aggregators, and third-party software vendors who will build, deliver, and support solutions engineered around Oracle's framework. At the time of this writing, more than 20 vendors have joined the partner program.

Based on the framework and its third-party contributions, Oracle expects to come up with a range of packaged portal solutions, especially for B2B and CRM applications, with an understanding that these packaged portals can be, and probably will be, customized using the concept of portlets to meet individual needs.

Implementing the Corporate Portal Framework

Chapters 6 and 7 were devoted to the subject of framework-oriented portal solutions and their potential benefits. They focused specifically on articulating the main objective of such technologies—to provide an enterprisewide backbone for the unification and integration of user access to multiple, disparate data sources and applications, such as business intelligence, database query and reporting, dynamic content generation, and all on-line interactions with an exponentially increasing number of business users.

This chapter presents a set of important recommendations outlining the best practices to be adopted in implementing the corporate portal framework (CPF) architecture and framework-oriented offerings. These recommendations have been formulated with a view toward enabling the creation of enterprisewide corporate portals, which have to address immediate business requirements and whose content, appearance, and functionality may be cost-effectively preserved over the longer term. Only a subset of these recommendations may be relevant to any single portal implementation or e-business initiative, depending on the portal's role and its intended objectives. The recommendations, therefore, can be viewed, to a certain degree, as generic. They should be used with the case studies and bibliography, resources, and references, which provide pointers to detailed guidance and application-specific practices.

Assessing Feasibility

All strategic initiatives, particularly those that are primarily driven by new technology, no matter what their underpinnings and area of imterest, have in common the need to assess the feasibility of implementing the new technology under consideration. Such a need is especially evident in projects that attempt to deliver an enterprise portal platform as a potentially single, integrated means of access to corporate information and services. Portal implementations frequently require substantial commitments of an enterprise's most valuable resources. Without an appropriate feasibility study or, more precisely, the planning of a "success model," key investments in human or financial capital are placed at increasing risk. In today's dynamics, this could be detrimental.

What is the planning of a "success model" in relation to enterprisewide portal implementations? In this context, it is the one specific initial step that a company completes as part of its strategic technology planning process for e-business. With more traditional technology initiatives (for example, enterprise resource planning implementations), most organizations go straight to full implementation planning, including return-on-investment (ROI) analyses. In the case of portals, it is highly beneficial to embark upon a feasibility study, treating it as a front-end exercise for full implementation planning. In undertaking this study, it is important to target the following specific objectives:

- Assessing and prioritizing business requirements

- Determining the feasibility of the fundamental concept

- Identifying and weighing the issues surrounding the implementation

- Identifying critical success factors

- Determining the likely costs of meeting business requirements based on the priority scheme

One of the best approaches for demonstrating the feasibility of the concept of portals is prototyping. Depending on the scope of the overall initiative and the company size, it is often beneficial to carry out prototyping in two stages:

- **Stage 1:** Providing a simple, cheaply implemented "demonstration" portal site with a single function or service for assessment by two or three focus groups, which will present an early view of how the corporatewide portal might look and operate. This pilot should be expected to be operational within two months.`

- **Stage 2:** Implementing a fuller pilot that can act as a more comprehensive evaluation` of standards, architecture (the technical architecture for the pilot should be a cut-down version of the final implementation), user activity and interaction levels, and user reaction/feedback. This pilot should also be suitable for noteworthy large-scale tests; it should carry several functions and be intended for use by a significantly larger user base; and it should be expected to be operational within six months.

The stage 2 pilot should test the core principles embedded within the full implementation, especially from the presentation (navigation and customization) and application integration perspectives. Consequently, one of the key criteria for determining the functions to be piloted is the complexity and diversity of interfacing to legacy systems. More importantly, the stage 2 pilot should help achieve a really crisp understanding of what success "looks like." Modeling the success of portal implementations means comparing the results of the stage 2 pilot against anticipated benefits and best-in-class implementations. Clearly, success in different kinds of portals (for example, an enterprise information portal versus a B2B/B2C portal versus a B2E portal) may demand different prototyping approaches and may have different result metrics. With B2B/B2C portals, for example, organizations may be inclined to prioritize transaction capabilities over collaborative or business intelligence features.

For each step of the feasibility assessment process, it is very important to document and summarize findings. These summaries could be just a few notes regarding what worked well and what did not. It is equally important to ensure communication and discussion about the findings in small management focus groups. The main goal here is to stimulate a great deal of discussion about the potential implications of enterprisewide portals for operational and decision-making processes, and to begin developing all the necessary strategies for the enterprisewide implementation. Such discussions will help build synergy among key stakeholders, create momentum and excitement about corporate portals, and, most importantly, force management to analyze the organization's opportunities and potential threats.

In terms of the people resources for the feasibility study, organizations should consider partnering with a consulting or systems integration vendor, preferably the framework owner or one directly affiliated with the framework program offering. When evaluating such vendors, attention should be given to their experience in working with other companies on similar endeavors as well as to their prototyping capabilities.

Identifying Critical Success Factors

Enterprisewide portal implementations based on framework-oriented approaches are giving rise to a new set of critical success factors that are important to the organization. Some of these success factors are extensions or, more precisely, reiterations of well-known factors that are characteristic to any enterprisewide application initiative. These so-called must haves include clear, well-understood business requirements, commitment and support from top management, strong championship of the process, a culture that supports collaboration and teamwork, an enterprise focus, and inclusion of key business area representatives on the feasibility study and implementation teams.

Scores of successful enterprisewide portal implementations at leading e-business transformation companies, such as Ford Motor Company, Intel, DaimlerChrysler, Wells Fargo, and many others, have advanced the case for establishing a number of factors. In combination with classical "must haves," these factors may substantially complicate the implementation of the concept of portals in large enterprises, if not addressed properly. What follows is a list of success factors that highlight important considerations for an enterprisewide portal initiative. The list is by no means all-inclusive. It covers primarily the most interesting and key issues:

- *The ability to create an integrated business and technology vision, providing the basis for integrating and leveraging the existing and new IT capabilities throughout the enterprise.* Having an integrated business and technology focus (as opposed to a pure technology or a pure business focus) is essential in order to provide the proper context for forging a keen understanding of how emerging technology can be applied to define new business capabilities (for example, enabling e-marketplaces).

- *The ability to realize the significance of architecture-driven approaches.* First and foremost, a successful corporate portal implementation means achieving an integrated set of multiple independent dimensions, such as information sources, business processes, and applications, that are predicated upon a unifying technology view or road map to guide the definition and implementation of related IT features throughout the enterprise. Only well-defined and articulated architecture definition can provide such a view. The enterprise's architecture establishes the principles and standards governing the technical aspects of portal implementations (for example, types of platforms for application servers, database servers, and desktop or mobile workstations; services, internal and external interfaces, and protocols for business and support applications; and application and network topology). The enterprise's architecture should be compared with the architectural concepts and constructs of the chosen framework-oriented offering (for example, the target architecture for the implementation). This comparison allows an enterprise to use the architecture relationships to determine the impact of the decision and the scope of the enterprise affected, especially the impact on the existing IT environment.

- *The ability to connect strategic business objectives regarding portals, and primarily to establish a single point of access to information and applications that relate to everyday operating activities.* In other words, it is essential to be able to translate the "grand" themes into everyday reality at the operating level of the organization (ask yourself, for example, how big the impact is of all these dispersed intranet sites on the stringent operational processes).

- *Planning for change.* Dynamics of the new economy and a rapid rate of change in technology are forceful reasons to consider both current and future needs when designing the portal's features and capabilities and determining its technical infrastructure and application structure. The approach to implementation planning for corporate portals must consider short-term as well as long-term business and adjunct technical requirements. With proper layering of the enterprise architecture and "componentization" of the enabling software, the most concrete portions of the portal's environment may change (for example, specific vendor products), while more abstract layers of the technical infrastructure remain more stable (for example, the types of services, the types of interfaces between applications and databases, the "look and feel," and so on).

- *The ability to achieve the right balance between centralization and decentralization in enterprisewide portal initiatives.* Implementations of corporate portals, by their very nature, generate activities that are cross-functional and span multiple business processes and organizational units. A key success factor is to achieve the right balance between centralization and decentralization in corporate portal implementations. Centralization, an ultimate goal for portals, allows the realization of a single access point to the universe, but may be difficult and cost- or time-prohibitive from the implementation perspective—it may be easier to create a couple of smaller-coverage portals to start with.

- *The ability to achieve the right balance between ease of use and security and confidentiality of information.* Corporate portals must universally meet the following requirements: they must have easy-to-use user interfaces; solid reliability; access to information sources, applications, and collaboration facilities; and adequate security and confidentiality of information. The security and confidentiality expectations of the target user base (for example, employees, customers, partners, investors, prospects, and so on) must be carefully taken into account during the requirement analysis/evaluation and design steps.

- *Putting community first.* No matter how "grandiose" the vision and implementation plans are, the success of a corporate portal starts with communities, groups of users who share common interests and objectives. Recognizing this fact, and tailoring approaches and plans accordingly, encourages collaboration and better information sharing; this, in turn, delivers success.

Within large global enterprises, many internal and (more importantly) external stakeholders involved at some stages of a corporate portal's life cycle may confront or need to implement strategies that deal with the above success factors. These provide particular challenges when human and financial resources, which are often managed locally (in a decentralized fashion), need to be integrated from an enterprisewide and inter-enterprisewide point of view. In such cases, successful implementation management typically entails a binding agreement between all stakeholders about minimum levels of resource commitment, management support, and delivery principles and practices.

Business Priorities Dilemma

It will probably not be a big surprise for many readers at this point to encounter the next statement, because its message will be very familiar.

Enterprisewide integration, which is the centerpiece of the concept of portals, has always posed a major challenge to IT organizations' staff, those who translate business requirements into systems specifications that govern the development, construction, installation, and operation of enterprise applications and their interfaces to all kinds of legacy systems. It is getting more and more challenging to deal with business requirements for enterprise integration projects.

The main reason for this is that newly implemented applications and legacy applications operate in a nonstable environment of rapidly changing business requirements to accommodate competitive pressures, the dynamics of e-business, customer demands, the unbundling of functional requirements, and dramatic changes in technology.

In portal-related projects, the above difficulties, coupled with the fact that these activities are highly cross-functional (this, in turn, adds an additional layer of complexity if full consensus is lacking across the company), can result in inadequate time to decide upon and prioritize business requirements. The question of when to perform the detailed requirements analysis step, too, is often a subject of controversy: Should it be completed before, during, or after the feasibility study, assuming the study produces favorable results?

The jury is still out on the best practices in defining business requirements for large-scale, enterprisewide portal initiatives. Many approaches are used, from traditional one-on-one interviews to full-blown business process reengineering and joint application development. What is becoming evident, however, is that more and more companies work on capturing the requirements in an iterative fashion. First, prior to engaging in the feasibility study, they are developing the macrolevel guidelines (the high-level, "rule-of-thumb"-type requirements) required in making key business decisions during the feasibility stage. Second, they are defining the detailed business requirements after this stage is complete, and before the full implementation is undertaken.

In addition, it is important not to come up with requirements that are overspecified, too detailed, and too prescriptive. This discourages creativity, which is instrumental to the success of portals.

But what about roles and responsibilities? Who is responsible for the requirements? A traditional assumption is that business users (key stakeholders) are responsible for defining clear business objectives, and IT organizations are responsible for coming up with a technical solution that meets all the business requirements. Such an assumption may not be the best approach in the case of portals. Portals are community efforts. Business requirements are results of collaborative work involving all key stakeholders and technology people in the requirements definition process. IT organizations are taking the lead in coming up with macrolevel guidelines; focus groups involved in the feasibility study are leading the detailed requirements analysis process.

There is one more important issue that needs to be addressed within the context of this discussion. For companies that are taking a decentralized approach to corporate portals, the question of how to identify the best target of opportunity for the initial implementation (basically, Where do you begin?) is often difficult to answer because of conflicting priorities (for example, urgent electronic commerce needs, information overload, collaboration and community needs, and so on). Brainstorming and best-practices analyses are useful methods for answering this question, but the best solution will come from combining these methods with an approach that is based on the inspiration and motivation of the most vocal members of the focus groups.

A look at the growing number of all kinds of Web sites residing on large companies' intranets, and the use patterns of these sites, suggests an attractive business case for leveraging portal capabilities within that area as a starting point to help conceptualize and structure a compelling "supplier-purchaser" relationship between information users and content providers within such companies.

Starting from the Intranet

Most corporate intranets are a result of evolution rather than planning and design. These shared resources evolved from earlier attempts to connect LANs, WANs, and mainframes in response to the demand for greater access to information. Dealing with the information sources on the intranet itself, however, can be a major challenge.

Companies today maintain many of their key business assets in electronic form on their intranets. These assets consist of collections of memos, reports, drawings, manuals, specifications, and so on, stored in all kinds of formats, including page description languages, markup languages, word processor files, spreadsheets and CAD/CAM files, and so on. Corporate intranets also reference a wide variety of on-line services and tools available from the Internet, such as news and weather. As a result, when reviewing many large companies' intranets, it is not uncommon to encounter hundreds of thousands and even sometimes more than a million URLs, with hundreds of new Web sites introduced every month.

The following is a short list of reasons why today's intranet is a challenge to those who must deliver the necessary levels of access to corporate information in a timely manner:

- Information is scattered throughout the intranet in a multitude of sources and in all kinds of formats.

- Information published on-line is often structured in a disorganized way.

- Finding relevant, accurate information is difficult (if not impossible), and often requires searching multiple systems.

- Information is accessed through different methods, such as Web browsers, e-mail clients, and groupware applications (for example, Lotus Notes).

- There are no established standards for navigation and overall visual design for the intranet, much less industrywide guidelines for procedures or policies for the development and publication of documents on the intranet's sites.

- Very seldom are interfaces provided to connect the intranet with on-line databases of critical corporate operational information, such as enterprise resource planning (ERP) and customer relationship management (CRM) applications.

- Extensive, manual, labor-oriented content publishing processes exist at a time when even large companies typically run their intranets with a minuscule staff.

These combined issues have a significant usability impact in regard to the intranet that translates directly to a company's bottom line, since any usability problems mean an immediate loss of employee productivity. As highlighted in the Alertbox report authored by Jakob Nielsen, "Intranet Portals: The Corporate Information Infrastructure,"[1] for example, for a company with 10,000 employees, the cost of a single poorly written headline on an intranet home page is almost $5,000.

It makes a lot of sense to improve and streamline the basic architecture and operational aspects of existing intranet environments as a starting point for the implementation of corporate portals, considering that the following critical factors are at stake:

- Employee productivity

- Increased likelihood of making decisions based on incomplete and inaccurate data

- Potential for a failure to effectively respond to important messages and information

A corporate portal creates a uniform design style for the intranet itself, complete with a navigational scheme that allows a customized home page layout, an easily recognizable color code, special graphics, and icons tailored to each particular audience group. It allows compartmentalization of the information for easier retrievability.

To sum up, intranets' problems are the results of success of electronic media and Internet-based information dissemination practices. Nevertheless, while intranets offer challenges, their payback is great. Bringing corporate portals to intranets within their existing functional landscape now seems sure to elevate e-business activities on every corner of the enterprise.

How to Encourage Users to Use the Portal

Encouraging members of focus groups to use the portal extensively during the feasibility study, and the general user population during the full implementation, is key to putting this technology in the hands of every employee and every customer and partner, and key to integrating it into the enterprise environment. So that users are better prepared to conduct business with portals, IT organizations need to be better prepared to teach the technology and its principles, and, more importantly, to encourage its usage. As user educators, IT organizations must be concerned with enabling users to use portal technology on the job and off the job and to clearly understand portals' role in the future.

The following are three suggested approaches for encouraging portal technology learning and subsequent extensive use by business users; they have been successfully used by several leading e-business organizations:

- Finding the self in the technology (this is equally important for both IT staff and user education).

- "If you build it with them, they will come"—directly involving users in the development of early prototypes (the previously referred-to stage 1 prototypes).

- Helping users build a vision of themselves as a technology-driving constituency (creating the "technology obsession" bridge between IT organizations and business units).

Finding the self in the technology means, first and foremost, perceiving technology as essential to everyone's life at the present time. The training modeled toward this specific issue must address ways to assist business users with their current challenges as Internet users (for example, when they are looking for a loan, or when they are trying to find information about UFOs). IT staff members engaged in the training of business users must be aware of their needs in everyday events (for example, how much their children are using the Internet for school work) and encourage them to use newly acquired portal technology skills to help their children finish class assignments. Encouraging business users to use the technology as a means of self-expression could be very effective. One example of this is to encourage users to use the portal's screenshots in their PowerPoint presentations early on.

Involving business users as developers in early prototype and development phases of a corporate portal tool designed to meet their specific needs will definitely change their perceptions and attitudes toward this technology. Their direct involvement in the portal's development enables users to envision the capabilities of the technology. The portal becomes more meaningful as the users experience a real sense of ownership. The users' input into the prototyping and development processes also assures a more accurate representation and alignment with their needs. These points illustrate the overall significance of having users' feedback recognized as a critical component of the portal implementation process.

In addition, it is important to help members of the user focus groups develop a vision of themselves as "technology teachers." By helping them "practice" developing effective ways to implement portals in their future business activities, this category of users will begin to build an approach for using portals effectively with their coworkers and as a tool in their cross-functional work processes. Making the concept of "teaching the teachers" as effective as possible to ensure that early adopters of this technology can situate themselves in the role of a "portal evangelist" is a necessary element for creating a successful, exciting, and active corporate portal environment.

Moreover, the above approach needs to be taken even further, transforming these groups of "technology teachers" into a technology-driving constituency. By openly pinpointing along the way the existing shortcomings of the technology and highlighting what new releases will be bringing in the near future, users will begin to construct the "bridge" for ongoing communications with the IT organization in terms of requirements for enhancement, new tools, and so on. As they place themselves in the role of an IT specialist, they will be trying to specify the best ways to use this technology within its current limitations. Other activities may include having users plan "technology-enhancing" projects as if they were members of a development team. Decisions about functions, portal services, budgets, and even architectural components should be discussed within these user focus groups. This type of "IT role playing" not only gives users the opportunity to understand how to play the role of business analyst effectively, but it also demonstrates the importance of collaborating and negotiating with colleagues from the IT organizations.

Supporting Corporate-Employee Communications with Portals

Previously, an appealing case was made for leveraging portal capabilities within the intranet space as a starting point in the evolution of an enterprisewide, all-encompassing portal environment. One of the most important functions of the concept of portals, particularly B2E-type portals, within that space is to establish a trusted, on-going communications channel with companies' employees. B2E portals increase productivity by providing employees with the information they need and keeping them well informed.

Although this subject was previously addressed in Chapters 3 and 5, it is so important for the overall success of portals in the corporate environment that further discussion can be extremely helpful.

Let's start with support of corporate-employee communications (for example, employee communications, manager communications, administration and benefits selection, training, and so on) enabled by a B2E portal. The primary focus of this type of organizational information sharing is providing personalized human resource (HR) information or knowledge through technology (for example, personalizing health care plan data, or helping individual employees, managers, and retirees find answers, make informed decisions, or take specific actions related to their own medical benefits). In other words, it means providing support for any activity that requires immediate, personalized attention. This varies from the classic definition of "communications" in the context of Internet-based information dissemination. Corporate-employee communications via B2E portals are dynamic and highly situational. The context to support such communications is not best stored per se in static text files or documents on a Web site. Rather, such context has to be built "on the fly" from many corporate documents and presented to users in a variety of forms (for example, a simple paragraph of text or a comparison chart). Such use of corporate information vastly extends the services a company can offer employees, capitalizing on the expertise HR applies in day-to-day activities and on the capabilities for delivering that expertise through portal-enabled self-service.

One area in which B2E portals can make a real impact on the company's bottom line is their ability to connect the learning capabilities of the HR organization to the change agenda. Such a "connection" will allow the elimination of administrative overhead and transform the HR organization (department) into a strategic partner for the employee-manager relationship in order for employees to better control key parts of their life at work.

How can this "connection" be achieved? It requires the active involvement of the human resources staff in the process of translating key challenges for business-driven employee learning, and it requires the specific business skills needed to address those challenges.

The main benefits of portals for business learning are as follows:

- Delivering all the necessary learning resources and support directly to the point of use in the workplace.

- Customizing learner support via libraries (searchable databases), forums (meeting places), and the user interface to on-line courseware applications.

- Providing all the administrative functions needed for user registration and authorization and the dissemination of needed training material within the company to sustain momentum in learning at work.

- Enabling "just-in-time" training, an effective mechanism for applying new knowledge to new tasks.

- Allowing the development of focused, large-scale, customized, on-line action-learning, hands-on, application-driven workshops based on the actual business challenges facing an organization—and giving portal users an opportunity to actively discuss, diagnose, and recommend solutions to real-life business challenges.

Nevertheless, in terms of enabling on-line learning, portals are not necessarily effective in every case, or in any company. In order for portals to be effective in this area, companies must have a number of characteristic features, the significance of which cannot be understated[2]:

- Emphasis on team structures for learning

- Well-developed communication and collaboration skills across functional areas

- Emphasis on shared learning and networking

- Emphasis on employees' interest in maximizing personal capability and creativity and in their willingness to sponsor career self-management

As we can see, the success of B2E portals is very much dependent on the broad cultural change needed to implement on-line communications throughout an organization.

And now a word on the key elements of technology infrastructure needed to support and deliver a comprehensive B2E-based solution. First, the core portal technologies are needed—searching, categorization, personalization, and content publishing tools. Second, applications and other sources of information have to be included—back-end system sources (for example, human resource management and ERP systems), on-line courseware applications, and, perhaps, an HR-specific data warehouse. In addition to these core technologies, the scope of the technology infrastructure includes the integration technologies or mechanisms—primarily middleware and application server technology, plus, in many cases, groupware applications and call center/voice response systems. Together all of these technologies and support tools for the development comprise an infrastructure for implementing a robust communications environment that can serve employees, managers, and other categories of intranet users effectively.

The Corporate Portal: Customer Service Center on the Web

Chapters 3 and 5 introduced another role of corporate portals, one that is getting more attention nowadays, and, as a result, deserves further exploration in terms of the best practices of portal implementations. This role is the so-called customer service portal, a kind of B2C portal fully dedicated to providing basic and extended customer services, including the following:

- On-line catalogs, containing product information and order-facilitating services.

- Direct product order capabilities.

- Technical update/support services for customers (especially large corporate customers).

- Personalized customer service related to a specific business relationship (similar, for example, to call-center services, such as for banking, order delivery inquiries, and so on).

- Personalized communications with customers (for example, opinion polling and customer satisfaction tracking via regular e-mails and on-line "assistants").

- Problem tracking and resolution, and customer assistance in relation to reported problems, both before and after a sale.

- Configuration services that enable customers to perform sophisticated tasks that would otherwise require an experienced sales associate or even a sales engineer, particularly configuring complex products (for example, computer systems) whose components are constrained by complex rules and bill-of-materials relationships.

Customer service and customer assistance on the Internet have become the most important factors in building customer satisfaction and customer loyalty for many industries, including retail, financial services, and brokerage. Even though it is done on the Internet, great service creates brand recognition and customer loyalty at such levels that such service is spreading out, covering "brick-and-mortar" outlets of the same brand.

In terms of services, customer service portals are focusing heavily on enabling personalization, collaborative filtering, and flexible access to customer service applications. This type of corporate portal extends the intranet into the "extranet" concept, where Web technology is used to build a rich interface between companies, their customers, and partners.

There are three approaches to delivering customer assistance on the Internet that could be significantly enhanced by using portals:

- **Self-Help Assistance**—The customer searches the portal and obtains relevant information; if the information matches the customer's request, this form of assistance could be sufficient.

- **Queued Assistance**—After the customer fills out a form to answer a series of questions, the form is put into a queue for follow-up processing, generally by a customer service representative, and a response is sent to the customer via e-mail.

- **Interactive Assistance**—Personal assistance to customers around the clock, at any time; the customer interacts on line with a problem resolution application that compares the customer's request against a database of resolved problems, product information, operational instructions, and so on, picking up the one or two reports which are likely to solve the customer's problem.

Whatever approach one employs, the key to providing a consistent customer experience is the ability to integrate back-end corporate systems with the portal. This integration ensures availability and consistency of customer information at the time of the customer contact. The next important point is the ability to apply user-designated business rules to all customer interactions in a consistent manner.

Providing a comprehensive set of customer service capabilities requires concentrating on many aspects that are characteristic of corporate portals. The majority of these aspects have been already depicted in this book. It is necessary to highlight the following characteristics in the context of this discussion, however, because of their importance:

- Customer-centric design, including flexible search and site navigation, targeted customization, and personalization based on user profiling and preferencing.

- Continuous and consistent information request tracking, and automated publishing of content according to tracked requests.

- Rules-based management, which is the ability to implement consistent business rules that enable companies to provide individualized services to customers.

- Multimode, level-based support services, which allow problem resolution applications to work in levels (general problems get addressed by "level one" service, and, if the customer's request did not receive satisfactory assistance, it is raised to the next level of service).

- Decision-support systems and data-mining applications, which assimilate and analyze user queries, understand customer request patterns, prepare sample replies, and so on.

The implementation of customer service portals, despite many complex issues and "hefty" requirements such as the above functions, is actually a very achievable goal. Recently, on-line customer service portal site FeedbackDirect Inc.[3] released the "Feedback 50," a directory of the 50 companies with the highest ratings in Internet-based customer service, as compiled from a study of several hundred firms conducted by FeedbackDirect analysts. Among the most highly rated were AT&T Residential Services, Charles Schwab, Lands' End, and L.L. Bean.

How Leading Companies Use Portal Technologies to Improve Customer Service: Cases in Point

While the corporate portal phenomenon is still relatively new, many leading e-business companies in a variety of industries have already demonstrated that automated, portal-based customer service environments can produce significant results. Two representative examples of such companies and brief descriptions of their achievements in customer support areas are described next.

Staples, Inc.

Staples, Inc., a $9 billion retailer of office supplies, furniture, and technology to consumers and businesses, is probably the best example of a company that has achieved substantial results with Internet-based customer service. The company has over 46,000 employees serving customers in the United States, Canada, the United Kingdom, Germany, the Netherlands, and Portugal through more than 1,100 office superstores, mail order catalogs, e-commerce, and a contract business.[4]

For Staples, customer service is number one. In this regard, the company's mission statement, posted at its Web site, says it all—"Great service every day in every way!" In order to realize every aspect of this mission, the company has built a multifaceted EIP-type portal (Staples calls it "Staples@work") to be used as the interface to key business processes and applications, especially for customer service functions.

The portal is used by executive management, contracts, procurement, sales and marketing, human resources, and managers of all U.S. retail stores, as well as for internal business by Staples' three business-to-business e-commerce sites: Staples.com, which serves the home-office and small-business customer, Quillcorp.com, which targets small- to medium-sized businesses, and StaplesLink.com, serving midsize to large businesses. It offers e-mail, scheduling, headlines and news, product information, and many other features.[5]

Using Plumtree's portal product and other technologies, Staples has developed a Web-based application that is an "easy to use and manage" platform application for customer service delivery. Staples' portal consolidates all customer information and customer contact points (phone, fax, e-mail, and Web) to provide a well-managed customer experience, where upsell, cross-sell, and relationship-building activities can be maximized. In particular, it allows customers to communicate with the company interactively via on-line chat. It also makes it easier for customers to navigate Staples' numerous product offerings. It offers extensive customer service/ help content, including how to place an order, what forms of payment the company accepts, what to do if a product the customer orders is not in stock, how to check the status of an order, the replacement policy, how to contact a sales representative, and much more. Store managers use the portal to access customer order information and associated specification sheets.

But the company goes beyond that, focusing on making the portal a much more proactive approach for delivering customer service and increasing customer satisfaction through self-service and personalized Web pages, customized to provide all the information, history, and knowledge that customers need for purchase decisions, account management, or customer service and support.

Dell Computer Corporation

Dell Computer Corporation is one of the leading direct computer systems companies in the world, with a yearly revenue of around $30 billion. Dell is No. 2 worldwide in market share and consistently the leader in liquidity, profitability, and growth among all major computer systems companies, with approximately 37,000 employees around the globe.[6]

The company's dedication to customer service is legendary. Its entire business model is based on the customer-oriented concept that in selling personal computer systems directly to customers, Dell can best understand their needs, and can efficiently provide the most effective computing solutions to meet those needs.[7] Consequently, through this model, Dell offers personal relationships with corporate and institutional customers, including phone and Internet purchasing, customized access to services, on-line and phone technical support, and self-serve problem resolution.

Dell is one of the leading e-business companies in exploiting the competitive advantages of the Internet by increasingly applying e-business technologies to its entire business. About 50 percent of Dell's sales are Web-enabled, and about 50 percent of Dell's technical support activities and about 76 percent of Dell's order-status transactions occur on-line.[8]

Dell is one of the first PC companies to embrace customer service portals and has incorporated this technology into its e-business environment, specifically for support services for Dell products. Dell is working closely with many leading customer service software vendors, such as Motive Communications, Inc.,[9] to provide interactive, automated customer support services using portals. Technical support portals will provide real-time data exchange and enable remote systems to diagnose the trouble with a consumer PC and automatically download a fix for the problem (or at least for simple, routine problems). More complex problems will roll into the technical support centers, which will be positioned to address such problems in a speedy fashion, since they will have been relieved of all kinds of routine calls. In addition, support portals offer attractive cross-selling opportunities, because with customers coming to a centralized spot to access support offerings, a company can promote highly targeted services or products.

But Dell is looking even further to turn corporate technical support portals into enablers of e-support marketplaces. Recently, the company provided financial backing for All.com, a start-up provider of Internet-based infrastructure to connect people who need technical support with those who have the expertise to resolve problems.[10] All.com uses a model in which support agents interact with customers over the Internet using diagnostic software from Motive Communications. With All.com, Dell is planning to extend the support it offers its customers to cover non-Dell products.

Managing the Portal as an Organization

Corporate portals are presently being investigated and described intensively across multiple disciplines. Technology-related topics capture most of the attention, while organizational issues are little described and little talked about. However, in order to achieve truly revolutionary results using the concepts of portals, we have to realize that rather than looking at the portal as a specific technology, it is necessary to place the portal in the context of organizational forms spurred by the Internet.

As companies progress with the CPF toward their ultimate goals, they will need to deal with the fact that organizational changes (especially in their IT organizations) are necessary, and they should be studied along with technology aspects. Which work organizations, structures, cultures, and political surroundings suit portals? Which interorganizational arrangements? What operating costs do portals bear? These are all important questions. Every large-scale implementation of corporate portals (presently being conducted or planned) has to be dealt with in such a way that it is allowed to begin answering some of these questions.

The changes in organizational aspects surrounding the corporate portal parallel trends in the wider portal world. General public portals, such as Yahoo!, Alta Vista, and so on, are independent companies, and in fact they are quite successful ones. They have demonstrated that the concept of portals is affecting the organization of work, organizational structures, technology, professional skills, the distribution of power, and cultural values.

In the context of the above issues, the main factor in relation to the organizational impact of portals is that, in essence, the user is provided the effect of a library, which is a synergy created by bringing together technologically the resources of many, many libraries and information services. Consequently, portal companies contend that the success of the concept is rooted in the notion of the "networked library," a notion that implies such values as:

- The core assets should be a collection of predominantly content material and access tools to that material.

- The portal organization should be structurally autonomous.

- The portal's social role is to organize and distribute knowledge.

- The portal has to provide this knowledge to users at no cost, and content providers have to pay for content dissemination privileges.

Common to all these "values" is the assumption that collaboration between portals and content providers is what makes it possible to expand access to, and delivery of, relevant information and analysis tools beyond the traditional limitations of efficiency and effectiveness of the intranet. And there is yet another way of looking at portals in even the broader context of the information industry. For example, corporate portals may reach out into the domain of publishing, so that almost every company becomes an information center serving various clients and selling information. The implications of such ideas for corporate portals represent an important question.

To study organizational issues related to portals, several "macro" models could be proposed that are based on the models that have been put forward by researches of the concept of "virtual digital libraries."[11] In turn, each of the macro models could be instantiated in a number of special models. The possible macro models are as follows:

- **Subsystem Model**—The portal is considered to be a new subsystem in existing IT organizations, built around appropriate technologies that are embedded in appropriate organizational arrangements (this model represents the prevalent thinking today, which is focused on technology).

- **System Model**—The portal can be envisioned as a new organizational design within the traditional company structure, centered around notions of more effective access to, and delivery of, holdings, closer support of users' work, and so on.

- **Independent Organizational Model**—The portal can be envisioned as a new, independent business unit with its own profit-and-loss responsibilities in order to economically leverage the value of the concept.

These macro and corresponding special models can serve as organizational development devices to support the evolution of the concept into the future.

Challenges for the Future

This chapter concludes our discussion of portals. From the title of this chapter, it is apparent that the discussion is looking forward. This inevitably entails predictions that, in turn, mean risk, and in such situations, it is very wise to remember how dangerous forecasting can be.

On the other hand, it is also important to realize that the move toward e-business has resulted in a strong shift from the situation only one to two years ago, when the implementations of "bleeding edge" technologies were normally seen as problems and risk factors by companies, to a situation in which they are also seen as opportunities—sources of efficiency improvement and competitive advantage. The progressive companies have understood this and they are grabbing the opportunities.

This perspective justifies a more enthusiastic look at several technology trends that are going to be instrumental to the future of portal technologies, specifically intelligent agent technology, the integration of XML with portals, and peer-to-peer computing. These new, highly promising technologies will be constantly forming and reforming the concept of portals, with far-reaching implications. The challenge for all of us is to see beyond the hype and to position ourselves for the full implementation of these new technical and associated organizational ideas.

Intelligent Portals: Delegating Front-End Web Functionality to Intelligent Agent Technology

Intelligent agent technology has evolved as a part of artificial intelligence— a field of computer science that for more than 30 years has dealt with the subject of enabling computers to perform brain-driven human functions (for example, to visualize, compare, make decisions, react, learn, collaborate, and so on). Intelligent agents are executable software entities that can implement these functions in an autonomous, proactive, social, and adaptive fashion. In practical terms, an agent is a self-aware program that can start a thread of execution, stop itself, move to another computer through the network (if necessary), and continue where it left off. It carries its own state along with it to maintain persistence and reacts to external stimulation according to its logic.[1]

The term *intelligence* and the related term *intelligent agent* are difficult to define. Researchers in the field of artificial intelligence to this day have radically differing views on the definitions, and whole papers have been written just to argue their views. At a minimum, an intelligent agent has to be able to accept the user's statement of goals and underlying preferences (rules) and carry out the task delegated to it, applying an inference engine or some other reasoning mechanism to act on these preferences.

The underlying technique of the agent—for example, a C/C++ program, a Visual Basic script, or a Java program—is irrelevant as long as the agent is capable of displaying intelligent behavior, meaning that the software entity is capable of a certain degree of reasoning as well as of learning and adapting to the environment.

With regard to the Internet, theory and development on the use of intelligent agents have focused on two areas: making agents "smarter" (that is, enabling them to replicate the experience of a human agent, for example, a travel or real estate agent) and creating a robust executable environment in which intelligent agents can operate. As was already stated (see Chapter 5 for a related discussion), with the explosive growth of information available through the Internet, users have been attempting to carry out tasks that traditionally have been given to hired human agents to execute, especially in terms of information searching and interpreting the results. Such self-service lacks efficiency and effectiveness. Without the use of software agents, the tasks of information searching and result interpretation become as overwhelming as they are in the conventional, physical world. Subsequently, the goal is to create a virtual world in which agents act as human representatives, making humans' professional and personal lives simpler.

In the corporate portal field, there is a solid consensus about how to differentiate between "unintelligent" and "intelligent" portals. "Unintelligent" portals emphasize broadly based and generalized mass dissemination of infor-mation. On the contrary, "intelligent" portals emphasize collaboration and highly targeted and personalized distribution of content, bundled with multiple types of specialized, expertise-oriented services that have been provided by top human agents over the years. Although the current intelligent agent applications are rather experimental and ad hoc, primarily targeting information searching and collaborative filtering aspects, it is only a matter of time before intelligent agents will play a decisive role in all aspects of corporate portals, specifically:

- **Searching**—Information filtering and analysis.

- **Learning**—Information needs identification and assessment, on-line training, and personal assistance (for example, Microsoft's Agent tech-nology, a set of programmable software services that support the presen-tation of interactive, animated characters within the Microsoft Windows interface).

- **Comparing**—Experience-based information brokering.

- **Negotiating**—Purchase and delivery of content and services.

- **Collaborating**—Workflow management, collaborative (on-demand) application integration, and risk management.

One type of portal-oriented application that immediately springs to mind is the use of intelligent agents in role-oriented portals, such as CRM portals, particularly for functions geared toward obtaining a competitive advantage. In the new economy, companies gain competitive advantage by exploring and exploiting the decentralized points of control under condi-tions of abundant resources and scarce human attention. Here, the most powerful technologies are those that extend, augment, and develop rela-tionships. As the relationships between enterprises and their customers become more complex, the enterprises need more information and advice on what these relationships mean and how to exploit them. Intelligent agent technology offers some very interesting options for addressing such needs. Consider just one example: Customers set certain priorities in their demands for products and services; these priorities lead to purchase-deci-sion rankings based on price, service, delivery time, and quality. Intelligent agents can master individual customers' or customer groups' demand pri-orities by learning from experience with them, and can quantitatively and qualitatively analyze those priorities, providing, for example, a very precise list of recommended models based on individual preferences and priorities when searching for a car.

There is a vast range of services required by customers that intelligent agents can address. Some of these services may include the following:

- Customized customer assistance with on-line services: news filtering, messaging, scheduling, and making arrangements for gatherings, ordering, and so on.

- Customer profiling, including inferring information about customer behavior based on business experiences with the particular customer.

- Integrating profiles of customers into a group of marketing activities.

- Predicting customer requirements.

- Negotiating prices and payment schedules.

- Executing financial transactions on the customer's behalf.

Another type of portal-oriented application that can benefit significantly from intelligent agents is the area of information dissemination in a corporate computing environment, particularly gathering information, packaging it, and presenting it to management for their day-to-day decision-making process. There are several advantages to the use of agents for these purposes. First, they can traverse the Internet and internal corporate data sources (for example, relational and legacy databases) without having a permanent network connection. Second, they have built-in intelligence to perform the time-consuming repetitive tasks of finding and filtering the information. Third, they can package that information into an acceptable form before returning it to the user. This type of application is already one of the most common uses of agents in commercial portal products, deriving from the use of "spiders" or "bots" to crawl the Web and search for information in general public portals.

These examples represent a spectrum of applications from the somewhat modest, low-level news filtering applications to the more advanced and complicated customer relationship management applications that focus on predicting customer requirements. The main point is that an intelligent agent within the context of corporate portals is an intermediary between the enterprise and its customer, and a source of effective, utilitarian information encountered at different virtual destinations.

Outside of the applications arena, there is one area within the scope of functionality of corporate portals in which intelligent agents are urgently needed: enabling dynamic (on-demand) application integration. Using agents for application integration extends the capabilities provided by distributed object technology and enables the direct manipulation of interfaces (for example, the disconnection or redirection of an interface; see Chapter 4 for related information regarding the topic of dynamic integration).

In terms of the state of the technology, the main obstacle to mass adaptation of intelligent agents is the lack of agreed-upon standards, especially for agent communication language. A first step in this direction has been made with the development of Knowledge Query Manipulation Language (KQML), a language and protocol for exchanging information and knowledge. KQML is most useful for communication among autonomous and asynchronous programs, such as agents, especially in cases in which agents have different and even conflicting agendas. Thus, the meaning of a KQML message is defined in terms of constraints on the message sender rather than the message receiver. This allows the message receiver to choose a course of action that is compatible with other aspects of its function. A lot of work has to be done in this area, as most of the current agent systems do not comply with KQML. Organizations such as the Internet Engineering Task Force (IETF) and its working groups are addressing the agent communication language issue.

Among leading software vendors, IBM is playing a significant role in the adaptation of intelligent agent technology for several high-profile applications, including corporate portals. IBM has introduced the Aglet Software Development Kit (ASDK), also known as the Aglets Workbench. This workbench introduces the notion of an *aglet*, a mobile (agile) agent written in Java. ASDK is a visual environment for building network-based applications that use intelligent agents to search for, access, and manage corporate data and other information. These agents can be constructed using the following default properties and functions provided by ASDK:

- Globally unique naming scheme for agents.

- Traversing patterns for specifying complex network "traveling" patterns with multiple destinations and automatic failure handling.

- "White board" mechanisms that allow multiple agents to collaborate and share information asynchronously.

- Agent message-passing schemes that support loosely coupled asynchronous as well as synchronous peer-to-peer communication between agents.

- Network agent class loaders that allow an agent's Java byte code and state information to travel across the network.

- An execution context that provides agents with a uniform environment independent of the actual computer system on which they are executing.

- Standard application-level protocol and Agent Transfer Protocol (ATP) for transferring agents over the network in a general and uniform way.

To sum up, it should be noted that the current state of research in the area of intelligent agents is furiously fast and quickly evolving, especially within the context of large-scale portal platforms. Although no commercial system is currently fully implementing intelligent agent technology, many products implement partial functionalities of agent technologies already. Perhaps, in the next couple of years, agent technology will be fully exploited in portal products, and we will see an explosion in its use.

XML Story—Working the Language End

Although Extensible Markup Language (XML) has been viewed primarily as the emerging language standard for information exchange between applications and trading partners, the XML story that users can apply most directly comes from the concept of portals. Portals offer the opportunity for the entire enterprise architecture to be based on XML. With such an architecture, companies will be able to significantly lower operating expenses and streamline technology infrastructure.

The first place a company can benefit from a portal solution based on XML is in application integration. XML can be used for two key integration tasks:

- To connect all kinds of systems to the portal, for example, enterprise resource planning (ERP), internal legacy systems, external systems, content syndication systems, and so on.

- To forge integration links between applications that were impossible to integrate in the past, for example, in manufacturing, an ERP system that runs on one platform, a manufacturing-plant operations application on a second, and a supply-chain application on a third platform.

Of course, the use of a common language such as XML doesn't guarantee interoperability. A standard document exchange model is needed. At the time of this writing, several consortiums, standards bodies, organizations, and steering committees are focusing on providing information to companies that are using XML for application integration purposes. One such group is headed by Microsoft, with its BizTalk Framework.[2]

The BizTalk Framework provides, among many important features, a platform for modifying an existing set of industry interchange standards to use XML. The BizTalk steering committee is working with application software vendors (for example, SAP, PeopleSoft, Siebel, and J.D. Edwards), industry standards groups (for example, the Data Interchange Standards Association and the Open Applications Group), developers, and customers to create a framework for defining XML schemas that serve as the basis for information interchange between applications. The association of the Biztalk framework with the Open Applications Group (OAG) is especially promising from the standpoint of corporate portal implementations because companies can start implementing OAG's specifications, which currently include financial, human resources, manufacturing, and logistics interoperability aspects.

However, the use of XML for integration does not stop with integrating business applications and related data sources. It will become vitally important to integrate people into the corporate portal environment through the inclusion of knowledge management tools and applications in the portal, especially all kinds of collaboration tools (for example, groupware, e-mail, and so on).

One of the most resource-consuming tasks companies face when dealing with corporate portals in large-scale implementations is organizing the content publishing process to work in conjunction with existing or newly installed internal document management systems and external content syndication systems. XML may play multiple roles in the streamlining of that process by:

- Unifying content definitions based on XML tags, especially for unstructured text, graphics, images, and so on.

- Unifying search mechanisms and search engines, allowing for the rapid identification of XML-annotated content and its location.

- Enabling flexible and speedy content syndication by making it easier to perform dynamic page programming.

- Enabling the definition of shared Web pages (for example, a single copy of an object that is replicated for use in collaboration services such as chat rooms) as generally shared applets capable of maintaining a consistent state of replicas for purposes of implementing both asynchronous (portal) and synchronous collaboration.

- Enabling content brokering and intelligent content assembly.

In terms of portals' architecture, however, XML's greatest impact may be in how it can facilitate service orientation. XML replaces the idea of predefined portal services with the concept of a flexible set of service definitions that can be read by every portal component involved in creating and using a given service, such as access devices (workstations, handheld devices, cellular phones, and so on) and application components (agents, portlets, stand-alone complete systems, and so on). A service can be defined in an XML page (let's call it the "feature XML page") that links to other XML pages in order to define service features. Each feature XML page can define "behaviors" for each corresponding component in the portal platform.

Behaviors that affect the user, such as how portals' home pages are constructed, search preferences, notification rules, and so on, can be created by users themselves. With simple XML authoring tools now becoming widely available, users can change service profiles easily, deciding what behaviors they want the portal to exhibit.

In order to achieve significant results in portal implementations using XML, however, there are still standardization issues to face. Most importantly, portals must be capable of accessing and querying databases for structured and unstructured information using XML. Industry groups are currently working on a standard for the XML Query Language (XQL). Another important standardization effort involves the XML meta-data exchange format (XMI). XMI is a standard proposal that would combine XML's benefits with object-oriented frameworks, specifically the Unified Modeling Language (UML) and OMG's Meta Object Facility (MOF). The XMI standard will allow the exchange of object descriptions, portlet definitions, and models between portals.

The main point behind the efforts to fully implement XML within portals' architecture is to provide an environment for the enterprise's ability to support portal implementations in a systematic way, guaranteeing uniform access, maintainability, and autonomy. By emphasizing service rather than technology, XML is forcing companies to focus on transforming the existing IT environment, which is primarily transaction-oriented, to a service orientation that is surely one of the most important outcomes and benefits of portal-based solutions.

Corporate Portals and Peer-to-Peer Computing

Peer-to-peer computing (P2PC), popularized recently by Napster, a controversial music file-sharing service over the Internet, is a new paradigm of distributed computing that involves the exchange of information or computing resources between multiple computers connected over a network. With the P2PC concept, computing devices (desktop PCs, servers, and notebooks, for example) become "peers" that share resources, such as processing power, storage space, databases, and applications.

The potential benefits of P2PC are mind-boggling, and go far beyond the obvious, tremendous cost savings gained by taking advantage of unused processing power and storage resources residing in computers on companies' networks and on the Internet. The new paradigm allows the introduction of new types of services and applications that will revolutionize the Internet. Let's consider two examples. First, P2PC can enable gigantic, dynamic on-line auctions, without any intermediary, in which people will be able to use their own computers to list items they have for sale and complete transactions with people looking for bargains. Second, it can enable the establishment of Internet-based, highly distributed, searchable public databases with up-to-date information aggregated from all kinds of Web and non-Web sources, such as databases maintained by companies or individuals.

P2PC is quickly becoming the hottest technology trend in the Internet space. Numerous companies are engaged in individual or alliance-based P2PC efforts. At the time of this writing, for example, IBM has started to work with Microsoft and other partners on a project called UDDI (Universal Description, Discovery, and Integration), which aims to standardize business-to-business Web services using the P2PC concept. Intel has spearheaded a multifaceted research and development (and capital investment) initiative to assess, and help develop, P2PC technologies that it believes are essential both to the new economy and to its own internal operations. There are indications that several important P2PC components are getting very close to being ready for prime time, including next-generation Linux desktops that connect users to a "cloud" of services and general-purpose instant-messaging systems capable of distributing XML-formatted meta-data among connected PCs.

The idea of P2PC makes the concept of portal networks possible. Consider searching. In a small company network, any user and any information resource can directly connect to a single, centralized portal. But at a certain scale, this could become administratively infeasible. Instead, an environment can be constructed in which a user specifies a searching request to his or her primary portal, which belongs to a peer network. The portal consults its network of peers to find out how to move the search request closer to the required information source.

The same is true when orchestrating virtual enterprises. It would not be feasible to have a single, all-powerful, intercorporate portal that knows how to serve everyone. Rather, there will be a peer-to-peer network of portals that cooperatively serve all constituencies.

From this perspective, portals will broker connections not only among information sources, but also among people. Architecturally, the peer-to-peer networks and portal applications layered on top of them will be able to model complex social interactions.

Without portals, P2PC is, to a large degree, a device-specific connection framework. The connection requests are strictly hardware-related, based only upon resource "attractiveness" on the other side. If portals were introduced into P2PC, something different would be going on. Resource attractiveness would no longer be the main factor for initiating a connection request. It might be based entirely on the fact that a particular person is present on one or another of the devices participating in a P2PC network.

This capability, which is referred to as "presence management," is one of the new developments making P2PC an exciting and highly attractive technology. In many cases, companies need to be able to find and contact people in real time. The telephone does not provide that, and neither does e-mail. The combination of portals and P2PC can significantly enhance a variety of applications that depend on effective presence management, such as CRM and SCM. But more importantly, this combination allows the connection of people to people—making it possible to establish ad hoc subspaces (ad hoc "intranets") in which teams can collaborate on project-specific work without requiring central coordination.

This raises an important point. As e-business becomes the predominant business paradigm and virtual enterprises are the norm, we'll find that large numbers of "nodes" (devices and users) have to actively participate in inter-enterprise networks. Managing such networks is going to be a huge challenge. P2PC is a set of architectures, technologies, and strategies that will help companies meet that challenge.

Competing for Leadership with Portal Organizations

According to many leading academic researchers and industry decision makers, in this decade and the next, the sources of strategic advantage are going to be intracompany integration issues and organizational issues—including how to create new forms of organizations that permit a company to do inconsistent things (for example, "playing" in different areas) simultaneously.[3,4]

Intraorganizational architecture based on a unified technical environment is the thing that will hold a multifaceted organization together—without it, it will "fly" apart. The key elements here include intraorganizational, architecture-building processes and structures, competencies and cultures, and mechanisms and approaches for consistent execution of strategies. Portal technologies and associated organizational structures will play a significant role in such architectures.

There are two primary reasons to justify this notion. First, while the dominant new forms for gaining a strategic advantage have not yet been fully defined, it is likely that many of the new forms will be driven by changes brought by Internet and e-business technologies. These technologies, among which corporate portals occupy the central stage, facilitate different types of innovation that are at the roots of sustaining competitive advantage:

- Architectural—different ways of linking existing systems together, enabling information exchange and collaboration, and repackaging of existing products and services to take them to different markets.

- Generational or modular—adding or subtracting system capabilities, enabling an evolution (progression) toward new generations of products and services.

- Cultural—moving toward empowerment of the individual, including customers as well as managers and employees, and using technology to offer new ways to involve individuals in smaller teams with the capability to innovate.

- Collaborative—transforming the concept of "community" at the same time as individuals are attaining new power.

- Forming networks and webs of alliances between communities of similar interests, creating access to unprecedented information dissemination opportunities.

- Capitalizing on those networks to achieve a competitive advantage using advanced communication and collaboration technologies.

Second, the biggest challenge that companies face in enabling the above types of innovation is managing intellectual diversity: shifting from information to knowledge to insight. As a result, the basis for infrastructure building will also be changing as companies move from tightly coupled centralized architectures based on transaction orientation to cooperative federated architectures based on service orientation in order to enable the fundamental shift of the notion of strategic advantage—from "market share" to "competency share" to "share of mind."[5]

Creating an intellectual framework that is widely shared requires a unified integration platform and a single access point to information resources and systems. Clearly, portals are going to be important.

But what can be said about the organizational side of portals? Will companies be using portals to establish the organizational forms of the future? There are plenty of indications that they will.

At the core of the organizational forms of the future is the high-level, network-oriented business design that imposes a network look at an organization, in which relationships between organizational elements are defined as an outcome—not an activity or communication but a deliverable between a supplier role and a customer role. This way of looking at an organization requires having a well-established "dispatcher" function (like a client executive) that lines up unanticipated requests from the customer with organizational capabilities to create a customer-specific value chain. Establishing an organizational structure aligned around portal technology allows for the development of a general, universal, and rigorous way of managing the dispatch function (for example, the negotiation and creation of commitments, keeping track of the current status of the interconnections, and dynamically changing commitments between organizational roles). Basically, a portal organization enables the establishment of a commitment management system that coordinates the behavior of organizational capabilities and technical infrastructure across the organization. It is also allows the adoption of a collaborative decision-making process that systematically integrates all kinds of views of how to create value in an enterprise by providing a vehicle for capturing and aggregating individual perspectives.

Conclusion

Despite the best practices discussed in this book, one should not conclude there is a totally clear vision as to what is imminent on the e-business front.

Any discussion about e-business at the beginning of the twenty-first century would be incomplete without noting that the Internet and related technologies continue to change and evolve at an enormous speed, constantly providing new services and new applications (for example, Internet television, broadband residential access to satellites, and so on). The availability of pervasive networking, along with powerful affordable computing and communications devices in portable form (including laptop computers, two-way pagers, personal digital assistants (PDAs), cellular phones, and so on), is making possible a new paradigm of "roving" forms of computing and communications. The Internet's connection paradigm is changing to accommodate yet another generation of underlying network technologies with different characteristics and requirements—P2PC. This evolution will permit more sophisticated forms of access and services based on new modes of interactions, transaction management, pricing, and cost recovery that will spawn new applications, which in turn will drive further evolution of the Internet itself.

The most pressing question for the future of the Internet and e-business is not how the technology will change, but how the process of change and evolution will be managed, and how much companies will be able to continually innovate and provide better and better service to their customers, partners, and suppliers. It is innovations like the ones mentioned at various points in this book, especially corporate portals, that will make conducting business on the Internet as easy, convenient, and profitable as possible.

It must be clearly understood that today's e-business offerings are piecemeal solutions, requiring much better methods upon which to actually perform real comprehensive business activities at the level of electronically mediated communications between people and systems. The concept of portals moves e-business beyond "point" solutions, making real e-business in terms of two-way communications (B2C, B2B, and B2E) a reality by providing the advantages of a strong unification and service-orientation scheme.

Many leading industry analysts, such as The Patricia Seybold Group, Forrester Research, and The Gartner Group, strongly believe that the e-business flow of interactions and transactions, in which users and businesses can interact with each other to achieve their common objectives, will be transformed into a "multiportal" form of interactions. Under this form, a customer's interaction is a set of seamless "handoffs" from one company's portal site to another. The multiportal form of interactions creates an environment in which many companies become responsible for fulfilling their part of the particular transaction. In this type of environment, companies have to develop their core competencies to a finer and finer degree, becoming "experts" on their particular portion of the customer experience.

There are several fundamental obstacles and barriers to widespread portal implementations that must be removed before any real e-business can develop.

First, we need a complete e-business infrastructure that is global in nature and is capable of enabling the management of accountability and liability in providing significant levels of quality of service (QoS), especially customer security and scalability.

Second, we need to fully embrace component-based development practices. Better use of components and better definitions of their relationships will make all kinds of mission-critical systems, such as ERP, CRM, and SCM, more consistent and much easier to implement and interface within the corporate portal framework in the future. On the technical side, it should not matter which component technology is chosen as a base for development. Deciding between Microsoft COM/COM+/DCOM and Sun/IBM EJB may not be as important as deciding on a development strategy that will force a focus on service orientation.

Third, we need to change systems engineering methodologies. We are taught in engineering to design systems so that they are optimized for performance, cost, and fault tolerance. These factors continue to be important, but none of these three will be crucial for achieving success in the new economy. What will be crucial is system flexibility in this new dynamic environment. First and foremost, system flexibility means ensuring that any system is an evolvable system. It means ensuring the ability to disconnect any point in the system and put something brand new in it. It means ensuring the ability to isolate changes and to specialize any part of the system without bringing the whole thing down. It means allowing for experimentation.

Finally, we have to remember that technology is the second most important consideration, but it is not sufficient in itself to drive a strategy as big and serious as e-business transformation. Solid business strategy is needed. But is technology a driver or a tool? Both. It all depends on how effective a company is in managing the transformation process and associated risk. Some companies, especially ones without a solid risk management approach, should decide their business strategy first, and then select a technology they will use as a tool. Others can decide upon technology first, and then decide what type of business models they want to enable with it. Nevertheless, only the combination of the two can truly enrich the enterprise.

All in all, predicting tomorrow's Internet development depends strongly on understanding all about one of today's leading developments: the portal.

Endnotes

CHAPTER 2

1. M. B. Sarkar, B. Butler, and C. Steinfield, "Intermediaries and Cybermediaries: A Continuing Role for Mediating Players in the Electronic Marketplace," *Journal of Computer Mediated Communication*, 1: 3, December 1995

2. META Delta, "Electronic Business Strategies," *EBS Delta*, 852, September 7, 1999

3. Sterling Software ADG, "eCommerce: Components for the Internet," White Paper, 1999

4. Hewlett-Packard, *An E-Services Strategy Book: Ideas, Strategies, and a Few Frameworks about Where the Internet Ventures Next—The Internet*, Chapter 2, May 19, 1999, www.hp.com/e-services

5. John D. Brennan, "Service Centric Computing," Hewlett-Packard, White Paper, 1999

6. Hewlett-Packard, "Appliance Computing Environment: Architecture Overview," White Paper, 1999, www.cooltown.hp.com/papers/jam/ApplianceComputingArchitecture.htm

7. J. A. Zachman, "A Framework for Information Systems Architecture," *IBM Systems Journal*, 26: 3, 1987, IBM Publication G321—5298

8. W. Selkow, *Something Old, Something New*, The Zachman Institute for Framework Advancement (ZIFA) 1997 Annual Forum, Chicago, May 7–9, 1997

9. R. Evernden, "The Information Framework," *IBM Systems Journal*, 35: 1, 1996
10. Architecture and Project Management, Ltd., *Advanced Architectures and Design Frameworks, Technical Report TR. 38.00*, Cambridge, UK: Architecture and Project Management, Ltd., 1993
11. Nippon Telegraph and Telephone Corporation, *Multisystem Integration Architecture: Concepts and Design Philosophy*, Tokyo: Nippon Telegraph and Telephone Corporation, 1992
12. J. Hong and M. Bauer, *Design and Implementation of a Generic Distributed Applications Management Framework*, Toronto: IBM Center for Advanced Studies, 1992
13. Product Information–www-4.ibm.com/software/ebusiness/

CHAPTER 3

1. Hewlett-Packard, *An E-Services Strategy Book: Ideas, Strategies, and a Few Frameworks about Where the Internet Ventures Next—The Internet.* Chapter 2, May 19, 1999, www.hp.com/e-services
2. Ibid. 1
3. P. F. Linnington, *Introduction to the Open Distributed Processing Basic Reference Model*, International Federation for Information Processing TC6 : Communication Systems (IFIP TC6) International Workshop on Open Distributed Processing, 1991, Elsevier/North-Holland (Information Systems Series), 1991
4. F. Hamilton, *Current Awareness, Current Techniques*, Aldershot, UK: Gower Publishing, Ltd., 1995
5. Richard M. Tong and David H. Holtzman, *Knowledge-Based Access to Heterogeneous Information Sources*, Advanced Decision Systems, Division of Booz, Allen & Hamilton, Inc., 1994, www.csdl.tamu.edu/DL94/paper/tong.html
6. M. Beyerlein and D. Johnson, *Theories of Self-Managing Work Teams*, Stamford, CT: JAI Press, 1994
7. J. Camillus, "Crafting the Competitive Corporation: Management Systems for Future Organizations," in P. Lorange, B. Chakravarthy, J. Roos, and A. Van De Ven (eds.), *Implementing Strategic Process: Change, Learning, and Cooperation*, Oxford, UK: Blackwell, 1993
8. Robert Tolksdorf, Gustaf Neumann, Wolfram Conen, Peter Bertok, and Matthew Fuchs (eds.), *Web Infrastructure for Collaborative Applications*, Proceedings of the 5th Workshop on Enabling Technologies: Infrastructure for Collaborative Enterprises (WETICE '96), 1996, grunge.cs.tu-berlin.de/~tolk/wsreport/wsreport.html
9. CASAHL Technology, "ecKnowledge: Providing the Backbone for B2B Collaborative Commerce," A White Paper on Capabilities and Architecture, 2000

10. Larry Lapide, *Are We Moving from Buyers and Sellers to Collaborators?* AMR Research, Inc., 1999, www.amrresearch.com/

CHAPTER 4

1. Katy Ring and Neil Ward-Dutton, "Enterprise Application Integration: Making the Right Connections," White Paper, Ovum Consulting Group, May 1999
2. White Paper, "Application Integration: A Management Guide," Butler Group, 1999
3. Mark M. Davydov, "Catching the Next Wave of EAI Evolution," *IntelligentEAI*, April 2000
4. Mark M. Davydov, "In Living Colors," *Intelligent Enterprise*, August 2000
5. Ibid. 4
6. Mark M. Davydov, "Getting ERPs on the Same Page," *IntelligentERP*, October 2000
7. Ibid. 6
8. Mike Beasley, Jane Cameron, Gray Girling, Yigal Hoffner, Ron van der Linden, and Gomer Thomas, "Establishing Co-operation in Federated Systems," *ICL Systems Journal*, 9: 2, 1994
9. Christos Nikolaou, Manolis Marazakis, and Dimitri Papadakis, *Synthesis of Services in Open Commerce Environments*, 1998, www.ics.forth.gr/ pleiades/documents/euromed98/euromed98.html
10. Dan Rogers, "The BizTalk Philosophy," White Paper from Microsoft Corporation, *BizTalk.Org*, 2000

CHAPTER 5

1. Christopher Shilakes and Julie Tylman, "Enterprise Information Portals," Research Report, Merrill Lynch, 16, November 1998
2. Avi Saha, "Application Framework for e-business: Portals," IBM Software Strategy White Paper, November 1999, www-4.ibm.com/software/devel-oper/library/portals/index.html
3. White Paper, "Enterprise Portals for E-Business," Portal Wave, Inc., 1999
4. *Corporate Portals Report*, The Delphi Group, April 1999, www.delphi-group.com/
5. Ibid. 1
6. Joseph M. Firestone, DKMS Brief No. Ten: *Benefits of Enterprise Information Portals and Corporate Goals*, DKMS Corp, 1999, www.dkms.com/EIPBenefits.html
7. White Paper, "Enterprise Information Portal Strategy," IBM Global Services, 2000, www-4.ibm.com/software/data/eip/services.html
8. Ibid. 7
9. Ibid. 7
10. Charles Steinfield and Chyng-Yang Jang, *Supporting Virtual Team*

Collaboration: The TeamSCOPE System, the Proceedings of GROUP'99, International ACM SIGGROUP Conference on Supporting Group, 1999

CHAPTER 6

1. White Paper, "The e-Business Portal—Door to Internet-Scale Revenues and 21st Century Computing," Intraware, Inc., 2000
2. White Paper, "E-Portal Framework—An Enterprise Information Portal Architecture," Viador, Inc., May 2000, www.viador.com/
3. Ibid. 1
4. Thomas H. Davenport, "Putting the Enterprise into the Enterprise System," *Harvard Business Review*, July–August, 1998
5. Randy Eckel, "Architecture for Federated Portals," White Paper, *Business Forum*, 1999

CHAPTER 7

1. *Secrets of the Web Design Masters*, CNET, Inc., 2000
2. Product Information—www.autonomy.com/
3. Product Information—www.brio.com/
4. Product Information—www.opentext.com/
5. Product Information—www.plumtree.com/
6. Product Information—www.portalwave.com/
7. Product Information—www.sagemaker.com/
8. Product Information—www.toptier.com/
9. Product Information—www.verity.com/
10. Product Information—www.viador.com/
11. Product Information—www.glyphica.com/
12. Product Information—www.inxight.com/
13. Product Information—www-4.ibm.com/software/data/eip/
14. Product Information—www.oracle.com/
15. Product Information/Oracle Technology Network—www.technet.oracle.com/
16. Kelli Wiseth, *Portal Power*, Oracle Publishing, 1999—www.oracle.com/oramag/

CHAPTER 8

1. Jakob Nielsen, "Intranet Portals: The Corporate Information Infrastructure," *Alertbox*, April, 1999
2. Richard Teare, *Designing your Corporate Virtual University*, Association of International Management Centers, University of Action Learning, 1998, www.imc.org.uk/
3. Company Information—www.feedbackdirect.com/
4. Company Information—www.staples.com/

5. Steve Konicki, "The New Desktop: Staples' Corporate-Portal Strategy Spells Productivity," *Informationweek News*, May, 2000

6. Company Information—www.dell.com/

7. Ibid. 6

8. Ibid. 6

9. Press Release, "Motive Customers Will Achieve Dramatic Results from Online Customer-Care Initiatives, Thanks to Motive-Synet Partnership," Motive Communications, Inc., August 2000, www.motive.com/

10. Todd Spangler, "Help Goes Direct: Dell Backs E-Support Venture," *Inter@ctive Week*, December, 1999

11. B. Travica, *The Design of the Virtual Organization: A Research Model*, Proceedings of the Association for Information Systems Conference (AIS'97), Indianapolis, IN, August, 1997

CHAPTER 9

1. Chang Sau Shooug, *Intelligent Agents in Business Computing*, National Computer Board, Singapore, 1999, www.ncb.gov.sg/

2. Biztalk Information—www.biztalk.org/

3. Working Papers, *The Wharton Impact Conference*—"New Forms of Organizations," University of Pennsylvania, March, 1999

4. George Day and Paul Schoemaker (coeds.), *Wharton on Managing Emerging Technologies*, New York, NY: John Wiley & Sons, April, 2000

5. Ibid. 4

Bibliography and Resources

Don Tapscott, *Blueprint to the Digital Economy: Creating Wealth in the Era of E-Business*, New York, NY: McGraw-Hill, 1998

W. E Deming, *The New Economics*, 2d ed., Potomac, MD: W. Edward Deming Institute, 1994

B. Konsynski, *Electronic Commerce and the Extended Enterprise in Competing in the Information Age*, J. N. Luftman (ed..), New York, NY: Oxford University Press, 1996

G. Hamel and C. K. Prahalad, *Competing for the Future*, Cambridge, MA: Harvard University Press, 1994

W. C. Kim and R. Mauborgne, "Value Innovation: The Strategic Logic of High Growth," *Harvard Business Review*, January–February 1997

J. F. Rayport and J. J. Sviokla, "Exploiting the Virtual Value Chain," *Harvard Business Review*, 73: 6, November–December 1995

Richard Martin and Edward L. Robertson, "Formalization of Multi-level Zachman Frameworks," *IUCS Technical Reports*, TR522, April 1999

Tom Loos, "A New Model for Solving the Data Distribution Problem," *IUCS Technical Reports*, TR471, December 1996, [Ph.D. Dissertation]

Vassilis Prevelakis, "A Framework for the Organisation and Dynamic Reconfiguration of the World Wide Web," Fifth Hellenic Conference on Informatics, Athens, Greece, 1995

White Paper, "SonicMQ—The Role of Java Messaging and XML in Enterprise Application Integration," Progress Software Corporation, Hurwitz Group, Inc., 1999

Judith Gebauer and Arno Scharl, "Between Flexibility and Automation: An Evaluation of Web Technology from a Business Process Perspective," *Journal of Computer-Mediated Communication (JCMC)*, 5: 2, December 1999, www.ascusc.org/jcmc/vol5/issue2/gebauer.html

C. Beam and A. Segev, "Automated Negotiations: A Survey of the State of the Art," *Wirtschaftsinformatik*, 39: 3, 1997

Judith Gebauer, "Modeling the IT-Infrastructure of Inter-Organizational Processes—Automation vs. Flexibility," Proceedings of the Fourth Conference of the International Society for Decision Support Systems (ISDSS'97), July 1997, inforge.unil.ch/isdss97/papers/61.htm

White Paper, "Beyond EAI: Strategic Business Integration," Hurwitz Group, Inc., June 2000

Mark F. Creamer, "When Message Brokers Won't Work," *EAI Journal*, July–August 1999

Oxford Summer Program, "Engineering and Managing the Extended Enterprise," George Mason University, The Institute of Public Policy & the School of Information Technology & Engineering, July 1999, www.pac.gmu.edu/Special_Prog/lectures/lecture4a/sld001.htm

Reference Architecture for iMarkets, Part 1 Overview, Ontology. Org, September 1998, www.ontology.org/

Paul M. A. Baker, "Governance, Policy, and Place in an Age of Technologically Mediated Interaction," Presentation at the 1999 APSA Conference, mason.gmu.edu/~pbaker/apsa99.html

Steven G. Jones (ed.), *CyberSociety: Computer Mediated Communication and Community*, Thousand Oaks, CA: Sage Publications, 1995

Brian Kahin and Charles Nesson (eds.), *Borders in Cyberspace: Information Policy and The Global Information Infrastructure*, Cambridge, MA: MIT Press, 1997

M. West, *A Framework for Enterprise Portal Simplifies Intranets*, The Gartner Group, April 1999, gartner3.gartnerweb.com/

Atul Aneja, Chia Rowan, and Brian Brooksby, "Corporate Portal Framework for Transforming Content Chaos on Intranets," *Intel Technology Journal*, Q1, 2000

"Portals in the Organization," The Delphi Group, April 1999, www.delphi-group.com/

White Paper, "Elevate Your State of Mind—Successful Strategies for Building an Effective Corporate Portal," Semio Corporation, 1999

Dana Mason, "eBusiness Strategy Development," Strategic Technology White Paper Series, BASE Consulting Group, Inc., 2000

Richard Karpinski, "Rethinking Enterprise Portals," *PlanetIT*, April 1999, www.planetit.com/techcenters/docs/e-commerce/opinion/PIT19990414S0008

Stefano Ceri, Piero Fraternali, Stefano Gevinti, and Stefano Paraboschi, "Building a Database Design Laboratory on the Internet," *Internet Computing*, 12: 5, September–October 1998

Sumner Blount, "The Problem with Portals," IT Quadrant, Inc., 2000, www.ebizquadrant.com/e_commerce/blount_1.html

White Paper, "e-Documents for e-Business: IBM's Enterprise Information Portal Takes Aim at e-Business," Bruce Silver Associates, Industry Trend Reports, January 2000

C. Siemens, "The Knowledge Center and Its Business Applications: Practical Applications and Benefits of Corporate Portals in the Enterprise," White Paper, KnowledgeTrack Corporation, 1999

White Paper, "Brio. Portal Enterprise Information Portal," Brio Technology, 1999

David Folger, "Enterprise Portal Frameworks," META Group, Inc., December 1999, www.metagroup.com/

Matt Chain, "Workgroup Computing Strategies," META Group, Inc., April 1999, www.metagroup.com/

M. West, "A Framework for Enterprise Portal Simplifies Intranets," The Gartner Group, April 1999, gartner3.gartnerweb.com/

Garry Murray, *Automating Content Integration with Autonomy*, IDC, 2000

Teri Robinson, "A Doorway through the Data Dimension: A Close Look at Enterprise Information Portals," *PlanetIT*, June 29, 1999

Martin White, "Enterprise Information Portals—An Information Industry Perspective," Intranet Focus, Ltd., January 2000, www.intranetfocus.com/

Rodney Bienvenu, "Longing for Copernicus," SageMaker, Inc., July 2000, www.sagemaker.com/

White Paper, "A Blueprint for Building Web Sites Using the Microsoft Windows DNA Platform, Version 9," Microsoft Corporation, January 2000, microsoft.com/business/products/webplatform/

White Paper, "Corporate Portal Scalability," Plumtree Corporation, June 2000, www.plumtree.com/

Gene Phifer, "Enterprise Portals: Ready or Not, Here They Come," The Gartner Group Symposium/IT Expo presentation, October 1999, gartner3.gartnerweb.com/

Greg Gianforte, "The Insider's Guide to Customer Service on the Web—Eight Secrets for Successful e-Service," White Paper, RightNow Technologies, 2000

B. Travica, "Information Technology and the Non-Traditional Organization: An Exploratory Study into Accounting Organizations," The Doctoral Dissertation defended at Syracuse University, 1995

Abbreviations

A

A2A—Application-to-Application
ABC—Appliance-Based Computing
AI—Application Integration
API—Application Programming Interface
ASP—Active Server Page
ASP—Application Service Provider
ATP—Application Transfer Protocol

B

B2B—Business-to-Business
B2C—Business-to-Consumer
B2E—Business-to-Employee
BI—Business Intelligence
BIP—Business Intelligence Portal
BO—Business Object
BOCA—Business Object Component Architecture
BPR—Business Process Reengineering

C

CBT—Computer-Based Training
CGI—Common Gateway Interface
COM—Component Object Model

CORBA—Common Object Request Broker Architecture
CPF—Corporate Portal Framework
CRM—Customer Relationship Management
CSF—Critical Success Factor
CTI—Computer-Telephony Integration

D

DCE—Distributed Computing Environment
DCOM—Distributed Component Object Model
DHTML—Dynamic HTML
DOM—Document Object Model
DW—Data Warehousing

E

EAI—Enterprise Application Integration
EBSTA—E-Business Strategic Technology Architecture
e-Business—Electronic Business
e-Commerce—Electronic Commerce
EDI—Electronic Data Interchange
EII—Electronic Information Intermediation
EIP—Enterprise Information Portal
EJB—Enterprise Java Beans
e-Marketplace—Electronic Marketplace
ERP—Enterprise Resource Planning
e-Service—Electronic Service

F

FSA—Federated System Architecture
FTP—File Transfer Protocol

G

GUI—Graphical User Interface

H

HTML—HyperText Markup Language
HTTP—HyperText Transfer Protocol

I

IA—Information Appliance
IBE—Integrated Business Environment
IDC—Integrated Development and Construction
IDL—Interface Definition Language
IE—Information Engineering
IETF—Internet Engineering Task Force
IIOP—Internet Inter-Object Protocol
IP—Internet Protocol
IPDM—In-Place Data Mining
ISO—International Standards Organization
IT—Information Technology
IVR—Interactive Voice Response

J

JDBC—Java Database Connectivity

K

KM—Knowledge Management
KQML—Knowledge Query Manipulation Language
KRC—Knowledge Resource Center

L

LAN—Local Area Network
LDAP—Lightweight Directory Access Protocol

M

MOM—Messaging-Oriented Middleware
MTS—Microsoft Transaction Server

O

OAG—Open Applications Group
ODBC—Open Database Connectivity
ODS—Operational Data Store
OLAP—On-Line Analytical Processing
OMG—Object Management Group
OO—Object Orientation

P

P2P— Peer-to-Peer
P2PC—Peer-to-Peer Computing
PDA—Personal Digital Assistant
PID—Personal Information Device
PKC—Public Key Cryptography
PKI—Public Key Infrastructure

R

RPC—Remote Procedure Call
RMI—Remote Method Invocation
ROI—Return on Investment

S

SCM—Supply Chain Management
SGML—Standard Generalized Markup Language
SOAP—Simple Object Access Protocol
SOI—Service-Oriented Integration
SQL—Structured Query Language
SSL—Secure Sockets Layer

T

TCP/IP—Transmission Control Protocol/Internet Protocol

U

UIP—Unifying Integration Platform
UML—Unified Modeling Language
URL—Uniform Resource Locator

V

VB—Visual Basic
VBScript—Visual Basic Script
VE—Virtual Enterprise
VM—Virtual Machine
VPN—Virtual Private Network

W

WAN—Wide Area Network

WAP—Wireless Application Protocol
WWW—World Wide Web

X

XMI—XML Meta-Data Interchange
XML—eXtensible Markup Language
XQL—XML Query Language
XSL—XML Style Sheet

Glossary

A

Active Server Page—a Web-based file/page that includes one or more scripts (small embedded programs), which are processed on a Web server before the page is sent to the client.

ActiveX—a technology developed by Microsoft that provides tools for directly linking desktop applications to Web browsers.

Agent—a self-aware program that acts as an intermediary for another program by performing some activity (for example, starting a thread of execution, stopping itself, moving to another computer through the network, and so on).

Agent Transfer Protocol—an application-level protocol for transferring agents over the network.

Appliance-Based Computing—a type of distributed computing, in which the services traditionally provided by general-purpose PC-class computers (for example, laptop, desktop, and workstation computers) can be supported by a set of cooperating devices and services.

Application Programming Interface—a published description of the way one program asks another program to perform a service.

Application Service Provider—a firm that aggregates, facilitates, and brokers IT services to deliver IT-enabled business solutions across a network via subscription-based pricing.

B

Back-End Systems—applications that automate operational functions of a company, such as order processing, inventory, receivables, and so on.

"Brick-and-Mortar"—a term used to describe a traditional company with non-Web distribution and selling channels for its products or services.

Browser—a client program (software) that is used to access various kinds of Internet resources.

Business Intelligence—a concept of analysis and exploration of structured, domain-specific business information (often stored in a data warehouse) to determine trends or patterns, thereby deriving insights and drawing conclusions.

Business Object—a software component that encapsulates business rules and aims to provide secure sophisticated access to diverse electronic content and software applications.

Business Process Reengineering—a concept of analysis and radical redesign of business processes, including their supporting organizational structures, information systems, job responsibilities, and performance standards, to achieve significant performance improvements.

Business Rule—a specification of business regulations, principles, and requirements, and the relationships between them and operations applied to them, from the business enterprise viewpoint.

Business-to-Business—an electronic form of exchanging information and enacting commercial transactions between two businesses.

Business-to-Consumer—an electronic form of exchanging information and enacting commercial transactions between a business and an individual.

Business-to-Employee—an electronic form of exchanging information between a business and its employee.

Buy-Side Processes—business processes for companies to purchase products such as requisitioning, product catalogs, approvals, purchase order creation, payment processing, and so on.

C

Chat—a form of direct communication over the Internet with multiple persons.

"Click-and-Mortar"—a term used to describe a company with a combination of traditional and Web-based distribution and selling channels for its products or services.

Common Gateway Interface—a set of rules that describe how application programs communicate with a Web server.

Common Object Request Broker Architecture—a component-based architecture developed by the Object Management Group that defines functions and components of the open distributed object computing infrastructure, focusing on enabling object interoperability in a networked environment, regardless of the language in which they were developed or on which computers they reside.

Component-Based Development—a process of designing, assembling, and deploying systems from a variety of independent, functionally discrete pieces (components).

Component-Based Model—a graphical representation of a system in terms of its component parts. It enumerates the system infrastructure, including technology, information, and applications, at a high level of detail and shows how the component parts are arranged and configured for a system.

Component Object Model—the Microsoft component-based model and underlying software architecture for applications to be built from binary software components, leading to higher-level software services for various aspects of commonly needed system functions, including compound documents, custom controls, data transfer, and so on.

Componentware—a generic term used to describe a combination of models, methodology, sharable software (libraries), and development tools for enabling component-based development.

Computer-Based Training—a concept of learning based on the use of a specialized software package, offering information on a certain subject and a test for the pupil.

Content Provider—a firm whose products are information-based (content), including services to access and manage the content.

Cooperative Processing—a type of computing environment that permits cooperation between processes on different, interconnected information systems.

Corporate Portal Framework—a management approach for leveraging and extending companies' assets into the new digital economy through a unified set of technology and business processes.

Critical Success Factor—an item relating to an organization, person, or process that is key for ensuring the success of the organization, person, or process.

Customer Relationship Management—a technology-enabled strategy to cost-effectively acquire, retain, and grow customers based on converting data-driven decisions into business actions in response to, and in anticipation of, actual customer behavior.

Cyberspace—a term originated by author William Gibson in his novel *Neuromancer*, which is currently used to describe the whole range of information resources available through computer networks and associated activities.

D

Data Centricity—a characteristic of a system design based on an approach to systems analysis that focuses primarily on data rather than processes.

Data Mining—a concept of analyzing data for the purposes of identifying hidden patterns and relationships.

Data Warehousing—a concept of collecting business information from many sources in the enterprise into specialized databases (referenced to as "data warehouses"), organized for purposes of providing business users with a multidimensional view of the data they need to analyze business conditions.

Digital Certificate—a technology for attaching encrypted personal information to electronic communications, such as e-mail or Web pages.

Distributed Component Object Model—an extension of the Component Object Model developed by Microsoft to support objects distributed across a network.

Distributed Computing Environment—distributed systems architecture, and a prepackaged group of integrated interoperability components and applications created by the Open Software Foundation (OSF) to provide services and tools for implementing a distributed network.

Dynamic Binding—a capability of linking a message and invoking the appropriate method at run time.

Dynamic HTML—a programming method that combines HTML, style sheets, and scripts to make Web pages more interactive.

E

E-Business Ecosystem—a term used to describe a dynamic electronic business environment, in which all parties in the supply chain—manufacturers, distributors, and final customers—play an integral role in creating value for themselves and for their trading partners.

Electronic Application Integration—a general term for all plans, methods, and tools aimed at interlinking disparate information systems and processes.

Electronic Business—a concept of performing business and functional processes to deliver an organization's value over computer networks.

Electronic Business Portal—a mechanism (or a physical device) that provides access to a changing set of business services while providing access to specific information dissemination services that can be used to communicate or deliver information to a user.

Electronic Business Strategic Technology Architecture—a detailed definition of all the technologies, application systems, components, and interfaces that enable and support an e-business model.

Electronic Commerce—a concept of conducting financial transactions over computer networks.

Electronic Data Interchange—a set of specifications and associated technologies for exchanging transaction-related documents between businesses.

Electronic Marketplace—a Web-based environment that enables trading of goods and services between a broad range of buyers and sellers.

Electronic Service—any resource accessible on the Internet by people, businesses, or even "things," fulfilling a well-defined function.

Encryption—a process of changing data into a form that can be read only by the intended receiver.

Enterprise Java Beans—a Java-based, server-side component architecture for enabling rapid development of mission-critical applications.

Enterprise Portal—a centralized, companywide portal environment.

Enterprise Resource Planning—a technology-enabled business strategy designed to integrate mission-critical operational functions and processes to balance and optimize an enterprise's resources.

Extranet—a portion of a corporate network (intranet) that is open to customers, business partners, and anyone to whom the corporation grants access privileges.

F

Federated System Architecture—a system architecture that deals with the issues of facilitating cooperation between autonomous systems for the purpose of sharing services and resources.

File Transfer Protocol—a technology based on TCP/IP for moving files between nodes of a computer network.

Firewall—a technology that provides essential security for protected computer networks.

Framework (Technology)—an all-encompassing specification for the collective set of products, components, and procedures necessary to create and deploy an enterprisewide technology solution.

G

Graphical User Interface—a term that describes a graphical (rather than purely textual) user interface to a computer.

Groupware—a generic term used to describe a class of software for supporting common collaborative functions and application services, such as e-mail, calendaring, workflow management, and so on.

H

Home Page—a term that describes the starting (main) page of a Web site.

Hyperlink—a mechanism for navigating between text portions, or from an image map to a page or other type of file on the Web; used as a predefined connection from a Web page to another resource on the Web.

HyperText Markup Language—a markup language used to create hypertext documents for use on the Web.

HyperText Transfer Protocol—a format based on TCP/IP for exchanging HTML documents between a browser and Web server.

I

Information Appliance—a device that supports a concrete information-based function: text, graphics, image, video, or sound processing.

Information Object—a term used to describe an information entity that comprises some related data and associated processing software, such as active documents and Web page components.

Integrated Business Environment—an enterprisewide systems environment that enables the integration of back-end enterprise systems such as ERP with front-end, customer-facing systems and tools, mostly governed by Internet technologies.

Internet—the global information system that: (i) is logically linked together by a globally unique address space based on the Internet Protocol (IP) or its subsequent extensions/follow-ons; (ii) is able to support communications using the Transmission Control Protocol/Internet Protocol (TCP/IP) suite or its subsequent extensions/follow-ons, and/or other IP-compatible protocols; and (iii) provides, uses, or makes accessible, either publicly or privately, high-level services layered on the communications and related infrastructure described herein [The Federal Networking Council].

Internet Inter-Object Protocol—an industry-standardized protocol for communicating between objects on the Internet.

Internet Protocol—an industry-standardized, connectionless packet switching protocol used as the network layer in the TCP/IP Protocol suite.

Intranet—a private network inside a company or organization built using Internet technologies.

J

Java—a general-purpose programming language invented by Sun Microsystems that is specifically designed for writing portable programs.

Java Database Connectivity—a Java application-programming interface that enables Java programs to interact with any SQL-compliant database.

Java Script—a scripting language based on Java used to program execution tasks.

K

Knowledge Management—a business strategy that formalizes management and leverage of a firm's intellectual assets based on a collaborative and integrative approach to the creation, capture, organization, access, and use of information assets, including the tacit, noncaptured knowledge of people.

L

Lightweight Directory Access Protocol—a specification for directories that contain information about network resources, such as names, phone numbers, and addresses, and a protocol for updating and searching such directories, especially those on the Internet.

Local Area Network—a computer network limited to the immediate area, usually the same building or floor of a building.

M

M-Commerce—a term used to describe e-commerce carried out using mobile devices (typically WAP phones).

Messaging-Oriented Middleware—a technology for enabling communication and data exchange between disparate systems based on sending and receiving messages using some sort of queuing processing.

Meta-Data—information about data that describes the content, format, and meaning of a particular set of data.

Middleware—a generic term used to describe a class of software for supporting common infrastructure services executing on top of operating system services that enable applications and their components (for example, presentation, business logic, database access, and so on) to interact with each other across a computer network.

N

Network—a connection of two or more computers that enables exchange of information or sharing resources.

O

Object Management Group—a consortium founded in 1989 to promote the adoption of standards for managing distributed objects.

Open Database Connectivity—a common database access method developed by Microsoft for SQL-compliant databases.

P

Peer-to-Peer Computing—a type of distributed computing that involves exchanging information or computing resources among multiple computers connected over a network.

Personalization—a concept of using continually adjusted user profiles to match content or services to individuals.

Portal—a single, Web-based interface into the world of heterogeneous and incompatible information sources distributed across the network.

Public Key Cryptography—an encryption method for message exchange that uses two types of mathematically related keys (public and private).

Public Key Infrastructure—a technology that enables the use and management of public key cryptography within digital certificates.

Pull Technology—a technology used for distributing information to subscribers based on their requests.

Push Technology—a technology used for broadcasting information to subscribers.

R

Reference Architecture (relating to an enterprise)—a high-level systems design of the enterprisewide computing environment that is free of implementation details and consists of a high-level description of major components, definitions of relationships between those components, definitions of relationships between those components and elements external to the enterprise, high-level definitions of key data sources, data stores produced, interfaces between the components, and identification of performance drivers and capacity requirements.

Remote Method Invocation—a mechanism used by a Java object to invoke (pass control of execution to) another Java running on a different computer or under control of another Java virtual machine.

Remote Procedure Call—a mechanism used by a program to invoke (pass control of execution to) another program running on a different computer.

S

Search Engine—a Web-based service that allows users to express a request for information and obtain that information.

Secure Sockets Layer —a protocol based on a public key that allows for the secure transmission of confidential information between a client and a server.

Sell Side—business processes for companies to sell their products and services such as catalogs, transaction processors, payment processors, and so on.

Shared Web Page—a term used to describe a mechanism for implementing both asynchronous (portal) and synchronous collaboration using replicated objects in chat-room applications.

"Shopping Cart"—a term used to describe a mechanism for keeping track of all the items that a customer wants to buy, allowing the shopper to pay for the whole order at once.

Simple Object Access Protocol—an XML-based, platform-agnostic communication protocol that allows significantly improved Internet interoperability.

Spider—a term used to describe a class of agent-base software that explores the Web by retrieving a document and following all the hyperlinks in it.

Structured Query Language— a standard interactive and programming language for defining the structure of relational databases, and manipulating data stored in such databases.

*Supply Chain Management—*a technology-enabled business strategy that encompasses a trading-partner community engaged in a common goal of satisfying the end customer and focuses on optimizing delivery of goods, services, and information from supplier to customer.

T

*Taxonomy—*a classification system for items based on their relationship to one another.

*Transmission Control Protocol/Internet Protocol—*an industry-standard protocol that enables networked computers and other devices to communicate.

U

*Unified Modeling Language—*an object methodology-oriented language for specifying, visualizing, constructing, and documenting the artifacts of software systems.

*Uniform Resource Locator —*an industry-standard specification format that defines an exact location of a resource on the Internet.

*Unifying Integration Platform—*an integration concept aimed at delivering increased levels of coherence between multiple technologies while keeping application development efficiency at a high level.

V

*Virtual Enterprise—*an organizational model that binds a fragmented and geographically spread set of partners collaborating together.

*Virtual Machine—*an abstract specification for a computing environment capable of executing a language-specific instruction set using the instruction set of a processor.

*Virtual Private Network—*a network in which some of the parts are connected using the public Internet, but the data sent across the Internet is encrypted so that the entire network is considered "virtually" private.

*Visual Basic—*a high-level programming language developed by Microsoft that is graphically oriented and relatively easy to learn.

*Visual Basic Script—*a scripting language based on Visual Basic used to program execution tasks.

Vortal—a Web site that provides a gateway to information (for example, unique editorial content, product reviews, and so on) related to a particular industry (for example, consumer goods manufacturing, health care, insurance, and so on) or to a group of people sharing an interest in buying, selling, or exchanging information about that particular industry.

W

Web Crawler —a term used to describe a Web service that scans Web documents, builds indexes, including for all associated links, and adds them to a database.

Web Hosting —a set of business activities that involve providing, maintaining, and managing hardware, applications, content integrity, security, and the high-speed Internet connection for a Web site.

Web Page—a file with embedded HTML tags, scripts, images, and other elements to make it accessible by Web browsers.

Web Server —software that accepts an HTTP request from a browser and returns HTML pages in response to the request.

Web Server Platform—a combination of hardware, operating system, Web server software, communications protocols, and content that is used to serve Web browsers' requests.

Web Site—a collection of Web pages associated with a particular location on the Web.

Wide Area Network —a network that covers an area larger than a single building or campus.

Wireless Application Protocol—a set of communication protocols for wireless devices designed to enable access to the Internet and advanced telephony services.

World Wide Web—an environment that exists on top of the Internet and combines the entire set of accessible Internet resources and related tools.

X

eXtensible Markup Language—a self-describing markup language that extends capabilities of the Hypertext Markup Language for describing data objects imbedded in hypertext documents by providing meta-data tags.

XML Meta-Data Interchange—a work-in-progress proposal for the use of the eXtensible Markup Language (XML) to provide a standard way for programmers and other users to exchange information about meta-data.

Index

About the Author

Mark M. Davydov, Ph.D., Technical Cybernetics and Software Engineering, is an internationally recognized expert in systems architecture, application integration, and advanced data management solutions. Currently he is chief architect of Galileo International, LLC. During his extensive career as a management consultant and senior IT executive, he has planned and implemented enterprisewide strategic technology initiatives for more than 30 Fortune 500 companies. He has chaired and developed many technical sessions/symposia in national and international conferences. He has more than 80 publications in refereed journals and industry-leading magazines.